The Battle for Wall Street

Behind the Lines in the Struggle that Pushed an Industry into Turmoil

Richard Goldberg

WILEY

John Wiley & Sons, Inc.

Published by John Wiley & Sons, Inc., Hoboken, New Jersey.

Published simultaneously in Canada.

For general information on our other products and services or for technical support, please contact our Customer Care Department within the United States at (800) 762-2974, outside the United States at (317) 572-3993 or fax (317) 572-4002.

Wiley also publishes its books in a variety of electronic formats. Some content that appears in print may not be available in electronic books. For more information about Wiley products, visit our web site at www.wiley.com.

Library of Congress Cataloging-in-Publication Data:

Goldberg, Richard (Richard S.)
    The battle for Wall Street : behind the lines in the struggle that pushed an industry into turmoil / Richard Goldberg.
        p.   cm.
    Includes bibliographical references and index.
    ISBN 978-0-470-22279-9 (cloth) ISBN 978-1-118-83675-0 (paperback)
        1. Investment advisors—United States.   2. Investments—United States.   3. Finance—United States.   4. Stock exchanges—New York (State)—New York.   I. Title.
    HG4928.5.G65   2009
    332.64'273—dc22
                                                                            2008038662

10 9 8 7 6 5 4 3 2 1

To my wife, Jill, and my children, Brett and Nikki
For their love, encouragement and endless patience.

Contents

Acknowledgments

My ineffable gratitude to James Mossman, a brilliant tactician and a better friend, Michael Kraines, an instrumental colleague in bringing this book to life, and Ed Hajim and Bruce Wasserstein, the driving influences of my Wall Street career.

I will always be indebted to Dean John Coatsworth, Rob Garris and Katharine Morgan from Columbia University; Dean Andy Boynton, Edie Hotchkiss, and Hassan Tehranian from Boston College; and Edward Bayone from Brandeis University for making my dream of a "second act" come true.

My deepest appreciation to Kelly O'Connor, the hardest-working development editor; Dave Pugh, a reassuring senior editor; Stacey Fischkelta, a patient senior production editor; and Alan Horowitz and Neil Plakcy for their guidance in navigating me through the rocky terrain of pushing a book forward. Matthew Berninger, Jessica Hunt, and Christopher Kaminker also provided invaluable assistance in research.

I am humbled and inspired by Steve Begleiter, Buzzy Geduld, Jeff Lane, Greg Meredith, Ben Phillips, Lou Ricciardelli, Gary Talarico, Catherine Taylor, and Mark Utay for sharing their financial pearls of wisdom which substantially increased the book's intellectual heft.

My loyalty and admiration to a cadre of friends who endured my obsessing over writing and rewriting this continually evolving drama: Ricardo Gomez Acebo, Reuben Auspitz, Joe Carson, Steve Feldman, Phil Friedman, David Goldhill, Matt Kissner, Barry Klein, Sherri Mahne, Bill Manning, Peter Marber, Jeff Silver, Joe Stein, and Joe Yurcik.

I would be remiss to exclude a special thanks to my wife, Jill, for being an invaluable set of eyes and ears, John Prior for his time and practical expertise, Chris Toro for her kind gestures, and Father James Woods for making the world a better place.

Finally, my parents and my in-laws instilled in me the value of a good education, specifically the importance of studying history and learning from it. To the above mentioned and many more, thank you for helping lead the charge of *The Battle for Wall Street*.

Introduction

Let the Battle for Wall Street Begin

The Battle for Wall Street.

I chose this phrase as the title for my book because, over the past two decades, a battle of major financial proportions has commenced on Wall Street, and as everyone is all too aware, it continues to rage as I write.

The battle is primarily between two giant armies—the buyers, whose soldiers come from such places as hedge funds; and the sellers, whose armed forces come from such places as hybrid commercial/investment banks. In addition, other participants—like exchanges, sovereign wealth funds, endowment funds and financial entrepreneurs—have joined the battle along the way.

In 2008, the battle for the Street found its way into my classroom. Just as the rise of the free agent changed the game of baseball, the new roles that aspiring Wall Street types are interested in today are very different than the ones I used to play when I was firmly planted as an investment banker.

In class, I discuss the theories behind global markets and financial institutions, along with the practical applications I've learned during my 25-year career. I share personal anecdotes and war stories and try to narrate the excitement of a career spent on the front lines of finance.

My students, though, are interested in something else entirely—it's as though I'm recounting tales of what it was like when the World Series was played during the daytime. However, all they care about is how the New York Yankees are financing their new stadium in 2009. They also wonder what the playing field will look like now that the credit crisis of 2007–2008 has forever altered the lay of the land.

They want to know what's going on behind today's headlines—not the traditional or new roles of investment bankers.

"Tell us about the buy side. Tell us about alternative asset managers, hedge funds and private equity groups," they ask. "What's happening to the stock exchanges? What's up with sovereign wealth funds? Who are these financial entrepreneurs we're seeing? Who's going to survive the shakeout between the nimble and the flatfooted?"

My students want to know where the action is today, and where it will be tomorrow. Hmm, I wonder. Am I a dinosaur?

When I was sitting in their seats, my professors came from commercial banking. They, too, shared war stories and personal anecdotes. All I wanted to hear about, though, was investment banking, because that was grabbing headlines back then—and I could feel the action shifting in that direction. Did my professors, I wonder, feel like dinosaurs?

It's not only the students who are feeling the ground shift under Wall Street. I recently spoke with a friend who told me about a retreat that a well-regarded sell-side bank held offsite, away from the clatter and hustle of the trading floor, for the members of its fixed income group. The topic? How a classic sell-side institution like theirs should respond to the rising clout of the hedge funds.

The sell side is seeing what the students are seeing: They're feeling the action crossing over to the buy side. Not surprisingly, they're searching for ways to respond. After all, they don't want to turn into dinosaurs.

How the Battle Lines Were Drawn

This battle, of course, is about power. As the story unfolds, you'll see that it's also about winning the hearts, minds, and—yes, the wallets—of the investment community.

For many years—one could say hundreds of years—the sell side held most of the power. Whether you were an individual investor or a major institution, what you knew about the market was largely limited to what the sell side told you.

If, as an individual, you wanted to know the price of a stock or corporate bond—or the direction the market was headed—you asked your broker. You only knew what your broker told you.

If you were a corporate executive considering taking your company public, you consulted with investment bankers, who advised you on what to expect from the market.

What buyers knew came largely, if not entirely, from what sellers told them—they had limited access to independent information.

Sellers created markets, made markets, controlled access to markets, controlled information about markets and largely managed markets. Buyers were participants with limited power or influence—or none at all.

And information wasn't the only thing in limited supply to the buy side—so was access to money. The market's liquidity came largely from the sell side. Money—capital—mainly flowed from the spigots of commercial and investment banks.

For a long time, that was just the way things worked. The sell side had the advantage. And then everything began to change. Like so many other revolutions, this change was partly due to technology, which has played a key role in leveling the playing field between the buy and sell sides.

For the first time, buyers, through their computer screens, could see who was making markets and at what prices. All of a sudden, they had access to more information than ever before. Over time, the gatekeepers of information, the sell side, lost much of their power. Others were providing large amounts of data—the very thing that had given them the upper hand for so long.

Technology also put the power of computation at the buy side's fingertips. Complex algorithmic analyses that looked for exploitable anomalies within the market became possible as computers became more powerful, software become more sophisticated, users became more knowledgeable and the cost of both hardware and software fell.

Another element added to the Wall Street landscape is an over-abundance of green. Money has always been floating up and down the Street, and has always been the key ingredient in the mix. But what I'm referring to here is liquidity: the availability of money, and lots of it.

In the last 10 years, there was more money available to Wall Street's players than ever before. It used to be that the mention of "a few billion dollars" was a tip-off that something important was being discussed. Over the past five years, however, you heard conversations about tens of billions of dollars. In fact, when discussing how much hedge funds have grown in recent years, people started talking about trillions.

The money available to play with grew as dramatically as the increase in the availability of sand from a backyard sandbox to the beach. It was all sand—and all money—but the increase in scale changed the way the game was being played.

Borrowers could tap into pools of liquidity—from pensions, endowments, wealthy individuals, banks, and, yes, electronic versions of exchanges—that were either nonexistent or largely inaccessible in the past.

And as the pools of liquidity expanded in number and size, more and more wealth was created, which just increased the amount of liquidity even more. This circularity fed on itself.

As we've seen during the credit crisis, we are currently in a different part of the liquidity cycle. While there is still money available, those who have it are currently less likely to lend it or will lend it on terms that the borrowers would have turned their backs on not so long ago—witness Warren Buffett's $5 billion investment in Goldman Sachs in September 2008. While Goldman was no doubt happy to have the cash infusion, it obtained it at a hefty cost. As Oppenheimer analyst Meredith Whitney said in a report to clients: " . . . the terms of this deal seem exorbitantly expensive and provide insight into how truly challenging current market conditions are."[1]

The increase in pools of liquidity caused the rise of new asset classes. Mutual funds may have seemed exotic in the 1960s and

1970s, but by the 1990s they were fully mainstream and quite ho-hum.

The buy side, always aggressive when looking for an edge against the sell side, created new asset classes, including hedge funds and other alternative management funds. The sell side, however, was slow on the draw. The buy side got the jump, an advantage it holds to this day.

With the evolution of asset classes, more new players entered the scene: university endowments and public pension funds. For years, these funds had been relatively small and were run by civil servants. Rare was the university with $1 billion; $100 million seemed like the pot of gold at the end of the rainbow.

Today, the folks running these funds have become a professional match for anyone on Wall Street. And in addition to brains and sophistication, they have more money than ever. For example, at the end of fiscal 2007, Yale's endowment had $22 billion in the till[2]—and there are other funds, like the California Public Employees' Retirement System (CalPERS)— with much, much more. As of September 2008, CalPERS had $223 billion in assets.[3] That's big money—and big power—by any definition.

These pensions and endowments boosted their returns by investing in buy-side asset classes like hedge funds and private equity firms— something unheard of 20 years ago. The shift toward these unconventional asset classes helped fuel their growth and their wealth. In turn, they fueled the growth of the buy side on one hand, while the sell side had to do battle with them on the other.

Sovereign wealth funds represent another new player shaking up the financial landscape. These funds, such as the Abu Dhabi Investment Authority, are pools of liquidity from a country's reserves, and they poured money into institutions that found themselves in need of a capital lifeline. When those folks needed a life preserver, who did they call? 1-800-SOVEREIGN-WEALTH-FUNDS.

And I'm not talking about little known, mom-and-pop type institutions that sometimes need a lifeline, but some of the biggest names on Wall Street, including Citigroup, Morgan Stanley, and UBS. Out of seemingly nowhere, sovereign wealth funds have taken a seat at the financial power table.

As the credit crisis has unfolded, we've seen the resurgence of another financial power broker—the Japanese sell-side institutions. Ironically, they weren't involved with the risky asset classes of the 2000s because they were navigating through their country's own financial crisis during the 1990s.

While these liquidity players were entering the battlefield, the sell side didn't exactly sit around waiting to be ambushed. While many of the advantages of the Battle for Wall Street have gone to the buy side, the sell side has developed weapons of its own. Prime brokerage and private equity/company buyout financing are examples of how the sell side has provided services to the buy side and profited nicely as a result.

But the sell side has met with mixed results. In 2007–2008, turmoil has been embroiling Wall Street. I'm referring, of course, to the subprime mortgage crisis and the resulting credit crunch, the likes of which hasn't been seen since the 1930s. In March 2008, Bear Stearns, one of Wall Street's mainstays, quickly disappeared into the hands of JPMorgan.

It wasn't just the credit crunch that brought down Bear Stearns; the firm also collapsed due to the weight of its own internal hedge funds, and its reliance on external hedge fund clients. This 85-year-old firm sunk in heavy seas as quickly and completely as a freighter could in a perfect storm: here one minute and totally gone from sight the next, as it drifts downward through the water to a deep, invisible, grave.

Of course, we now know that it was only the first of several major financial freighters to go down or be tossed about in heavy seas. In the fateful months of September and October 2008, the credit crisis escalated to the point where the financial markets capsized, having disastrous effects on three sell-side sectors.

In the investment banking sector, four principal U.S.-based investment banks were meaningfully affected. Lehman Brothers went out of business; Merrill Lynch had little choice but to fall into the arms of Bank of America; and Goldman Sachs and Morgan Stanley were reorganized into bank holding companies in order to weather the crisis.

In the insurance sector, giant AIG required an approximately $85 billion federal bailout; and in the depository sector, Washington Mutual and Wachovia stumbled into the hands of JPMorgan and Wells Fargo, respectively.

As the financial sector was faltering, the U.S. government joined the battle. Congress approved an unprecedented multibillion-dollar bailout of the financial industry in late 2008, aiming to loosen up credit markets that had tightened up severely as the cascade of bad news unfolded.

Casualties in the Battle for Wall Street suddenly became heavier than anyone had imagined.

The Generals Leading the Battle

While I've been talking about liquidity, technology, and asset classes, the driving force behind any firm or community is its people.

Therefore, throughout this book, I discuss many of those who have left their mark in the Battle for Wall Street. Some are entrepreneurs who have created electronic markets or information technology or other products or services that have helped change the balance of power on the Street. Others lead firms that were influential or otherwise important to the development of the financial community. As with military battles, where generals play key roles in the outcomes, Wall Street is filled with individuals who play essential roles. You'll meet a number of these folks during the course of this book, and in particular in the case studies that I include in each chapter.

On the sell side, I would liken these executives to nine position players in baseball, who pitch and hit all the time.

On the buy side, I would compare them to designated hitters, waiting for their pitch and driving the ball.

The Battle Plan

Neither side is capable of a New York Yankees–worthy dynasty (or, in my particular case, a Boston Red Sox–style dynasty), which is why I think this book is so timely. This is not a history book. It is a book about the wrestling for power that is going on today and likely to continue for some time to come.

Join me as we travel through the ever-shifting, always tumultuous world of Wall Street. We'll track the forces that have swept through this terrain, from rivers of liquidity to crashing waves of risk. We'll gaze out over the rocky cliffs of the credit crisis of 2007–2008 and visit the uncharted territory staked out by entrepreneurs. As our compass leads us from the sell side to the buy side, from the past to the future, we'll draw a comprehensive map of the Wall Street landscape and drill down to the bottom line of each battle. And at the end of each chapter, I will discuss the implications of each battle as well as declare which side seems to be gloriously winning.

So buckle your seat belts and get ready for an insider's journey— you're about to watch the Battle for Wall Street unfold.

Part One

INSTRUMENTS OF CHANGE

Chapter 1

Sea of Liquidity

C an you have too much money, so much that you spend it
unwisely? Can having less money give you a competitive
advantage over those with more?

I think the answer to these questions is "definitely yes." And before
you tell me that I'm crazy, I'll explain. No, I'm not turning in my Wall
Street name tag just yet and taking a vow of poverty.

It's just that money, in the form of the sell side's balance sheet and
liquidity, can make the sell side act in ways that are open to debate.

One of the strengths of the sell side has been its lofty liquidity position, specifically its access to capital. That's why the buy side has made
many withdrawals from the sell side's ATM since traders and specula-
tors first negotiated a truce they called the Buttonwood Agreement,
which laid the groundwork for the New York Stock Exchange.

The sell side readily financed the needs of the buy side because it
enjoyed the transaction fees it was getting in return. What it didn't fully
realize was that it was supercharging the buy side's growth by providing it
with the deadliest weapon—liquidity. With liquidity as their ammunition,
hedge funds and private equity funds became formidable competitors.

It was as though the sell side was providing weapons to the buy side, which the buy side used to its advantage to propel its growth. It was a battle the sell side didn't quite realize it was entering. Today, it's too late for the sell side to do anything about it—except play its own hand while emulating its progeny.

I saw the sell side from a front-row seat, and a question pops up. Did it act downright "liquidity silly" during the rise of the buy side? If you want to understand the Battle for Wall Street, liquidity is a good place to start.

Overplaying Your Ammunition

The summer of 2000 was filled with news about the presidential election as well as some heavy-hitting stories about sell-side firms merging with each other: UBS merged with Paine Webber;[1] JPMorgan merged with Chase;[2] and AXA Financial sold its majority stake in Donaldson, Lufkin & Jenrette (DLJ) to Credit Suisse.[3] These skirmishes within the larger Battle for Wall Street demonstrated sell-siders duking it out amongst themselves.

These deals filled not only the airwaves, but also the hallways of my old firm. We were involved particularly with AXA, which sold its majority stake in DLJ to Credit Suisse—a timely move, by my calculation.[4] By divesting itself of DLJ (which was a major sell-side player), AXA got out of one meaningful sell-side business just as the buy side was starting its ascendancy. It wisely decided to shift its focus toward the buy side.

A few months after AXA sold DLJ, it acquired Sanford Bernstein, a major money management firm, which it subsequently combined with its existing Alliance Capital Management.[5] Today, Alliance Bernstein is a major player in the buy-side business of money management.

Looking back at the Credit Suisse/DLJ transaction today, it paid about $13.7 billion for . . . what?[6]

That transaction—any transaction—is debatable. On one hand, Credit Suisse acquired a number of quality businesses. Three come to mind: a leverage finance business (funding companies with a greater-than-normal debt-to-equity ratio)[7]; a high-yield bond business (offering bonds rated below investment grade)[8]; and a merchant bank (providing investment bank services to multinational corporations).[9]

On the other hand, a good deal of what is bought on Wall Street is talent: the human capital at the firms being acquired. Yet, some of the talent Credit Suisse set out to acquire—the people who were part of the DLJ franchise—left after the merger.

And where did they go? A healthy number went to the buy side. After all, the size of a combined organization like Credit Suisse/DLJ may not have been a selling point. Two primary benefits offered by a big organization like Credit Suisse—technology and liquidity—were becoming more available to the buy side just as Credit Suisse was plunking down its billions.

Whereas the AXA buy-side expansion in the early 2000s was timely, the Credit Suisse/DLJ timing in 2000 may have been off from both a technology and a liquidity angle.

Technology was becoming less expensive and more powerful, and the information that could be gleaned from it was better and broader. One of the edges that investment bankers had—information—was being eroded by the technology, which made that information much more readily accessible. (I'll cover this explosion in technology in the next chapter. Actually, explosion is an understatement—it was more like a line of cannons blasting its way through a crumbling Maginot line.)

And the buy side was building up its liquidity. While the sell side still had an edge, it was quickly being eroded. The folks at the investment banks saw this happening and were heading for the doors. Those investment bankers who stayed home saw that the sell side had more liquidity than it could usefully deploy.

A quote that is often attributed to Wallis Simpson, Duchess of Windsor, says, "You can never be too rich or too thin." I don't know about the thin part, but I believe you can be too rich, and it is possible that the sell side was in this position, to its detriment.

For example, did NationsBank (now Bank of America) and General Electric overplay their balance-sheet and liquidity positions in acquiring sell-side firms? NationsBank bought Montgomery Securities,[10] while General Electric bought Kidder Peabody.[11] Today, both sell-side firms are history.

Let's look at the sell side's misusing its liquidity to win business. When giving advice on mergers and acquisitions or capital markets, a number of firms tend to give away liquidity as well. They do this by telling a prospective customer that, if hired to manage a deal, they will provide more attractive funding as well.

The buy side, however, doesn't get involved with those types of deals. It doesn't finance its customers, and can be smarter with decisions regarding its use of capital. As such, it can avoid this liquidity trap.

Bottom Line

In the liquidity race, the sell side should be a step ahead of the buy side, but recently it does not seem to be using this benefit to its advantage. When it stretches the liquidity band and/or the balance-sheet band, and tries to overreach for, say, market share or earnings, either band can snap back. When it does, the sell side stumbles; it falls a step behind the buy side.

I call that a fall from grace.

The King

There is an aphorism in the business world that has become so widely used that it's now a cliché: "Cash is king."

While this phrase may sound trite, no one I know on Wall Street disputes its accuracy or relevance. Cash, or should I say capital, is the lifeblood of every business. A company's growth, even survival, depends on it. This is one of the primary reasons that the sell side was the king of the financial world for so many years: It provided corporations with windows on capital or—to use the more technical term—*liquidity*.

Companies are always keen for fresh capital to increase their profits and, ultimately, their valuation—whether it's their stock price (if they're publicly traded) or their franchise value (if they're privately held).

Liquidity

"Liquidity, in the financial sense, is a measure of the ease with which one asset can be traded for another. Land . . . is usually considered the least liquid of investments. Alternatively, cash is the most liquid."

Source: John Steele Gordon, *The Great Game.* New York: Scribner, 1999, p. 186.

For a long time, it was impossible for companies to go directly to investors for capital because investors were often fragmented and scattered. Sell-side bankers justified their fees, in part, by being the ones who could coax money from investors, gather it all in one place, and make it available to corporations. They were like the generals of mercenary armies, able to bring together men and materiel—for a price. These investment banking generals are navigating through a very different battlefield in 2008, which I will cover later in the book.

They could have said, "We have the sales relationships, we know where those with money are located, we know who likes to invest in autos or aerospace or technology or whichever industry you are in, and we alone have the wherewithal to make your deal happen."

The investment bankers of the sell side held the keys to the vault—always a good position to be in. In this vault was access to the public and private markets, as well as the sell side's own capital, which the sell side used to create liquidity that, in turn, was used to hold sway over the buy side.

And these investment bankers had—and have—additional powers at their command. The brains, brawn, and capital to create secondary markets were theirs. They knew, better than anyone else, which investors held which stocks and bonds, and they had relationships with many of them. They understood the markets best, had the skills needed to value companies, and knew how various types of issues were traded. They had the sophistication and institutional structure required to raise money for virtually every type of company, using any type of asset class.

Sounds good, right? Wrong. And we can thank liquidity for that.

In this Battle for Wall Street, liquidity has played a major role. Historically, the sell side was a bridge to investors' capital. But with greater liquidity, the buy side has been able to gather an investor capital base that was unthinkable in the past.

Hedge Fund

"An aggressively managed portfolio of investments that uses advanced investment strategies such as leverage, long, short, and derivative positions in both domestic and international markets with the goal of generating high returns (either in an absolute sense or over a specified market benchmark)."

Source: Investopedia, www.investopedia .com/terms/h/hedgefund.asp.

For example, a half dozen guys could set up shop in Greenwich, Manhattan, or wherever, pull out their electronic Rolodexes, make some calls to moneyed folk they know, and raise hundreds of millions of dollars or more to start a hedge fund. Not that long ago, such an enterprise would have been impossible.

What was also at one time unthinkable—explosive hedge fund growth—is today a fact. In the last 20 years, the number of hedge funds has grown from 100 to approximately 10,000, and their assets under management have gone from $20 billion to several trillion dollars.[12] That's a lot of hedge funds and a lot of assets; thank you, liquidity.

As an example of how active—and important—hedge funds have become, there was a time when investment bankers, underwriting securities, refused to allocate part of their offerings to hedge funds because these funds were considered to be hot money, "flippers," rather than long-term players. Today, the investment bankers are singing a different tune: one of their first phone calls is to the hedge funds.

Bottom Line

The rise of hedge funds to their current pinnacle of prominence is due, in part, to the expansion of liquidity and the buy side's embrace of it, as well as its ability to use it to its advantage. There's more to liquidity than just the rise of hedge funds.

Long Live the King

Liquidity creates progeny. Collateralized mortgage obligations (CMOs) are an example. Before CMOs, commercial banks typically handled mortgages. Now, mortgages are sliced and diced into tranches (single stages within a series of staged investments) based on different risk and yield levels. This has had the effect of increasing the variety of risks and yields associated with mortgage investing.[13]

These new levels led to an expanded number of investors. More investors means more money, which increases liquidity. We're dealing with circularity here: Liquidity creates new products, and new products create more liquidity.

A second example of liquidity is dark pools. They match buyers and sellers in ways where neither knows the other's identity. This creates liquidity where it previously didn't exist. Investors are more willing to become players when they have the shield of anonymity—and the more players, the more liquidity.

Is the expansion of liquidity seen in the past decade or so likely to continue? Well, liquidity has always waxed and waned to some degree.

During my career, I've seen liquidity go through various cycles. The 1980s had a lot of it, until the stock market crash of October 1987, when liquidity contracted. It recovered, only to be sent into a reversal with the start of the first Gulf War in 1990, when it again went into a restrained mode. It loosened up again, and for the rest of the 1990s, liquidity was quite plentiful. But when the Internet bubble burst in 2000, liquidity went into a contraction phase again, then returned to an expansionary track until the credit meltdown of 2007.

That's one too many liquidity downturns for an old-timer like me.

Dark Pools

"A slang term that refers to the trading volume created from institutional orders, which are unavailable to the public. The bulk of dark pool liquidity is represented by block trades facilitated away from the central exchanges. Also referred to as the 'upstairs market.' The dark pool gets its name because details of these trades are concealed from the public, clouding the transactions like murky water. Some traders that use a strategy based on liquidity feel that dark pool liquidity should be publicized."

Source: Investopedia, www.investopedia.com/terms/d/dark_pool_liquidity.asp.

Bottom Line

The credit crunch of 2007–2008 showed that liquidity can contract dramatically and swiftly. But, because of the factors I've cited above, I have to say that the expansion of liquidity is permanent.

The globalization of the world economy has made it dramatically easier for investors around the world to get in the game. The more participants, the more money floats around, looking for investments to latch onto. This new army of investors is opening the battle to many new fronts.

Case Study: BlackRock—Liquidity as Friend

In 1988, a sell-sider named Larry Fink cofounded a management firm called Blackstone Financial, now called BlackRock. At First Boston (now Credit Suisse), Fink was instrumental in the development of mortgage-backed securities, which were sold to investors. Understanding the value proposition of these securities, he crossed the Street, became a buy-sider, and marketed these securities directly to investors.

Fink also has an eye for human talent, and the BlackRock team that joined him was like the roster of baseball's annual All-Star game— superstars, every one of them.

Back in 1988, where did that All-Star team come from? One place was Fink's former sell-side firm. One of them was Rob Kapito from the mortgage trading desk.[14] When Fink told Kapito he was leaving Credit Suisse (and had not yet asked Kapito to join his team), Kapito reportedly asked, "Where are we going?" That's trust. Also on the team was Barbara Novick[15] from structured products, and Ben Golub,[16] who recognized early the importance of financial technology. One of the keys to BlackRock's success is that, 20 years later as I write this book, all of these stars are still working alongside Fink.

Closed End Fund

"A fund that has a fixed amount of shares outstanding, unlike mutual funds, which are open-ended (allow new shares to be purchased). Closed-end funds behave more like stocks because they trade on an exchange and the price is determined by market demand after an initial public offering process. Closed-end funds can trade below their net asset value or above it."

Source: http://mutualfunds.about.com/od/glossaries/g/closed_end.htm

In addition, some members of the original BlackRock team hailed from the sell-side firm Lehman Brothers. (I will discuss a few of those All-Stars later in the book.)

Keep in mind that, when it opened for business in 1988, BlackRock had no assets and no buy-side track record to speak of. Fink and his team went to the sell side to raise investor capital—assets under management— in the form of closed-end funds.

The investment bankers, always hungry for fees, agreed to underwrite a fund for Fink. And then a second fund. And then a third. And more.

Instead of the sell side's salespeople selling, say, IBM to their customers, they sold the BlackRock family of investment funds. It was a classic case of the buy side's leveraging the sell side's liquidity—access to financial markets—to fuel its growth.

All of this was for one asset class: fixed-income mortgages.[17] Fink and his team understood the product and the technology behind it— but also understood the value of the sell side.

The result? As of December 31, 2007, BlackRock had over $1.3 trillion in assets under management.[18] That's a lot of money by any definition. I would say that BlackRock's success is one of Wall Street's great stories.

Interestingly, the sell side—namely, Merrill Lynch, now owned by Bank of America—sold its disappointing money management business (Merrill Lynch Investment Management) to BlackRock, in return for a 49 percent interest in the combined entity.[19] As I write this, the BlackRock investment is one of the truly bright spots in Merrill's portfolio.

The sell side, Merrill, looking to the buy side, BlackRock, as a partner for investment performance and returns? That's not the Wall Street I joined in the early 1980s.

Case Study: AIG—Liquidity as Foe

Before the credit crunch of 2007–2008, who would have thought the insurance giant AIG would face liquidity issues? Who would have imagined that given its size (market capitalization of $180 billion), AIG would fall under the knife of the mortgage debacle?

But fall they did. They fell into the hands of the U.S. government.

In September 2008, after severe losses and liquidity issues that drove it to the brink of collapse, AIG accepted a federal bailout that would give the company an approximately $85 billion line of credit, and would give the government about an 80 percent equity stake in AIG.[20]

Why did the Federal Reserve (Fed) step up with a lifeline?

Credit Default Swap

"A swap designed to transfer the credit exposure of fixed-income products between parties. The buyer of a credit swap receives credit protection, whereas the seller of the swap guarantees the creditworthiness of the product. By doing this, the risk of default is transferred from the holder of the fixed-income security to the seller of the swap."

Source: Investopedia, www.investopedia .com/terms/c/creditdefaultswap.asp.

The Fed determined a disorderly failure of AIG could create havoc in the global financial markets. To prevent this chaos and ensure an orderly process, the Fed provided a loan to cover AIG's liquidity needs until the company could sell enough assets to fill its capital hole.

Why was AIG in this precarious capital position?

Collateral Call

"Collateral is assets provided to secure an obligation. A more recent development is collateralization arrangements used to secure repo, securities lending, and derivatives transactions.

"Under such arrangement, a party who owes an obligation to another party posts collateral—typically consisting of cash or securities—to secure the obligation. In the event that the party defaults on the obligation, the secured party may seize the collateral. In this context, collateral is sometimes called margin.

"In a typical collateral arrangement, the secured obligation is periodically marked-to-market, and the collateral is adjusted to reflect changes in value."

Source: www.riskglossary.com/link/collateral.htm.

AIG was a provider of insurance guarantees on risky credit default swaps tied to the mortgage market. As the credit crisis of 2007–2008 intensified, AIG was caught in a liquidity death spiral. Those spiraling actions played out like this: AIG went one way on credit default swaps, and with the subprime crisis raging, the market went the other way. Not a good scenario for AIG.

As the credit crisis intensified, AIG incurred write-downs and losses. As a result, Moody's and Standard & Poor's (S&P) downgraded the company's credit ratings. Those credit reductions triggered collateral calls, and AIG was forced to post more capital.

At this point, counterparties (the other parties to these financial transactions) did not want to take AIG's risk. They wanted capital. AIG did not have the capital and could not get access to capital in time to offset the impairment of their assets. They had a severe liquidity issue.

Over its fateful last two weeks as an independent company, AIG's capital issues grew geometrically. According to an industry observer, during that time, AIG's capital requirements skyrocketed to the tune of tens of billions of dollars.

Why didn't AIG—an insurance company—recognize the probability of blowing up if the rating agencies downgraded them from AAA to A (S&P) and AAA to A2 (Moody's)?

I would suspect the answer is that they predicted the probability of a credit downgrade was a low event. But why take even a minimal chance, knowing that it could lead to catastrophic risk?

That risk took their stock down from dinner for two ($70 a share) to less than a Manhattan subway token ($1.50 a share).

The AIG story is rife with ironies. First, the company turned to the Fed after unsuccessful negotiations with the one and only Warren Buffett of Berkshire Hathaway[21]—the same Warren Buffett who invested in Goldman Sachs and General Electric at the height of the credit crisis of 2007–2008. As I write this book, Buffett may still be interested in "in acquiring a couple of AIG's assets depending on what the company was willing to sell."[22]

The second irony is that has been reported that the former AIG chief executive, Maurice Greenberg, would like the chance to bid on the assets that are going to be sold as AIG repays its multibillion-dollar bailout loan from the federal government.[23]

The third irony is that going into the credit crisis, AIG was the world's largest insurer. The AIG left standing at the end of the credit crisis will not be the same—it will be significantly smaller.

AIG—and for that matter, any financial institution falling on the battlefield during the credit crisis—is victim to the bullet called liquidity.

Implications

As I write this, a debate is going on over liquidity. Financing of commercial deals has pretty much come to a stop. Commercial lending has shriveled up. So is the credit crisis due to a lack of liquidity or because the credit window has virtually closed for the time being? This makes for an interesting debate in financial war rooms.

I would suggest it is because the credit window has closed for the time being. To illustrate my point, look no further than at a number of sell-side players, who in early 2008 had aggregate balance-sheet write-downs of approximately $85 billion.[24] Yet, in less than six months, virtually all of it had been replaced by raising new capital. Before the growth in liquidity, making up that sort of loss would have taken years. In the early stages of the subprime crisis, it could be done in a matter of months. In battle terms, this was a definite win for the sell-side team.

Most of the money came from players who, in the last half of the 2000s, became large enough to make a difference—sovereign wealth funds (foreign-owned investment entities). In the first part of 2008, we saw how much liquidity was available and how readily financial firms could get their hands on it. That much liquidity—and that kind of access to it—was new.

Shutting down the credit window, for the most part, has led to shocks within the system. Management and shareholders alike have to ask if the best and brightest on Wall Street really know what they're doing. Do they understand the instruments they've created? Do they have proper management systems in place? Do they understand the risks involved?

As we know, history repeats itself. We've had liquidity and credit crises before. In the 1980s, Japanese banks went crazy buying things, while the Nikkei average dropped about 65 percent during the 1990s, as a result.[25] Too much liquidity led to silly decisions, which led to a major fall. Sound familiar? Who would have imagined that too much liquidity could be your enemy?

What are the lessons to be learned here? Well, we're playing with more risk, which is good as long as we truly understand that risk.

What may not be as good (and here, history repeats itself yet again) is that Wall Street may once again overplay its liquidity hand when the devastating credit crisis of 2007–2008 is only a memory. "Why not?" it asks itself. "Meaningful pools of liquidity are out there in the form of petrodollars and sovereign wealth funds."

Vegas is known to give its high rollers, or "whales," a few extra chips to play with. Do the whales take the new liquidity to the checkout window? Not really. Do the whales overplay their bets? Most likely. The whales on the sell side could well behave the same way—focusing on the next set of gambles rather than future safety.

If history repeats itself, the pain will be worse than it is today—which is even worse than it was during the credit crunch of the early 1990s. That's because we will be playing with ever more liquidity. As the dollar figures become increasingly astronomical, the stakes get higher, and the losses are harder to bear.

If this scenario of repeating crises plays out, and the sell side continues to overplay its balance-sheet hand and toss liquidity around like popcorn, I see the Battle for Wall Street leaning more and more in favor of the buy side.

The buy side has time on its side. It can sit back and wait for opportunities, and can commit capital when it wants, not when the market wants. The buy side, for the most part, is also not tied to the timing of—or held captive to—public earnings. And, finally, the buy side provides capital to itself, in a sense, while the sell side provides capital to its clients.

This entire scenario will not just favor the buy side, but could further widen the gap between the two sides—which could lead to any number of sell-side firms disappearing. Bear Stearns or Lehman Brothers, anyone?

Battle Victorious: **Buy side.**

Chapter 2

Financial Information in a Digital Age

I t's time for a pop quiz.

Have you ever heard of the sell-side firm Dellsher Investment Company? My guess is that only a handful of you—in fact, only a handful of the most experienced Wall Street players—will have heard of this company. (If you answered correctly, give yourself 10 points.)

Next question: Who is Leo Melamed? This time, I'm guessing that most of you—and virtually all of the most experienced Wall Street players—will be in the know. Melamed, after all, is referred to as the godfather of financial futures and, arguably, one of the visionaries behind today's global exchanges.

But in case you were unable to answer these questions, let's step back in time for a moment—to the 1980s. Leo Melamed owned a small futures trading company called Dellsher Investment Company. In 1991, he sold a majority interest to Mitsui Taiyo Kobe Bank of Tokyo. [1]

This deal was emblematic of its time: a Japanese financial institution investing in a U.S. financial institution. Back in the 1980s and early 1990s, American financial institutions were selling minority or majority stakes to Japanese financial companies.

At that time, it was the Japanese players who had the deep pockets—the pools of liquidity. Back then, they were what sovereign wealth funds were to U.S. and European financial institutions for most of 2007–2008. (In subsequent chapters, I'll discuss sovereign wealth funds at some length and touch upon Japanese banks in their second tour of financial investments in late 2008.)

Sound familiar? During the credit crisis that began in 2007, numerous American (and European) financial institutions went looking for liquidity abroad, and found it with sovereign wealth funds and other foreign investors. The names of liquidity players may change—but not the waves of liquidity hitting the financial beaches.

One of the firms coming ashore by riding on the waves of liquidity was Mitsui. What was this Japanese firm buying when it bought Dellsher? At the time, the *New York Times* reported, "Mitsui will execute trades to hedge against losses on its investments."[2] Put another way, the Japanese bank wanted to take advantage of Dellsher's trading acumen.

Was it buying financial earnings? Not really. Earnings, I suspect, were fairly small.

Was it buying a strategic franchise? Not really. Dellsher was small and hardly a household name.

It was buying, in part, a "body of information." It was buying one person's insights, one person's access to information about the financial markets, specifically the futures markets.

It was buying Leo Melamed. Smart move or necessary move?

In the early stages of my career, market information was not readily available. One way to obtain such information was to acquire companies like Dellsher, or should I say, acquire Melamed's body of information. These were necessary moves then, but not today. With the emergence of technology, the need to buy companies just to access market information has dissipated.

But back in the days of Leo Melamed, information, one of the big guns of Wall Street, was then firmly in the hands of the sell side. What did the sell side do with that weapon? It sold it to buy side firms, who would pay wagons full of money for such information, which included market color, market pricing . . . market anything.

Another difference between then and now is that information used to be human driven, not technologically driven. People like Melamed had "a feel" for a market, an intuitive understanding that was unique and valuable. Not everyone had it. Today, thanks to technology, information is there for everyone, sell side and buy side alike.

Bottom Line

Technology gave the underdog access to a playing field it never had access to before. Think of this as akin to what technology, specifically the Internet, did for smaller retailers. Such companies could, for fairly small sums of money, create web sites that were as attractive, slick, and compelling as those of the largest retailers.

Likewise on Wall Street. Technology leveled the playing field between the buy and sell sides. Both sides could now sport the big gun that is information. Information now flows as easily to one side of Wall Street as to the other.

As a result, there is no information advantage any more—information is a weapon used by both sides. Therefore, the winner will be determined by which side uses it more strategically.

Broader, Cheaper, Faster

I don't want to sound like some graying geezer of Wall Street—I'm a Baby Boomer, and not that old by most accounts—but in my quarter century on the Street, the changes I've seen have been profound: namely, the power shift moving from sell side to buy side, thanks in part to financial technology.

For the buy side, financial technology was like Rip Van Winkle waking up to a new world after 20 years of deep slumber.

When I was starting out on Wall Street, information wasn't frequently refreshed. Days, even weeks, would pass before certain information was updated. You could spend a relaxing week or two in Europe, come back to work, and not see much of a difference.

Information was segmented by country, by company, by market. It was hard to link, it was hard to make connections, and it was hard, if not impossible, to bring it all together. That's why we generally saw information only from a U.S. perspective. London, Frankfurt, Tokyo, and Hong Kong weren't just physically removed from Wall Street—they were worlds away psychologically.

Information was also not as broad in scope as it is today—much of it wasn't available to anyone, even on the sell side. Other than raw trading information, like volume and price, information was cloaked in mystery. Who owned what may have been known on a piecemeal basis, but it really wasn't known in aggregate.

And what information existed was not readily accessible. My information sat in notebooks that lined my bookshelves. It was a paper world, and I lived in the middle of it.

But that has now all changed. Today, we live in an age of instant access, where great amounts of information are immediately available at the push of a button. When this rise in technology found its way into the financial world, it served as the powder keg that further sparked this epic Battle for Wall Street.

Nasdaq, especially, was key. With its creation in 1971, suddenly, there was a computerized system that allowed traders to instantaneously see markets, the market makers, the market's pricing, and how these evolved during the course of a trading day.[3] As a result, the buy side no longer had to call up the sell side—its broker—for a quote. It was all on the screen in front of the trader.

Nasdaq's computer screen then evolved to allow screen-based execution; you could trade from your desktop machine.[4] This only heated up the battle more! Electronic trading was now taking place away from traditional floor-based trading. What used to happen in a large, noisy room with traders doing face-to-face deals now was happening online, anonymously, and simultaneously in many different places in the United States and around the world. In Chapter 7, I'll drill down into the world of electronic versions of exchanges.

The emergence of technology on Wall Street also enabled people to see information from a global perspective. If you want to, you can access information about January's Asian trade flows in February. Twenty years ago, it would never have occurred to me that access to such distant and obscure data would be so readily and quickly available. Today it is, to the delight of both the sell and buy sides.

And we don't just have access to more information today: The information we have, such as price discovery, is much faster—no surprise, then, that it has more value. Like bananas, information has a short shelf life. It starts to ripen and smell and lose its desirability pretty quickly. The more rapidly information comes to us, the more useful it is. And the more rapidly we can use it to our advantage, the more value it has.

Just ask the buy-side trader where the value is. The buy-side trader now has the advantage of execution speed at his disposal, and those buy-side bananas have very little if any shelf life. Faster access to information has helped level the playing field between the buy and sell sides.

Again thanks to technology, while the information has become more global, useful, and valuable, it has also become cheaper. Both the buy and sell sides used to rely on small armies of analysts earning hefty incomes.

Now, there are off-the-shelf information software packages and subscription services like Bloomberg that provide enormous quantities of information to the buy and sell sides alike at a small fraction of the cost of an in-house staff. The buy side can only smile, knowing that technology has not only broadened and deepened the amount of data available, but allowed it to mine the data more profitably. This, too, helped level the playing field.

A third reason for the buy side to smile is that technology has created a cottage industry of entrepreneurs: a number of old soldiers from the 1990s and 2000s who have reinvented themselves. They now provide technology tools, services, and entirely new exchanges (of the virtual, electronic kind), including more cost-effective, efficient trading products and platforms.

This cottage industry, which is based on providing technology-based products and services, has been partly fueled and financed by private-equity firms. (In Chapter 6, I'll take a closer look at the entrepreneurs and private-equity firms behind this cottage industry.)

These new trading products, platforms, and assets have been marketed to the buy side—great news for them, because now they don't need the same costly infrastructure as the sell side. Thus, these financial entrepreneurs have leveled the playing field.

Bottom Line

There's no question that broader, cheaper, and faster technology has leveled the battleground for the buy and sell sides alike. I would suspect, however, that the buy side today views that playing field as tilted in its favor.

Both Sides of the Battlefield

Algorithm

"A well-defined procedure to solve a problem. The study of algorithms is a fundamental area of computer science. In writing a computer program to solve a problem, a programmer expresses in a computer language an algorithm that solves the problem, thereby turning the algorithm into a computer program."

Source: Sci-Tech Encyclopedia, www.answers.com/topic/algorithm?cat =biz-fin.

You probably thought the algorithms you learned in high school algebra had no value. Well, some folks are making millions today by using algorithms. The sell side and buy side have both embraced algorithmic trading. During the past few years, such trading has gained momentum and is today a major part of the trader's arsenal.

How major a part? A pretty big one. For example, an estimated 71 percent of fund managers and 93 percent of hedge funds used algorithms in 2006.[5]

Algorithmic trading is not just a U.S. story. The Deutsche Boerse says that about 40 percent of equity turnover in Germany is accounted for by algorithmic traders.[6]

It looks like algorithmic trading has become more than a niche strategy: it's a global phenomenon.

The sell side and buy side are equal opportunity users of algorithmic trading; it is a global phenomenon that crosses both sides of the Battle for Wall Street. The arsenals of traders on both side of the battlefield are filled with algorithms. Algorithms have become the trading weapon of choice, rather than human-dependent trading. Why? Because algorithmic trading provides two valuable benefits—speed and liquidity.

Thanks to algorithmic trading, the pace of trading has increased. Any new information that enters the market is picked up more quickly—and responded to faster than ever before. Reaction time of algorithms and the traders who manage them is now blindingly fast. Milliseconds fast. And if milliseconds are not fast enough, there have been reports of trading firms paying to have their computers located physically next to markets to help speed up trades. We can now talk about real estate in terms of both location and speed.

Algorithmic Trading

"Algorithmic trading is based on mathematical instructions, or algorithms, programmed into a computer that decides how and when to trade a stock."

Source: Tara Perkins, "Program Trading Goes Mainstream," *Toronto Star* (Canada), February 2, 2007; accessed via the Internet.

A December 2006 *Wall Street Journal* article cited dozens of firms, including Citadel Derivatives Group and a brokerage unit of JPMorgan, which moved their computers to buildings close to markets to facilitate this kind of split-second trading.[7]

In addition to speeding up trade, algorithms also improve the market's liquidity. They search markets and track where executions occur, and send out requests to traders willing to participate in their trades.

These algorithms, using real-time rather than historical data, can continually test a market and balance the price of a trade with the impact of that trade on the market. They adjust on the fly to maximize the price and minimize market affect.

The algorithms used by Wall Street search for liquidity and find it in many nontraditional, obscure corners of the market. Such liquidity can be found in dark pools, electronic trading platforms like BATS Trading,[8] and block trading networks such as ITG's Posit and Pipeline Trading Systems.[9]

Algorithmic trading and these alternative sources of liquidity are critical pieces in the Battle for Wall Street. Not that long ago, when the buy side needed liquidity, it went to the sell side firms while relying on the established exchanges to provide a marketplace.

Now the buy side can bypass both the sell-side bankers and such institutions as the New York Stock Exchange (NYSE) and find its own liquidity and markets.

The sell-side traders have their own motivation to use algorithmic trading. They are also looking to improve trade execution.

Thus, algorithmic trading has proven to be a good friend to both sides. As a result, neither side wins the algorithmic trading battle from a technology perspective.

But there is a human perspective, too. If one side has an advantage over the other, it relates to the people who create the algorithms. If one side can attract better programmers, analysts, and mathematicians—a more effective army behind their algorithms—then it could gain an advantage.

At this time, I am unaware that either side has such an advantage.

Bottom Line

Neither side has a notable advantage, either human or technological. In the Battle for Wall Street, algorithmic trading is a draw.

Front-End Sale, Back-End Execution

The current access to financial information via technology has numerous implications for the Battle for Wall Street. Not only has it taken away the advantage the sell side once had, but it gives the buy side an edge. Information is out there for the taking in the battlefield. But it appears the buy side is in a better position to use it more effectively today than the sell side.

That's because technology doesn't just make information more accessible, but speeds up our access to it. The buy side is more likely to take more advantage of this new speed than the sell side, given its mindset. The sell side could be referred to as a marketing machine. It looks for services to sell from which it can earn fees and commissions. Their mentality is, as it has been for decades, that information is a product to sell.

Not so for the buy side. This side of the Street does not rely on selling information or viewed information as a product. It uses information as a tool to put to work on its own behalf. Information is actionable, not salable; it is a tool that helps the buy side make money, not a commodity to sell. Thus, the ever-increasing speed of financial technology plays into the hands of the buy side a little more than the sell side.

Given the depth and speed of information available to Wall Street today, we should be better able to use this information—and we should better understand the risks, the markets, and the companies we are investing in. We should have a more profound appreciation of the assets we are investing in, too.

This seems to be lost on the sell side. After all, it's the sell side, not the buy side, we think of regarding the unappreciated risks associated with the subprime mortgage crisis of 2007–2008.

Why? Did they not effectively use the information at hand to calibrate risk? Maybe yes . . . maybe no. Did they ignore the information and think that the credit crisis was not in the cards? Maybe yes . . . maybe no. Did they see the high returns the buy side was raking in (as well as seeking high returns for themselves) and push the fee envelope? Maybe yes . . . maybe no.

See, yes or no means little to the buy side. What matters—what always matters—is performance, and the buy side has outperformed the sell side in the subprime crisis.

Bottom Line

I would say that the sell side and buy side, for the most part, use financial information in two very distinct ways. The sell side is a market-driven machine, crisscrossing the battlefield, looking for buyers with the mind-set that information is salable. The buy side is an idea-driven machine, crisscrossing the battlefield, looking for undervalued and turnaround situations with the mind-set that information is actionable.

Case Study: Michael R. Bloomberg— Democratization of Information

Before Michael Bloomberg's rise to political stardom as mayor of New York City, he was a major player on Wall Street. An indication of how well he did on the Street can be found on his balance sheet.

According to Forbes's 2007 ranking of the 400 wealthiest Americans, Bloomberg is the 25th-richest person in the country, with an estimated fortune of $11.5 billion.[10] He did not amass such wealth by being mayor of New York, that's for sure.

Bloomberg became phenomenally wealthy because he was, in the truest sense of the term, a visionary. He saw what was needed on Wall Street and created the means to provide it. What Wall Street players needed was information that was accessible, fast, complete, accurate, and actionable. As such, he was an important part of the Battle for Wall Street.

Bloomberg started a company, called Bloomberg LP, which created a desktop device called—what else?—the Bloomberg Terminal. This terminal helped alter the balance of power between the buy and sell sides. Through his adept use of technology, Bloomberg provided access to an enormous wealth of useful information to anyone who wanted it (and was willing to pay).

Bloomberg's Wall Street career began at Salomon Brothers, now part of Citigroup, which was a leading trading house with proprietary data, information, and technology. There, he became a general partner and head of equity trading and sales.[11]

In 1981, Salomon was purchased by Phibro Corporation, and Bloomberg left the firm with a hefty severance package reported to be $10 million.[12]

While he was at Salomon, a trading powerhouse in its day, I suspect that Bloomberg became a fan of the sources and uses of information—big enough of a fan, you could say, to start an information terminal of analytics, data services, and news named after himself.[13] Hats off to Merrill Lynch for agreeing to buy 20 Bloomberg Terminals in 1982[14] and seeing Bloomberg as a future navigator of financial information.

In 1990, Bloomberg expanded his offerings to include a financial news service now called Bloomberg News.[15] It provides business news as well as news about politics and sports. The company also publishes magazines and books and produces radio and television programming. Bloomberg LP now has terminals on desktops throughout the world. When Bloomberg began it, did he envision that his financial information portal would one day be such a status symbol?

And why has Bloomberg, the company, been so successful?

Well, Bloomberg was a trader, and he understood what traders wanted and needed.[16] One could surmise that he and his team built their offerings around just that. Their data was state of the art, as was their technology and customer service. The information they provided was targeted to what those on Wall Street really needed. It was, and is, information they can use and make money from. The Bloomberg service was, I assume, created by traders for traders.

It also helps that Bloomberg owns the content (information/data) and the machines.[17] If you try to replace your Bloomberg, chances are you will need more than one provider to give you all the information your terminal provided. Bloomberg turned its subscribers into junkies—they just can't live without their terminals.

The Bloomberg Terminal has become a portal to financial information and a tool for trading. Information that was once available only to the sell side is now available to anyone willing to be a Bloomberg subscriber.

Michael Bloomberg, a true visionary, saw the value of information and the power of technology to distribute that information. The result? A more even balance between the power of the buy and sell sides.

Research Goes Buy Side

Let's take a closer look at the effects of technology on research, as there has been a dramatic shift in sell-side and buy-side research. Historically, research (research analysts' reports and analyses of public companies), like market information, was once the captive of the sell side. Driven by the sell side's sales machine, research was sold to the buy side. In the Battle for Wall Street, this wasn't really a battle, but a romp. The sell side was the clear and consistent winner.

Then what happened? Inherent conflict. Who was the research for? Was it there to provide independent, unbiased advice to the investor, or was it designed to push product? We saw with the implosion of such companies as WorldCom and Enron in the early part of this decade, and the touting of Internet companies in the late 1990s, that the beneficiaries of research were not necessarily investors.[18]

The collapse of Internet and scandal-ridden companies resulted in actions by investors and regulators that led to the sell-side firms becoming more regulated. Because new laws required Wall Street firms to separate their research from their investment banking, research became a less lucrative career; it was no longer generating the information that could create deals. As a result, the pot of gold for the analysts became tarnished.

The research guys and gals, not surprisingly, were unhappy with the sell side's economics.

At the same time, the buy side was experiencing an improvement in its economics. The financial industry was exploding, not just domestically but globally. The financial pie was bigger, and the buy side was taking bigger and bigger bites of it. And the dollars upon dollars poured in.

But it wasn't just the dollars. The buy side endured less regulation, which provided buy-siders with a different job lifestyle than those on the sell side with its greater government oversight.

This freedom was fortuitous because it helped the buy side with idea generation—identifying and creating high-profit investment opportunities. The buy side was able to come up with more ideas because it now had more people attuned to generating ideas, namely, the sell-side folks it had attracted.

And the buy side needed more ideas to keep up with its client base. This client base, which included pension funds and wealthy individuals, now had access to more information, invested in more diverse assets, and thought globally. For example, global gross assets in hedge funds went from $30 billion to trillions of dollars in a few short years.[19]

The buy side couldn't stand still. Its clients wanted more and better ideas, and the buy side, by hiring former sell-side researchers, responded with better and better research.

This pendulum swing regarding research from the sell to the buy side has been quite dramatic, and it has the sell side trying to respond by reworking its model. Since they are losing the research battle, the sell side has had to rethink its model.

And there are signs that it's making the shift. For instance, a number of analysts on the sell side have become a lot less interested in chasing brand name stocks with recommendations, as they historically did. Instead, they are looking for unique plays and anomalies in the market, which they can exploit.

Good news for the investor. The sell side is going deeper into its analysis, and the investor is ultimately better served with more and better information.

Bottom Line

With the sell-side research folks walking across the Street, the buy side built up its own research capabilities and developed more idea generation, thus becoming less dependent on the sell side for information.

Less dependency and less dialogue with the buy side translates into diminished sell-side fees. What is the sell side to do? Try a new strategy. And the sell side is doing just that and becoming more of a business adviser. In fact, it is selling a service to help the buy side develop its own research. Why would the sell side help the buy side in this way?

It's the old story: If you can't beat 'em, join 'em.

Researcher Goes Entrepreneurial—Arming Both Sides

Another factor helping the buy side win the financial technology battle is the emergence of independent research shops. These might be considered allies of the buy side, though their services are available to anyone willing to pay.

Rather than being part of a large sell-side firm, these independent companies focus only on research. They differ from the research departments of sell-side firms in another important way—they specialize in one or a few specific industries, rather than covering a wide array of industries. As the sell side has shed some of its research capabilities, these entrepreneurs have picked up the slack.

In the old days, analysts and the research departments of the sell-side major brokerage firms tended to cover many industries with trained analysts. The new specialists are much more narrowly focused on one sector and have become true

(continued)

experts in their chosen markets. For example, a shop that focuses on health care might hire physicians and former regulators, or people with extensive technical expertise and experience, as research contributors instead of sell-side Wall Street analysts who never worked in those industries.

This is more good news for the investor—institutional and individual—who is now being armed with in-depth information.

Source: Rick Wayman, "The Changing Role of Equity Research." www.investopedia.com/articles/analyst/03/031803.asp. and Jon Merriman and William J. Febbo. "Due Diligence 2.0." *The Deal.* February 14, 2008.

Individual Investor Goes Buy Side

There's a direct link between the importance of the individual (also called the "retail") investor and the jockeying for position between the sell side and the buy side.

The sell side services two distinct sets of investors—an institutional base and a retail base.

For the longest time, the retail base was less interesting—these folks were historically low-fee generators. Of primary interest to the sell side was the institutional base, which included pension funds, insurance companies, and the like, who used the full spectrum of sell-side services and kept coming back for more.

This started to change in the 1980s, when we had a long bull market, a buildup of liquidity, low interest rates on money market funds, and the popularity of 401(k) retirement plans (where individuals could choose where to put their retirement savings). The result: Individual investors began flooding the stock market. This excitement of individual investors playing the market and making their own decisions increased the public's thirst for information.

We can see this with the development of online brokerages, CNBC, Bloomberg Television, and Fox Business Network—all of which were created, in part, to cater to the individual investor and provide that investor with information. Such information, now so freely available, was not available to these investors before the 1980s, and only in the last decade or so has it become really widely available.

As a retail customer, when you're armed with information, what happens? You control your destiny. You are not tied to a brand—you're free to choose. The fact that your sell-side broker has been your broker forever is not nearly as compelling as it once was. You're looking for performance.

Price becomes less important because you are now sophisticated enough to know that it's more important to have good performance than low price. Hedge funds keep attracting assets, not because they are cheap (they are, in fact, very expensive), but because a number of them produce better risk-adjusted returns. Choice and performance, to a degree, replaced brand and price, which is not the best of news for the sell side.

The sell side takes a financial hit because all this leads to mobility. The individual investor now has no need to stay with the sell side. The high-net-worth investor, in particular, is able to move between the buy and sell sides.

In fact, such customers are no longer an afterthought to the sell side, which is aggressively pursuing them with in-house hedge funds and other alternative investment products.

To keep up with the individual investor, who is hungry for information and knowledge, the buy side has also had to become a conduit of information so that when investors call for information, it has it.

Bottom Line

The sell side and the buy side are trying to win the hearts and minds of the individual investor. Today, individual investors have a choice, and with that choice, they'll play a pivotal role in the Battle for Wall Street.

Case Study: Barclays—Ahead of the Curve in Financial Technology and Information

In the 1990s, farsighted firms like Barclays, a giant British bank, saw that a younger, more sophisticated investor base was developing. It anticipated the need to align with these new clients, and realized that financial technology and information would play an important role in this alignment.

As investors began opting more and more for choice over brand loyalty, the old sell-side business model began to unravel. Instead of focusing on domestic products and traditional investment strategies, the sell side had to accommodate the new demand for international products and those with various levels of yield and risk.

The savviest sell-side CEOs got a jump on their rivals by embracing new financial technologies. Today, their firms have gone still further, and function as hybrid players, straddling the increasingly hazy line between buy and sell sides.

Let's take a closer look at Barclays.

Barclays had been a traditional sell-side British retail banking operation before it became a multifaceted force in the global arena. Building up an array of innovative products to offer to a new breed of investors, the bank began to provide value-added services for buy-side customers and positioned itself as the anti–hedge fund. It was born of the sell side, but took advantage of its access to markets to offer index funds, exchange-traded funds (ETFs)[20], and tech-driven mutual funds[21] to an expanding buy-side client base.[22]

Exchange-Traded Funds

"A fund that tracks an index but can be traded like a stock. ETFs always bundle together the securities that are in an index. Investors can do just about anything with an ETF that they can do with a normal stock, such as short selling. Because ETFs are traded on stock exchanges, they can be bought and sold at any time during the day (unlike most mutual funds)."

Source: "Exchange Traded Fund (ETF)." Investopedia, 2008; www.investopedia.com/terms/e/etf.asp.

My understanding is that it took mutual funds, which traditionally were actively managed by people—real human beings who made decisions and choices based on reasoning—and transformed them into a technology-driven asset class.[23]

Barclays had the foresight to leverage its distribution power to successfully market these tech-centric funds. In the process, it was able to capitalize on the power of being a buy-side player, providing innovative buy-side products while being housed inside a sell-side franchise: the best of both worlds.

Staying ahead of the curve in financial technology and information has its advantages.

As I write this, Barclays can lay claim to being one of the largest asset managers in the world. Not bad.

Case Study: Société Générale Group—Behind the Curve in Financial Technology and Information

If Barclays was ahead of the curve in technology and information, can we say the same for other sell-side banks like Société Générale (SocGen), France's second-largest bank?

As we live through multibillion-dollar subprime losses and an outright failing at a number of these global sell-side institutions, let's not lose sight of SocGen, which in early 2008 reportedly suffered a $7.2 billion market loss due to fraud by a rogue trader. This was in addition to a $3.8 billion loss as a result of the credit crisis.[24]

Regulators say the fraudulent loss was due to the bank's poor controls[25] and that similar acts of deception could occur at other banks. Of course, fraud has occurred elsewhere—perhaps most famously in 1995, when trader Nick Leeson lost $1.3 billion for Barings Bank, a British institution that has been in business since the 1700s. His losses on unauthorized trades caused Barings to collapse. But we have yet to see fraud on a scale that SocGen experienced. It could be called the *Titanic* of fraudulent losses.

Just as there have been movies and books about the *Titanic,* I can see movies and books being made about this monumental fraud. What makes this story fascinating is that the perpetrator, Jerome Kerviel, was no star trader. According to a number of press reports at the time, he went to a middling university, spent much time in the bank's back office, and then moved into trading, where he failed to distinguish himself [26] (that is, until he cost the bank over $7 billion). In fact, the bank's losses were entirely trading losses, as Kiervel seems not to have profited in the least by his trading.

Speculation at the time was that he was an ordinary trader who started taking extraordinary actions,[27] and his lack of experience and savvy did him in. He probably did not realize it, but he was playing with a formula for disaster, because he was betting (using leverage) on exotic instruments,[28] namely futures.

This may work well when the market is moving in your favor. But when the market moves against you, it is easy to be run over, especially if you are not battle-hardened with years of experience, which Kerviel was not. It appears he didn't know what to do when the market took a direction he did not expect, so he kept piling on his bets like a gambler doubling down, and lost big, very big.

The bank's co–chief executive was quoted in the *Wall Street Journal* as saying about Kerviel, "He was mentally weak."[29] My guess is that his personality meant he blended in and was therefore below the radar screen of the bank's managers.[30]

One way to look at this fraud is by focusing on the human element, namely, that the risk managers may have been distracted[31]— they had one eye looking at the bank's $3 billion loss due to the credit crisis, and another looking at the global credit as it played throughout the banking system, and there was no eye left to look at one rogue trader.

Why worry about a trader who was so colorless and seemed to be doing well for the bank? Kerviel has said, according to numerous press accounts, that the bank was happy with his trades for a couple of years because they generated large profits.[32]

But there is also the technology angle to this episode. One could speculate that technology may have been a contributing factor to the length of time the fraud was allowed to continue. Were their computer systems not up to the task of analyzing traders' activities, allowing the safeguards the bank had in place to miss Kerviel's shenanigans?

Is it possible that their in-house technology did not ring the warning bells loud enough to get anyone's attention, and management did not know anything needed to be fixed, so it did nothing?

In fairness to SocGen, questions tossed around on the adequacy of risk managers and technology/risk controls are not just company specific; rather, they are industry-wide in the credit crisis of 2007–2008.

Staying ahead of the curve in financial technology and information, not behind, is where you want to be.

As I write this, the latter half of 2008 is looking better for SocGen—positive third-quarter 2008 results.[33]

Implications

Financial information in the digital age is broader, faster, and cheaper than in the paper age that characterized Wall Street in the early 1990s and before. That is the good news. Not so good is the role of technology in the credit crisis of 2007–2008. There's been a lot of finger pointing as to what went wrong.

Let's keep the conversation going as it relates to technology's role on both sides of the Battle for Wall Street, as the credit crisis showed that much can still go wrong.

1. Will the buy side, in its battle to keep up with and even surpass the sell side, excessively misuse its technological arsenal?

This is a timely question. They have access to new oceans of information. They have new allies—sharp, smart, technology information entrepreneurs—knocking on their door every day with financial innovations. They have increased access to liquidity, through new types of investors. And their bets are larger and riskier than they have ever been before. All these factors may lead the buy side to overplay its technology hand.

However, I have faith in the buy side. I think they will step back, learn from the 2007–2008 credit crunch and its effect both on the sell side and the buy side, see the limitations of technology, and apply human judgment. The buy side will be excited by the promises of technology, but I don't think it will be seduced by them.

2. Will the sell side, in its power struggle with the buy side, retool its technological arsenal?

As opposed to the buy side, which freely uses third-party vendors, sell-siders tend to be wedded to their legacy mainframes and minicomputers, rather than open technology architecture and outside vendors. Think of the sell side as a battleship: It can change direction, but only slowly.

However, I have faith in the sell side and believe if 2007–2008 taught them anything, it is how volatile markets can be. I think they will change. In fact, I think they are already changing and embracing the buy-side world of an open (best-of-breed) technology arsenal.

Battle Victorious: Buy side.

Chapter 3

Prime Brokerage Meeting Hall

The Battle for Wall Street is occurring in the prime brokerage area as much as it is occurring with liquidity, financial information, and other areas covered in this book.

I'm willing to bet that when you think of prime brokers, you think of such sell-side powerhouses as Goldman Sachs and Deutsche Bank to name just two. But what about Furman Selz or Lou Ricciardelli? Have you even heard of either of them?

Most people haven't—but Ricciardelli and the investment banking boutique Furman Selz were early foot soldiers in the front lines of prime brokerage. So if you want a handle on this arena, allow me to introduce you to Ricciardelli, who is affectionately referred to by industry observers as "the father of prime brokerage"—with good reason.

Ricciardelli, in effect, connected the dots. Back in the mid-1970s, he saw the value of sell-side firms' positioning themselves to clear and settle

Prime Broker

"A soldier from the sell side:
a broker that acts as settlement
agent, provides custody for assets,
provides financing for leverage, and
prepares daily account statements
for its clients, who are money
managers, hedge funds, market
makers, arbitrageurs, specialists,
and other professional investors."

Source: InvestorWords.com, Web Finance,
Inc., www.investorwords.com/3835/
prime_broker.html.

trades for hedge funds, as well as providing them with financing. Thanks to
Ricciardelli and others, prime brokerage
proved to be a win-win for both the sell
side and buy side: It fueled sell-side earnings and buy-side growth.

Ricciardelli's prime brokerage moves
included a change from monthly to daily
record keeping, consolidated accounts, and
effective use of technology, as well as providing leverage and financing to the hedge
fund community.

The daily records allowed hedge funds
and their clients to better understand their
current positions. In today's computer age, such calculations are pretty
simple, but back in the mid-1970s they weren't.

Word got out among the members of the small hedge fund
community that Ricciardelli, his team, and Furman Selz could, to
the penny, tell clients their positions after every trade. Hiring Furman
Selz meant the hedge fund could improve its customer service.
It made life a lot easier and better for hedge funds, so they started
knocking on the door. As a result, business and those bottomline
profits boomed.

Eventually, Ricciardelli moved to Morgan Stanley, which I suspect—
like other major Wall Street firms—viewed prime brokerage as more
of a nice little hobby than a significant profit generator. Yet, over time,
the hedge fund world was on the upswing and added more and more
prime brokerage services. The net result: The prime brokerage market
expanded dramatically, to the delight of the sell side's cash register and
the buy side's ambitions.

Prime brokerage proved to be an important early engagement in
the Battle for Wall Street, and thanks to folks like Ricciardelli, the buy
side was off and running. In the early days of prime brokerage, the sell-
side firms called the plays, cut the deals, and had the upper hand. Over
time, the pendulum has swung in the other direction, and now hedge
funds are largely calling the shots.

What accounts for this switch in power? The increased competition
between prime brokers and the clout of hedge funds.

Without the prime brokerage movement, it would have been significantly more difficult for hedge funds to flourish. They would have needed infrastructure and expertise, which was expensive. The little guys would have struggled, and the big guys might not have gotten into the market at all. Providing prime brokerage services gave the hedge fund industry a jump start.

How big a jump start? Well, without prime brokerage, it's quite possible that the hedge fund industry that we know today would have sat in the starting gate for another 5 or more years.

Bottom Line

I guess you could say that Ricciardelli turbo-charged the industry. For the most part, the buy and sell sides have a divergence of interests—but trailblazers like Ricciardelli found a way for them to converge, for both sides to come together in the prime brokerage meeting hall.

That Was Then: Back-Office Money Machine

Think of the battle between the sell-side prime brokerage and the buy-side hedge funds unfolding in two distinct time periods. From the 1970s to the 1990s, the sell side held sway over the buy side. One way to look at this first time period is through the lens of an analogy: The sell side built a prime brokerage machine that was Wall Street's equivalent of a Wal-Mart—one-stop shopping for hedge funds. The hedge fund industry, wanting to move up the growth curve, filled their shopping carts with prime brokerage services, and the sell side's cash registers kept clanging with sales.

In the context of our analogy, I would say the sell side designed prime brokerage "stores" as management and financial service providers. Let's begin with managerial services.

A good example comes to mind. Hedge funds love to use multiple brokers to spread their trades around in order to get better pricing, as well as to camouflage the trader's identity.

Sell-side prime brokerage entered the scene and turned to the hedge funds, and could have said something like, "You like multiple trades? Let us make it easier for you—we'll create a centralized account, with all the record keeping in one place for all those multiple trades."

"Think of it this way," they could have said. "All your trades will be executed at multiple brokers, but will be treated as if they were done through your prime broker. Leave the heavy lifting to us." Hedge funds were more than happy to say, "Okay."

It didn't stop there. The sell side offered a gamut of back-office services including custody.[1]

The hedge funds now came to rely on prime brokers for more than just avoiding the expense and time of setting up all the back-office systems and infrastructure. Prime brokers could now allow hedge funds to focus on what they do well—namely, trading—and let the hedge funds outsource back-office services that are not core to their business.

Let's turn our attention from management products to financial products. From the sell-side perspective, why not offer our financial bread and butter—liquidity. The prime broker stepped up and more than likely said to the hedge funds, "We can offer bank lines of credit and access to a variety of funds."

Hedge funds said, "Sign me up." They now had funding to facilitate two things hedge funds like to do, short selling and leverage, which are key ingredients in their financial bread and butter.

The prime brokerage and hedge fund alignment was going strong, not so much as a back-office game or management services, but rather prime brokerage was now feeding the hedge funds' appetite by funding their financing needs.

Prime brokerage fees attracted sell-side firms to this corner of the market. But more than that, as one of my prime brokerage observers notes, prime brokerage is a hook into a client. By providing prime brokerage services, the sell-side gains the trust of the hedge fund and might be able to leverage that into additional business and keep building out the prime brokerage store.

Bottom Line

Hedge funds are often long on ideas, but short on capital and infrastructure. Prime brokerage is there to pick up the slack. The payday for prime brokers lending their liquidity along with back office support is big—very big.

This Is Now: The Pendulum Shifts

Until the late 1990s, prime brokerages' advantage in the Battle for Wall Street went entirely to the sell side. The big payoff came to the firms providing prime brokerage services, more than to the firms using it. No longer.

Beginning in the 2000s, the pendulum has swung to the hedge fund side, and they could enter the prime brokerage store with size and pricing advantages.

Originally, when a hedge fund worked with a prime broker, all of its business went to that prime broker. Today, with many hedge funds being so large, the fund's business is likely split among multiple prime brokers. The funds like this situation because they have greater access to financing.

When prime brokerage began, this type of relationship was not even feasible. I suspect the costs and complexity of tracking a hedge fund's trades made it impossible to spread such activity over multiple prime brokers. But today's technology allows it.

Historically, the computer programs used had to be developed in-house. Now, third-party software developers are building and marketing prime brokerage systems off the shelf. A fund or other organization that wants to go into prime brokerage no longer has to spend millions and millions of dollars. Instead, it can lease a system for six or seven figures. This opens the market to smaller sell-side firms. The oligopoly position of the large sell-side firms is being partly eroded.

Also, given their modern size and volume, hedge funds can negotiate for better pricing and execution. And they are large enough today to take their own portfolios and lend their own securities to short sellers, circumventing the sell side and going directly to institutions.

Bottom Line

Hedge funds of 2008 are very different from hedge funds of 1998. They are now living in a world where technology is cheaper and better, the competition for their business is fiercer, and the size of their funds has grown so dramatically that power has shifted to them and away from the sell side.

Case Study: Deutsche Bank—The Accidental Prime Broker

Let's look at sell-sider Deutsche Bank's acquisition of NatWest's derivatives business. Fortuitously, a back-office support operation came along with the deal.[2] That back-office operation, according to industry observers, helped position Deutsche to become a significant prime brokerage player.

Prior to the NatWest purchase in 1997,[3] Deutsche Bank faced a number of issues in its U.S. operations.[4] Around the same time, U.K.-based sell-side bank NatWest was facing its own difficulties. NatWest found itself with meaningful financial losses and decided to sell a number of businesses.[5]

I wonder if NatWest asked itself the classic, sell-side survivability question: "Okay, we've been torpedoed and are taking on water. Let's throw assets overboard and try to stay afloat." A few years later, another torpedo was launched, this from a fellow sell-side U.K. bank, Royal Bank of Scotland, and NatWest finally sank, as it was taken over by RBS.

Deutsche Bank, it appears, saw a strategic opportunity with NatWest's financial woes. Deutsche was quite clever and ended up buying not just a derivatives business but landed a true plug-and-play operational capacity. Deutsche was now able to drop NatWest's expertise into its own system.

This was great timing, since the prime brokerage revolution was well under way. Deutsche was now able to connect its stellar new back office with the growing needs of hedge funds.

In 2008, Deutsche Bank is one of the top global prime brokerage firms, because it recognizes the importance of these new products as well as the value of operational efficiencies (clearing and settling trades).

Implications

Prime brokerage was developed by the sell side. The buy side, particularly hedge funds, utilized prime brokerage services, and the sell side was only too happy to provide them because such services generated consistent and considerable profits. It was a win-win all around.

By providing such services, including financing, the sell side freed up buy-side players to do what they do best, namely trade and make money. Prime brokerage allowed the hedge funds to hone their skills and build up their track records, which ultimately enabled them to attract billions of dollars of investors' money.

During the latter half of the 2000s, it seems like the buy side has been winning the Battle. Simple arithmetic tells the story. On one side of the equation, prime brokerage has directly put millions and millions of dollars in hundreds and hundreds of sell-side cash tills. And on the other side of the equation, prime brokerage has led to the creation of approximately 10,000 hedge funds and several trillion dollars of assets under management. So who won?

When I think about prime brokerage both today and tomorrow, four questions come to mind:

1. Can hedge funds, and the buy side in general, disintermediate the sell side and become prime brokers for others?

Disintermediation

"Disintermediation is the removal of the intermediary or middleman. In the case of hedge funds and prime brokerage, for example, disintermediation would be the removal the prime broker and having the hedge fund conduct prime brokerage internally. In the world of trading, disintermediation is an investor buying an asset directly rather than going through a broker."

Source: InvestorWords.com, WebFinance, Inc., www.investorwords.com/1488/disintermediation.html.

Whether the buy side can handle prime brokerage business for others is still open to question—and it may, in fact, be a bad idea. The buy side would have to construct a Chinese Wall (a barrier to the flow of information between two different parts of a firm's business) between its fund and prime brokerage businesses to avoid conflicts of interest—not easy. Competitors would worry that the hedge fund/prime broker might use their information or ideas. They could ask, "If it becomes difficult to borrow securities, who gets first shot at the securities that are available? Me or them?"

There are inherent conflicts of interest here, and because of them, I don't see hedge funds, for the most part, providing prime brokerage to other hedge funds.

It's true that companies like Goldman Sachs have their own hedge funds, while still providing prime brokerage services to others. But big firms like these have many other businesses, creating lots of potential for conflicts of interest—and they have the systems in place to keep apart the functions that need to be separated. They would be out of business if they didn't have the trust of their clients.

But hedge funds, which to date have only one primary business, have not gained such trust. Therefore, I suspect that hedge funds will most likely stick to what they know best and leave prime brokerage services to the sell side. The sell side can breathe easy; the buy side is not likely to seriously challenge it on the prime brokerage battlefield.

2. Can hedge funds bring the prime brokerage function in-house?

You could argue that a firm like Goldman Sachs is both a hedge fund—one of the world's largest—and a prime broker, and is able to do both. Now, of course, it is also a bank holding company, having to restructure during the height of the credit crisis of 2007–2008.

But Goldman is diversified, and it has scale that a stand-alone hedge fund probably could never match. Also, it has already built its prime brokerage infrastructure, a cost any stand-alone hedge fund will have to foot if it decides to prime broker for itself. So Goldman Sachs doesn't really represent your typical prime broker.

Although it might work in some cases, such as at Goldman, this is generally not a good idea. To be an effective prime broker, a hedge fund would need sufficient size, since there are economies of scale at play here. The vast majority of hedge funds lack this kind of size.

Therefore, hedge funds will continue to explore the opportunity of in-house prime brokerage. I suspect that a number of the larger hedge funds will establish a prime brokerage function, while a majority of hedge fund players will keep their interest level on the back burner, to the delight of the sell side.

3. How does the sell side respond to the fact that it's helping the buy side win the Battle for Wall Street by fueling the growth of the hedge funds? Does it say goodbye to prime brokerage?

The existing sell-side prime brokers enjoy too much of a cost advantage over everyone else to shut down such a profitable business, even if they are helping their competition.

There are also profit advantages—prime brokerage makes the sell side serious money. According to industry observers, prime brokerage, for the most part, sits inside the traditional equities business and supports the equity business's lower and lower returns. If you take away those prime brokerage soldiers, who defend the sell side, the equities business may well lose money. You won't see the sell side surrendering this way.

4. How will the 2007 and 2008 credit crunch affect the prime brokerage space?

Sell-side firms are struggling with overwhelming balance sheet and earnings issues. At the same time, hedge funds will most likely pull in their horns because of the crisis. Prime brokers will have less business, and the uncertain investment and economic climate will lead them to use less leverage (I hope) in order to reduce their risks. In fact, because the credit window is effectively closed, I think there will be contraction by both sell-side and buy-side firms.

For example, as I write this, some sell-side firms, like Morgan Stanley,[6] are witnessing meaningful hedge fund outflows in light of the credit crisis. Such firms may consider scaling back or exiting prime brokerage.

But, despite the credit crisis, growing hedge fund power, and the fact that it's helping the competition, a majority of the sell side will want to keep prime brokerage going. Why? Dollars, dollars, and more dollars for the till.

The sell side is well aware that it would be difficult for the buy side to enter prime brokerage because of the start-up costs, the need for scale, and the fact that the sell side, with its first-mover advantage, is so well established. So as I see it, the sell side will continue to provide prime brokerage services, while the buy side continues to gain power as a result of its best friend, prime brokerage.

Battle Victorious: Buy side.

Part Two

AGENTS OF CHANGE

Chapter 4

Hedge Funds: Buy-Side Player, Sell-Side Foe

In the early 1980s, where did those of us who wanted to make a few extra dollars on Wall Street go? Straight into investment banking. It was simple: That was where the money was.

By the 1990s, though, things had changed. Venture capital was the place to be. And by the time the 2000s had rolled around, another shift was occurring: first to private equity, then to hedge funds. Today, those looking for "a few dollars more" and the ability to be "financially creative" head to the buy side.

An overlooked factor in the migration of the talent pool from the sell side to the buy side is what I call "follow the money." Historically, the sell side's big money machine was client driven—capital raising and advisory services—and the individual investment banker's and trader's compensation was pretty good. But over the past 10 or 15 years, the sell side has developed even larger money machines.

These larger money machines can be referred to as principal or proprietary trading.[1] This type of trading produced out-of-this world returns. Wall Street traders found their compensation exploding, not just a million here or a million there, but several million, even tens of millions.[2]

On the sell side, these traders had to share their spoils with the house, while on the buy side the profits, for the most part, stayed with the traders. Proprietary trading (like research) is portable. It can readily be taken to the other side of the Street. And the walk to the other side isn't long. Just follow the money.

This is not a trivial matter. The Battle for Wall Street, to an extent, is defined by the fight for talented employees and which side of the battle they decide to call home.

The Analysts Are Coming

In the last chapter I discussed how the sell side inadvertently helped fuel the growth of the buy side by offering prime brokerage services. Now, again, the sell side inadvertently spurred buy-side growth, this time by supplying experienced talent.

Let's take this idea of the migration of the talent pool one step further. Think of the sell side as the equivalent of an incubator, a farm system for the buy side. You could also think of a farm system as a place to practice your swing before hitting a trade out of the ballpark. And, to be a bit commercial, think of the sell-side farm system as a training ground to dress up your resume before knocking on the investors' doors for those billion-dollar funds.

This farm system was not your run-of-the-mill sell-side network. It was made up of household names (Goldman Sachs, Morgan Stanley, etc.), and they were training those who would create tomorrow's brand name funds.

For example, Goldman Sachs developed Leo Cooperman, who started the hedge fund Omega. In fact, Goldman has been a major incubator, having developed the folks who started such hedge funds as AQR Capital Management,[3] Eton Park Capital Management,[4] Farallon

Capital Management,[5] Fortress Investment Group,[6] GLG Partners,[7] Och-Ziff Capital Management Group,[8] Perry Capital,[9] and Silverpoint Capital,[10] to name just a few.

And Goldman Sachs was not alone. JPMorgan was the fertile ground from which BlueCrest Capital Management[11] flowered; the Morgan Stanley farm system brought us FrontPoint Partners;[12] and Rothschild played a similar role with Atticus Capital.[13]

All of these hedge funds were started by people who followed the two-sided talisman of money and passion—the power to be fiscally creative, to be financially successful, and to make something of lasting value.

Hedge funds engender passion because they allow people to be creative. As a result, not all hedge funds are the same. Just as one novel or motion picture differs from another depending on the interests of the author or screenwriter, hedge funds differ depending on the interests of the people behind them. They can use very different strategies to achieve the same end, which is higher risk-adjusted returns for their investors.

Some invest primarily in commodities, while others rely heavily on quantitative strategies, and still others are long or short sellers. There are real differences between hedge funds, just as there are real differences between the books that line the shelves of a library.

Of course, not all hedge fund founders come from the sell side. Academia has produced its share, including the founders of D. E. Shaw and Renaissance Technologies.

I've been talking in generalities about a "talent pool," but let me make this a bit more personal by telling you the story of a research analyst who left the sell side. His story could be applied to any number of people who migrated over to the buy side, myself included, as we both embarked on Wall Street in the early 1980s, and we both crossed paths with one of the legendary sell-side and buy-side professionals.

Our analyst left the sell side as he came to better understand its business practices. In particular, on the sell side, the failures and successes of his research reports were public. Virtually all analysts make bad calls from time to time. And it's not the best of times to have your dirty laundry hanging alongside your clean white sheets.

He talked about how clients and management expected him never to be wrong, even though such expectations were, of course, unreasonable. Understandably, this did not sit well with him. He felt that on the buy side, he could make mistakes as long as his overall track record was good.

In addition, he says, the sell side was not about investing money: it was for the most part about selling ideas and generating commission dollars—pushing product, to put it bluntly. The sell side paid for research by using it to produce trading volume, which, in turn, produced commission dollars.

This analyst also felt a number of institutional constraints. The institution had too much control over an entrepreneurial guy like him.

In addition, his mind-set was to make above-average, risk-adjusted returns over a market cycle. At some time during a cycle, this meant he would have to hedge, and a hedge fund is a great instrument to hedge your investments.

Again, the sell-side was really a believer in long investing: buy, and buy some more. When you are thinking about traditional sell-side long-only investing,[14] you're thinking of a relative performance model rather than an absolute performance model. The move to the buy side hedge fund was a huge pendulum shift, where people wanted to manage money on an absolute, not relative, basis.

Bottom Line

It's quite simple, really: On the buy side, traders and researchers could keep just about all they made, rather than share it with a big sell-side firm, with all its overhead and bureaucracy. Therefore, running a hedge fund today is ideal for a person who wants to do exactly what he wants to do with his and his investors' money without the constraints of the sell-side institution.

With all the sources of talent now available to the buy side, and all the advantages the buy side presents to those with the gumption and drive to head out on their own, it's no wonder there is a battle for talent on Wall Street.

2 and 20

Risk and *reward* are two words not lost on the talent that migrated from the sell side to the buy side.

A surefire way to make a boatload of money without a lot of risk is to step into the hedge fund world of the standard 2 and 20.[15] A 2 percent management fee is paid by investors for management essentially turning on the lights. Management also earns 20 percent of the profits as a performance fee for simply doing their job. Nice gig.

Historically, what did people really risk when starting a hedge fund? Certainly, they invested some of their own money, which was at risk, but they were able to do this in a reasonably risk-controlled way, without mortgaging their homes.

When people say a hedge fund is performing poorly, they're usually talking about a fund down 10 percent or 20 percent, and we could be looking at even lower performance levels as the credit crisis rages on. Of course, spectacular blowups of hedge funds are not unknown.

Let's assume you put 60 percent of your net worth into your own hedge fund. If the fund falls 20 percent, your net worth drops 12 percent. That's a lot, but not a fatal blow to your personal wealth. And, besides, there's an upside to managing a hedge fund, even when it's not performing well. That upside is the management fee of 2 percent of assets. Or should I say, a 2 percent annual income stream earned by showing up for work.

Let's assume that a fund starts with $500 million under management, which was not uncommon. With typical management fees of 2 percent, the manager will get $10 million in fees in the fund's first year of operation, plus the usual 20 percent of any profit produced by the fund.

> ### *2 and 20*
> "In the hedge fund world, *2 and 20* is a term that is widely known, widely used, and perhaps widely debated. It refers to the fee structure of the typical hedge fund: the investor annually pays the hedge fund manager 2 percent of his or her investment as a management fee, plus 20 percent of any profits the fund produces for the investor."
>
> *Source:* Investopedia, www.investopedia.com/terms/t/two_and_twenty.asp.

Chances are good that any loss to a manager's net worth will be more than made up by management fees alone. Essentially, there's relatively little risk to the person starting the fund.

Good-bye sell-side farm system . . . hello hedge funds.

To put it bluntly, you didn't have to be a brilliant strategist to make money managing a hedge fund. You did, however, have to be able to raise money. And, counterintuitively, it seemed that the less experience you had, the more money you could raise. This was a function of all the money chasing hedge funds' high returns.

Admittedly, the entrepreneur who leaves the sell side to start a fund takes on some risk. There are opportunity costs—namely, giving up a job and a fairly secure income. A mental trade-off must also be made: You're going off on your own and no longer have the institutional power and organization of a sell-side firm behind you.

Another downside to starting a hedge fund is the actual associated costs—both external and internal.[16] These include external costs, such as start-up fees (including the expense of setting up a limited partnership), marketing fees (the expense of winning over the investors' capital), and prime brokerage fees (the expense of outsourcing back office). Then there are internal costs, including compensation (for traders, analysts, office help, and others), information technology (trading stations), and occupancy (believe me, hedge funds are rarely housed in inexpensive real estate).

But perhaps the biggest risk is related to job security. The cyclicality of jobs is simply a fact of life. Wall Street often hesitates to fire people, but once it starts firing, it goes at it with all guns blazing. It fires people in big waves when it goes through a massive retrenchment. But between waves, Wall Street carries people. It piles up deadwood faster than a forest. When times are neutral or good, people keep their jobs, but when things get bad, Wall Street fires folks by the thousands, as we are living through in the credit crunch of 2007–2008. The person thinking of starting a hedge fund knows this.

We've had other cycles, too. Go back to the late 1990s, where it seemed everyone had an Internet start-up. Then, in the early part of the 2000s, Nasdaq fell through the floor.[17] It has yet to return to its previous high, or even come close.[18] That was a cycle. For sure, a cycle will hit hedge funds, where things get bad and hedge funds contract.

But, for now, the benefits seem to outweigh the risks, especially to the sell-sider eager to break out on his or her own. Just as the risk may be greater than staying on the sell side, so are the returns. The net present value of the hedge fund founder's income stream should be higher over time than on the sell side. In most cases, you can simply take more off the table—easy math. There are also intangible benefits: the hedge fund is an environment you can control, without having to deal with the bureaucracy of the sell side.

In addition, I think people tend to overestimate the associated costs of starting a hedge fund. What does it really cost to run a hedge fund business? Hedge funds need less infrastructure (remember the last chapter, when we talked about prime brokerage—the sell side maintains infrastructure for hedge funds).

Most of the costs are variable, not fixed, because there's no reason for a hedge fund to carry a big overhead. Services, such as prime brokerage, can be outsourced. Excellent software can be bought off the shelf, rather than developed in-house. The head count can be kept low, too. This results in a lower cost structure, making hedge funds smaller and leaner than sell-side banks. This means that the folks who start hedge funds can often take home more money than their counterparts at sell-side banks.

> ### Short Selling
> "The selling of a security that the seller does not own, or any sale that is completed by the delivery of a security borrowed by the seller. Short sellers assume that they will be able to buy the stock at a lower amount than the price at which they sold short."
>
> *Source:* Investopedia, www.investopedia .com/terms/s/shortselling.asp.

Also—and this is a nice point for those with hedge funds—a number of organizational expenses are charged to the fund.[19] At that point, is it the hedge fund manager's money at risk or the investor's money?

Bottom Line

There has been little risk going to Greenwich or Boston or Manhattan to start a fund. With liquidity in the financial system, and exponentially more post the financial crisis of 2007–2008, all the hedge fund manager needs to do is slice off a tiny allocation from the investor community and he or she is off and running.

Good news for the buy side. Not the best of news for the sell side watching its talent exit stage left.

130/30—Magic Numbers

The search for something a little extra—something above and beyond the norm that doesn't incur additional costs—is never-ending. Think of it as getting something for nothing. This certainly holds true with investments, where investors look to have their returns boosted, while not taking on more risk. In fact, Wall Street has a name for the difference between normal returns and above-normal ones, at a given level of risk: alpha.

Alpha

"The mathematical estimate of the return on a security when the market return as a whole is zero. Alpha is derived from a in the formula $Ri = a + bRm$, which measures the return on a security (Ri) for a given return on the market (Rm) where b is beta."

Source: http://financial-dictionary.thefreedictionary.com/Alpha.

"The relationship which the return on a stock has with the return on the market as a whole, often described a 'stock-specific return.' Stocks which rise when the market as a whole is falling have 'positive alphas.' Stocks which fall when the market as a whole is rising have 'negative alphas.'"

Source: www.finance-glossary.com/terms/alpha.htm?ginPtrCode=00000&id=1566&PopupMode=.

Because alpha has such a hold on investors' imaginations (and their greed), Wall Street actively caters to this demand by creating products that claim to provide it. No surprise there. One of the more recent advances in the search for alpha, though, has come from a seemingly innocuous strategy that hedge funds and mutual funds are touting as a great way to boost returns while minimizing risk. The new product is usually referred to by the percentages used in its strategy: 130/30.

130/30 Funds

These funds go long 130 percent, while going short 30 percent, hence the 130/30 moniker. "A strategy that uses financial leverage by shorting poor performing stocks and purchasing shares that are expected to have high returns. A 130/30 ratio implies shorting stocks up to 30% of the portfolio value and then using the funds to take a long position in the stocks the investor feels will outperform the market. Often, investors will mimic an index such as the S&P 500 when choosing stocks for this strategy."

Source: Investopedia, www.investopedia.com/terms/1/130-30_strategy.asp.

The logistics: The fund buys 100 percent of a long position in a basket of stocks the fund manager thinks will rise in price, shorts 30 percent of the value of that basket in another basket of stocks the manager thinks will fall, and takes the money received from the short sale to add an additional 30 percent to the original long position, ending up with the 130/30 ratio of long to short. Some funds use variations on this theme, such as 120/20 and 140/40, but the goal is still the same—namely, to hedge part of a bet on an investment.

Why bother, you might ask. The bet here is that 130 percent of the portfolio will go up, while 30 percent falls. If the manager is good, in theory, extra returns can be earned from stocks heading in both directions, boosted by the fact that we have leverage at work here: stock borrowed for the short sale.

Fund managers say this approach is a winner because it allows them to employ not just those stocks they think will rise in price (the typical long trade), but also to bet against those stocks they believe will tumble. With this strategy, they can bet in both directions, where as a typical mutual fund only bets long. And that's where the alpha is supposed to come from.

Some observers are calling these hedge funds "lite," since hedge funds, of course, have used hedging strategies for a long

(continued)

time—but 130/30 greatly restricts the amount of hedging a fund can do, which isn't true for a conventional hedge fund. These instruments are still too new to know how well they'll perform in the long run—but they're certainly gaining in popularity, in the form of investor allocations drawn to alpha and lower leverage, a combination it's hard not to like.

Merrill Lynch, as reported in the *Wall Street Journal* in February 2008, predicted that 130/30 funds would have up to $1 trillion under management within three years.[20] That's a lot of money being bet on a strategy that has yet to prove its value. Nonetheless, expect to hear more about these 130/30 funds.

Problem of Large Numbers

If a turning point in the Battle for Wall Street will happen that slows down the hedge fund players' growth march, I suspect it won't be because of technology. Nor will it be because of the entrepreneurs who are backed by venture capital and private-equity firms and who are providing financial technology tools to the buy side. The turning point for hedge fund growth declines will more likely be due to changes in the investors themselves—specifically, how they employ capital allocations relative to expected returns.

There have been times when hedge fund performance has been poor, such as in 2008. Yet, we also know that hedge funds have generally outperformed the market, so a number of them still a better alternative to the options typically available in the low-interest-rate environment of 2008.

However, their slowing performance raises an important question: Will hedge

Hedge Fund Investors

"Investors in hedge funds are typically high-net-worth individuals, public pension funds, endowments, and corporate pension funds, both in the United States and around the world. The hedge fund industry has a global reach, attracting investors from around the world."

Source: Dave Valiante, "Hedge Funds Continue to Attract Investors but Face New Challenges." *Wall Street & Technology,* August 16, 2008; www .wallstreetandtech.com/advancedtrading/ showArticle.jhtml;jsessionid=CCA0NQ ELD5GZWQSNDLQSKHSCJUN N2JVN?articleID=210002918.

funds be able to maintain their better-than-the market returns in the future?

I think it'll be difficult for hedge funds to continue to produce better-than-market returns. The reason? The more money they attract, the bigger they get. The bigger they get, the lower their returns on average. This has to do with the law of large numbers. The correlation between size and return can be negative; the bigger you are, the lower the return you earn, with the reverse being true in more cases than not.

Simply put, they'll produce lower returns because they'll have fewer choices of investments, as a result of their having more money to invest. When you have a lot of money to move at any one time, you could well have a liquidity issue.

A hedge fund, when small, can consider investing in small-, medium-, and large-capitalization stocks. But when it's large, it will most likely be able to invest only in large-caps.

Others, including mutual funds, experience the same thing. In fact, in his 2007 letter to shareholders of Berkshire Hathaway, Warren Buffett made the same observation about his own company: "Berkshire's past record can't be duplicated or even approached. Our base of assets and earnings is now far too large for us to make outsized gains in the future."[21]

One could say that what affects mutual funds and Warren Buffett will affect hedge funds. Its range of investment opportunities shrinks as it grows. In that sense, it's a victim of its own success—and a potential victim in the Battle for Wall Street.

Let's look at how the law of large numbers affects talent migration from two perspectives. First, when hedge funds are relatively small, say $1 billion to $2 billion in assets under management, and earn handsome returns, those returns act as a lightning rod for investors' capital, which propels fund and earnings growth.

Growth requires more people on the payroll, a concept well recognized by sell-side professionals. Migration from the sell to the buy side, which starts slowly, picks up speed, as hedge funds become bigger and richer.

Second, this upward curve might well reach a point of inflection, at which it starts to turn downward. This is a function of the law of large numbers. Hedge funds may eventually get so big that their returns start to drop, which convinces some investors to turn the capital allocation spigot off.

The assets under management, as well as the partners' earnings, start to level off and/or decline. Partners and other senior professionals become antsy and maybe retire and even contemplate closing the fund down. Life was good. Party over. Time to go fishing.

Bottom Line

It's that law of large numbers again: The larger pools of assets to manage leaves the industry on the potential downside of returns. Lower returns translate to lower earnings, as well as less investor appetite for hedge funds. And potentially fewer battle-tested buy-side veterans. These breaks in the battle line provide hope for the sell side.

Case Study: Citadel Investment Group— The Demand Side of the Equation

About 10,000 hedge funds currently exist. One of the more innovative hedge fund managers is Kenneth Griffin, founder of Citadel Investment Group.[22] Think of Citadel as Goldman Sachs—only distilled.[23] I would say that Griffin has distilled the essential functions of the buy and sell sides into a concentrated form called Citadel.

Citadel could be characterized as a buy-side/sell-side hybrid, marching along both sides of the line.

The Citadel business model involves a multi-strategy approach. It's not just a hedge fund—it includes aspects of the sell side as well, like financing and back-office operations (á la prime brokerage), plus sophisticated in-house technology.[24]

Founded in 1990, Griffin-led Citadel has enjoyed considerable success based on a winning formula: diversifying into new investment strategies opportunistically over time, using a mix of relative-value, event-driven, and fundamental approaches.

Today, Citadel's operations include nine global proprietary hedge fund investing businesses including global credit, energy, equities, global markets (exchange-traded funds [ETFs], derivatives, fixed income, currencies, commodities), quantitative strategies, securitized products, and more.[25]

One could say that Ken Griffin and his team have been quite busy since 1990.

If that weren't enough to fill its dance card, Citadel also has non–hedge fund subsidiaries that include execution services, back-office functions, and asset management.

Citadel's employees are just as diverse and include former university professors, meteorologists, astrophysicists, mathematicians, and even experts in "string theory" (a unifying theory of physics). Not your run-of-the-mill employee roster, is it?

In the early to late 1990s, I could envision Citadel considering selling a minority share of itself to raise capital in order to turbo-charge their hedge fund growth plans. Looking forward, given what Citadel has accomplished, if they had pulled that hypothetical trigger for a minority investment, they would be kicking themselves.

If such a sale had occurred, it could have been to a sell-sider, and for the sell-sider, this would probably have been among its best investments.

Technology at Citadel[26] is paramount. Its information technology (IT) staff is small by Wall Street standards, but is about half of the firm's 1,200-person workforce. It builds nearly all of its applications in-house, because Citadel doesn't see an upside in teaching outsiders anything about the hedge fund game. Most likely, the firm views technology not as a cost, but as a revenue generator—the lens through which it spots opportunities others do not, and the means by which it capitalizes on opportunities faster and with fewer people than its competitors.

One of the keys to the firm's success is that it doesn't *need* Wall Street. Why? It's simple: Citadel, it appears, can take care of its own needs. The organization contains all of the necessary divisions, from a stock loans department to an elaborate back office, all the while remaining an innovative broker/dealer.[27] Citadel is a massive pool of capital, and it accounts for a large percentage of the daily trading on the New York Stock Exchange (NYSE).[28]

By bringing these support services in-house, Citadel is able to maintain its trading advantage, minimize expenses paid to sell-side banks, and realize additional revenue by providing the same services to others. Its focus on self-sufficiency is reaping rewards.

One of those rewards is migration of sell-side talent. If my students are any indication of Citadel's popularity—it is one of the companies they are most inquisitive about—the supply of talent outside Citadel's door is never ending.

Citadel is blurring the lines between the sell and buy sides and, in doing so, is shifting the power balance ever so slightly from the sell side to the buy side.

There's no doubt that Citadel is looking good, but there are still some issues. One arises from the problem with large numbers. Citadel is big and getting bigger, so earning higher returns could get increasingly tougher. Two, as it becomes more self-sufficient, it may lose its edge and gain a sell side–like bureaucracy. And three, Citadel, like others, finds itself in the turbulence of the 2007–2008 credit crisis storm.

That said—although there are no guarantees—Citadel certainly is impressive as I write this book.

Case Study: CalPERS—The Supply Side of the Equation

The Battle for Wall Street is made up of players who do not fit into the buy or sell side. For example, many institutional investors, such as public and private pension funds, are fueling the growth of Wall Street. One such player is CalPERS.

When the name CalPERS (California Public Employees' Retirement System) comes to mind, we think of the nation's largest pension fund (approximately $240 billion in total assets[29] for 1.5 million state employees[30]), and a key participant in the private-equity world: not only is CalPERS a major investor in private-equity funds, it has taken direct ownership in private-equity firms like Apollo Management,[31] Carlyle Capital,[32] and most recently, Silver Lake Partners[33] via minority stakes.

CalPERS was an early proponent of hedge funds as well, and began investing in them in 2002 with $50 million placed with five funds.[34] Since then, its commitment has grown significantly, and its position in hedge funds in late 2007 was $5 billion in 27 funds.[35]

CalPERS' hedge fund investments over the near term could grow to around $12 billion, since it has recently increased its allocation to these funds from 5 to 8 percent of its total global equity portfolio.[36]

Still, this is a small number compared to CalPERS' overall size of $240 billion. Some of the hedge funds receiving CalPERS investments include well-known names like Och-Ziff Capital and Farallon Capital.[37]

And CalPERS wasn't the only pension fund placing bets with hedge funds. The top 200 pension funds invested $76 billion in hedge funds as of September 2007, up from $51 billion a year earlier.[38] High returns were bringing pension funds to the hedge fund table.

Consider that General Motors pays its retirees billions every year.[39] To do so, it needs annual returns of 7-plus percent, which is hard to do in the 2007-2008 fixed-income environment.[40] With CalPERS reporting returns of approximately 10 percent from its hedge fund investments,[41] it's easy to see the appeal of hedge funds to pension funds.

It's possible that there might be regulatory pressure to limit pension fund investments in hedge funds, but I don't see that happening. For one thing, the investments being made by the pension funds are relatively small.

So where might there be regulatory pressure?

California's politicians are looking at CalPERS and others who are investing in private equity funds with ties to sovereign wealth funds (generally in cases where the sovereign wealth funds have ownership stakes in the private-equity firms). They may very well tell CalPERS and other state pension funds not to make any more such investments—or even to get out of these investments entirely.[42]

What could change the regulatory landscape? A hedge fund could blow up, affecting state pension funds—which, in turn, would affect retirees. After a lifetime of hard work, the Californian looking forward to quiet time with his grandchildren could possibly be left with nothing in his retirement fund. That would really get the attention of politicians.

But as long as hedge funds outperform other benchmarks and remain solvent, allocations will continue. This is good news for both sides, but more for the buy side hedge funds because this is their bread and butter. For the sell side, it is a smaller part of its total business.

Implications

Where does all this lead? To three questions, all centered around the hedge fund supply line of investors and talent, as well as the hedge fund's future prospects for growth.

1. Will hedge funds move the line on the fundamentals of market share gain?

I would say yes.

When we look at virtually any industry, we look at fundamentals. But that's not what we do with hedge funds. One reason why hedge funds are different is the lack of an acceptable substitute product. Another is that, despite their recent growth, hedge funds still constitute only a small percentage of total global financial assets, which can't be seen when analyzing them through a fundamentals lens.

It isn't necessary for hedge funds to capture a large piece of the world's financial pie to continue their march on market share. Therefore, buy-side hedge funds can relax a little, knowing that with no competing products and a fragmented global financial pie, the prospect of gaining market share looks promising.

2. Will the hedge funds hold the line on 2 and 20 and keep the turnstiles moving with sell-side talent?

I would say yes.

Their performance, as I've noted, is likely to decline, but it will still be better than most asset classes (which is why there's no good substitute for them). Should performance dip down, I can just hear investors piping up and saying, "Those fees you're charging are outrageous!"

But they're not outrageous enough that investors will decide that they're not worth paying. The fee situation is similar on the sell side, where investors and corporate managers have screamed for years about underwriting fees. As with hedge funds, the sell side can get away with a lot because there are no substitute products. All of these variables bode well for hedge funds. Therefore, the buy side hedge funds can breathe a little easier, knowing the formula of 2 and 20 will continue to draw sell-side talent to their side of the battlefield.

3. Will hedge funds continue to attract high levels of investor capital allocations?

I'm afraid not.

Investors in the future will be more selective as returns from virtually all types of hedge funds come back to earth. And as returns decline, investor allocations won't just be tied to returns, but safety. New funds, in particular, will be hit the hardest, since they're more likely to produce lower returns than established funds, while also lacking their liquidity.

Other shifts that may take place are in the market environment itself. If long-term rates go up, hedge fund growth will slow as investors put their money in safer asset classes that yield higher returns.

And there is also the credit crunch to consider. As I write this, the credit window is barely open. Hedge funds depend to a great degree on leverage to produce outsized returns. If credit is tighter and/ or more costly in the future, hedge funds won't be able to put their money to work like they have been, which will lead to lower returns.

Cheers to the buy-side hedge funds for the victorious battles relating to market share and talent attraction, as I mentioned above. But hold the champagne for the moment. The hedge funds may need to retreat somewhat. The hedge funds are looking at the current world and seeing lower leverage and lower returns.

Simple formula, really: Lower returns equal less investor capital.

The investment community does not stand still when it's a question of lower returns. It will be sweeping the Street for alternative investment opportunities. Hedge fund phones will still be ringing—just not ringing off the hook. The sell side may want to stay by the phones, too.

Battle Victorious: Buy side.

Chapter 5

Private Equity: Buy-Side Player, Sell-Side Friend

F or many years, private equity firms and financial services companies had little to do with one another. They were all on the same battleground—namely, that of financial dealings—but they served in different armies.

I worked with both groups, though. As an investment banker, I was trying to sell financial services ideas not just to financial institutions, but to the private equity world as well. Well, for the most part, the private equity world didn't want to hear about it. I might as well have been telling them that taking companies private was a bad idea.

That didn't stop me, even though my ideas were usually met with responses like, "Are you kidding?" Eventually, the private equity guys came around and became believers, but it took a long time for those ideas to stick, and to have staying power in the private equity world.

Private equity's unfavorable view of financial services was not entirely unfounded. Their traditional view was that financial services were overly regulated and highly volatile, and lacked traditional control over assets. After all, those assets were people, not widgets. Financial asset risk was seen as just being an elevator ride away—assets were said to "go home at night."

Since then, the private equity and financial services sectors have crossed paths and created fresh synergies—namely, financial technology. For the first time, we had a true nexus of finance and technology. It was as if two armies, which had been passing in the night, decided to join forces.

The private equity firms, already possessing long experience with technology investments, were no longer asking folks like me, "Why are you here?" Instead, they were asking, "Where have you been?" Today, financing for new financial services hardware and software products comes from private equity and venture capital firms.

Profitable Partnership

The sell side, eventually, was happy to have the private equity firms invest in new trading services and products. On the flip side, the private equity firms were happy that they could find another way to exit their investments, specifically financially technology investments. They could monetize their investments, first by selling to just the buy side, but over time, to both the buy and sell sides.

Admittedly, this was small potatoes, chump change for the private equity firms. But, in time, a more lucrative alignment of interests developed between private equity and the sell side. Both sides could make a boatload of money and become best friends.

The sell-side firms could provide financing to private equity firms. This gave the private equity firms the money they needed to do their thing, which was company buyouts—resulting in higher payouts for their investors and higher payouts for themselves. Happy days for private equity.

The private equity shops turned around and paid the sell side huge fees for arranging that financing, while, at the same time, the sell side was creating new debt securities for private equity firms to carry out company bayouts.[1] The sell side then sold these securities to the marketplace for even larger fees: a double payday. Happy days for the sell side.

The sell side's take from these transactions was so large that a number of private equity firms had to keep sophisticated spreadsheets and computer models just to track all the fees they paid them. It was the kind of money that would get even the most blasé commercial or investment banker's heart racing as he started to picture that little island in the Caribbean he was going to buy.

These fees were significant enough to account for a meaningful part of the sell side's total revenues. In fact, fees from private equity firms could be hundreds of millions of dollars a year—a big number by any standard. Very happy days for the sell side.

These deals were a sign of the times—the times being 2003 to 2007—and they would not have occurred without the sell side's huge financing commitment. Even in my little world of investment banking for financial institutions, I saw old-school private equity firms like Bain Capital,[2] Blackstone Group,[3] Kohlberg Kravis Roberts,[4] Texas Pacific Group (TPG),[5] and Warburg Pincus[6] place huge bets in the financial arena. For example, two financial technology buyouts, Sungard[7] and First Data,[8] were completed for $11 billion and $26 billion, respectively.

Bottom Line

The private equity shops and sell-side firms were fueling each other's growth, completely aligned and intertwined. An illustration of how close they are: Every September I go looking for U.S. Open Tennis tickets, which are rare commodities in New York. I don't bother calling ticket brokers. I call friends at private equity firms who, in turn, call sell-side firms. You see, sell-side firms have the best seats in the house and are more than willing to give their best seats to their private equity friends.

Once a year, it's a circle of friendship I'm happy to be part of.

Liquidity and Leverage

Liquidity and leverage is a combo made in heaven (or, more specifically, on Wall Street). No matter what private equity firms say they bring to the table—value-added services, such as management prowess, for instance—in my estimation, it is part two of the story. Yes, they do add some magic to the value of a deal, but what they add is secondary. Private equity deals, I would say, are more about leverage and liquidity. Sound familiar? I talk a lot about both in this book, and with good reason: They are the air that

Wall Street breathes. In fact, the Battle for Wall Street largely takes place over liquidity and leverage.

Let's say a private equity shop buys a company. We'll assume that the company has an average management team and is in a decent economic environment. The company, of course, has assets. Depending on the economic environment of the time, the private equity firm will leverage those assets at a hypothetical ratio of 6 to 1.

Why would the private equity firm go through all the trouble of buying the whole company and taking it private? Because it will make more money this way than by buying the company's publicly traded stock. It is the leverage that produces the delta—the difference between a typical investment and one that's a home run.

If you buy, say, a $1 billion company, and you use 6-to-1 leverage, you put up only $167 million to take control of the entire company and do with it whatever you want. If you buy stock in the open market, you cannot begin to get this kind of financial leverage or managerial control.

With leverage, you can buy something middle-of-the-road and, like our hypothetical company, make a lot of money. How much of the profits private equity firms generate from deals come from what they add to the company (such as management expertise) and how much from simple, commodity-type leverage?

My estimate: 50 percent–plus is financial leverage; the rest of it is managerial. Private equity firms say they bring a complete toolkit to a management buyout. I'm arguing that this toolkit is less than 50 percent of the equation. These private equity firms walk around saying, "We bring all these services; we add all this value; we know so much." And they do. But the key factor at play is leverage. Period.

What kind of weapons are in the arsenal of a typical private equity firm? Management skills, for one. The private equity firms say they know how to run a company more efficiently. It's supposed to include special operational managers, who really understand how to run a business, by having savvy relations with a company's board of directors and bringing know-how to that board. And let's not forget that a number of private equity firms also say that going private removes the pressures of being a public company and reporting to stockholders.

I smile when I hear that. And I hear that a good deal of the time. What's amusing is that while the private equity guys are taking away pressures of being publicly traded, they're really talking about taking away the pressures related to the reporting of quarterly and annual results.

What they don't say is that they're replacing this reporting with a new kind. Private equity firms ask their management teams to continually report back to them on the company's financial situation and other aspects of the business. Public-market reporting is replaced by reporting to the private equity firm, and I would suspect that this reporting is done with more detail. Claiming that going private removes reporting pressures from management is not accurate, at least when a private equity firm is involved.

The irony is that private equity firms themselves go public. I wonder if they had a temporary memory loss about those public-market pressures.

Bottom Line

The cat is out of the bag on what's inside the private equity arsenal. That arsenal's success is predicated more on leverage than on oversight. And the sell side is only too happy to provide the buy-side private equity firms with the weapon of leverage, when that weapon is available.

Losing Old Ground, Gaining New Territories

The private equity industry has been around about 25 to 30 years, and has experienced out-of-this-world growth. In 2008, the private equity world was brought back to earth. Its sources of money (investors) and opportunities to put that money to work (in the form of management buyouts) have diminished.

Let's first look at investors like pension funds, who are always seeking healthy returns. They typically won't buy into investments for just 25 or 30 basis points (one one-hundredth of one percent) over what Treasury bills pay. These investors want higher spreads. There's few penalty to the investor in taking on added risk when we're in an economic environment where there are few defaults.

Put another way, investors looking for high yield in these situations don't face a penalty for reaching for that yield. When we're in a good economic environment with few defaults, investors will open up the money spigots. When this happens, the availability of capital to private equity firms becomes enormous, which has led to an exponential growth in the private equity world.

What happens when we are in the credit crunch environment with significant defaults, as happened in 2007–2008? Investors are now facing a penalty (higher risk) for yield. The investment game in 2008 is not as easy as it was earlier in this decade. No surprise, investors in this environment start dialing down money flows going to private equity firms.

Another way to think of it: Those investors allocating capital to the private equity firms are the supply side of the equation. The demand side of the equation, which is the private equity firms themselves, put the capital they raised to work by going out and acquiring companies.

For the longest time, private equity firms were enjoying an abundance of riches—investors allocating capital and numerous acquisition opportunities to redeploy that capital. Let's look at how that capital was put into play to the private equity firms' advantage.

The idea that a private equity player—a leveraged financial player—had more attractive pricing than, say, an industry or strategic player was an oxymoron. In the old days, when folks like me sold a financial institution or an industrial concern, there were few private equity firms in sight. Back then, if you wanted to sell a company, who would show up to the dance?

Traditionally, it would be five or six strategic industry buyers. You would search everywhere for a private equity guy, and if you were lucky, you would find one to keep the strategic buyers honest. Strategic players could pay more, since they benefited from the synergies of combining two like companies. They also had management know-how because they were in the same industry.

But then, leverage has leveled the playing field between strategic and financial buyers. With the liquidity that washed over the markets during the past decade or so, private equity firms could pay a higher price. It got so crazy that the private equity versus strategy player relationship actually got flipped on its head.

The financial players, the private equity firms, surpassed the strategic buyers, so when selling a company, instead of finding five strategic buyers and one financial buyer, now you had three financial and two strategic, or something similar.

Why? Because suddenly, private equity firms had huge amounts of financing available and, thanks to leverage, they could pay more for a company than the strategic players.[9] In this side battle between industry players and private equity firms, power shifted to the financial side and away from the industry side.

As the sell side, my fellow investment banking colleagues, saw more competition among buyers, we started to receive higher prices. Also, there was a domino effect. More companies came up for sale, which translated into more deal flow. The private equity industry grew larger and larger as a result.

The pendulum was swinging in private equity's favor, and private equity firms were looking victorious on Wall Street. But nothing lasts forever. In 2008, the free-flowing liquidity of the past dramatically slowed. Private equity firms are now facing resistance with these type of investments because they can't get their hands on the leverage, the liquidity, even if the companies are still willing to make a deal.

Why? The sell side is holding bank loans. Remember, in this Wall Street battle, it was the sell side that helped fund the buy side's purchases. There are now tons of such loans on the sell side's balance sheets, which is tying up the money they would otherwise use to finance deals. These are loans, such as those involving leveraged finance, which the banks can't sell to investors because there is no real market for them. In 2008, the sell side will not make new loans until they get rid of their old ones.

To reiterate, no bank loans equates to no leverage. And with no leverage, there are no victory parades for the private equity world in their pursuit of acquiring companies of size.

The year 2008 is not the best of times for private equity firms, so they are finding new ways to reinvent themselves. One such way is to make direct equity investments in faltering financial institutions. An example is the private equity firm Warburg Pincus's major investment in the bond insurer MBIA.[10]

A second example actually speaks volumes of the turbulent financial times. In April 2008 the private equity firm TPG Group provided a significant capital infusion to the struggling sell-side institution Washington Mutual (WaMu). Within five months, TPG watched its investment in WaMu turn into a $1.25 billion loss when WaMu collapsed.[11]

Another way is to establish new funds whose strategy is to invest in distressed assets, which are fairly numerous in 2008. Think of these funds as opportunistic soldiers looking for the spoils of war. These spoils are nonmarketable, nonperforming assets that the private equity firms will acquire at a discount today and sell at a premium tomorrow.

Private equity firms with a surplus of uninvested capital will not need to look very far for distressed assets—just across the Street, inside the sell-side balance sheet. The sell-side firms, looking to shrink—or deleverage—their balance sheets can now package and sell multibillion-dollar bundles of leveraged assets that are currently unmarketable through traditional venues.

Sell-side and private equity firms are finding ways to temporarily band together in the Battle for Wall Street. A true band of soldiers in 2008.

Bottom Line

Remember the old adage that says you are no better or smarter than the times you live in. You can say that in the Battle for Wall Street, two sides—private equity firms and the sell side—continue to find common ground, even in difficult economic times.

Distressed Funds—A Product of Our Times

The credit crisis of 2007–2008 caused a lot of distress—to commercial banks, hedge funds, investment banks, and others who put together mortgage-backed securities. They got stuck as the market for such securities evaporated. Many other businesses also suffered as credit was tightened and became more expensive. There's a truckload of distress to go around.

But in every financial cloud there seems to be a silver lining, and clichés not withstanding, there is usually money to be made when others are suffering. I'm seeing this now with the establishment of buy-side firms whose strategy is to invest in distressed assets. *Opportunistic investing* and *vulture investing* are two terms also used to identify this strategy.[12]

An adage of the financial world is that the time to buy is when blood is running in the streets. And blood is currently running down Wall Street. Carlyle Group, a buy-side private equity firm, suffered the indignity of having a mortgage securities fund collapse due to the credit crisis. Yet, after this, Carlyle raised $1.35 billion in early 2008 to create a fund that will invest in distressed assets.[13]

Blackstone Group raised nearly $11 billion to buy the class of assets most hard hit during the crisis: real estate.[14] Apollo Management said in March 2008 that it will buy $1 billion in distressed debt.[15]

These distressed funds are a sign of the times. They appear when the going gets tough and the wounded have a hard time getting out of the way. The buy side, and in particular private equity firms, are among the most active players in this market. W. L. Ross & Company paid $2.6 billion for two mortgage servicers and a bond insurance company.[16] Citadel Investment Group bought $2.5 billion of online broker E*TRADE's asset-backed securities for $800 million, or 27 cents on the dollar, in November 2007.[17]

One of the more interesting skirmishes in the Battle for Wall Street is how private equity firms are buying the distressed assets of major sell-side players. Those assets, of all things, are the leveraged debt the sell side has issued on behalf of the private equity funds. The game plan was simple: Private equity firms had their financing to do their thing; the sell side had the debt for distribution. Well, as the saying goes, "The best-laid plans . . ."

Then, the credit crisis of 2007–2008 came into play, and everything changed. Now, the sell side is left holding the leveraged

(continued)

debt on their books. The media reported that the sell-side Deutsche Bank was selling $15 billion to $20 billion of high-risk debt to several private equity firms for less than 90 cents on the dollar in April 2008.[18]

Deutsche Bank was not alone in pursuing this strategy. The last I heard, Citigroup wanted to sell $12 billion of leveraged loans at 90 cents on the dollar.[19]

Those using the distressed investment strategy are counting on having bought debt at a low enough price that, in the future, they can sell the debt back to the marketplace at a profit. This isn't the first time that such a strategy has been used by savvy investors. Some bought distressed savings-and-loan assets from the Resolution Trust, which was created in response to the savings-and-loan crisis of the 1980s, and generally did very well with such investments.

Perhaps we'll see a replay with the distressed assets bought during the current credit crisis. More to the point, in the Battle for Wall Street, we now see the sell side selling distressed debt to the buy side at a discount.

A win for the private equity firms and buy side? Most definitely. No surprise: The private equity firms are in the game to make money, and these trades should prove profitable. And is it a win for the sell side? I would say yes, to a lesser extent. I applaud their efforts to sell assets and delever the balance sheet.

Battle Lines Converge

One phenomenon affecting the private equity industry—and the buy-side more generally—is convergence. Convergence refers to the blurring of the line between private equity and hedge funds, where each is getting into the other's business. Traditionally, hedge funds and private equity firms have been quite distinct. But today, some hedge funds are getting into the private equity business, such as D. E. Shaw[20] and Cerberus Capital Management,[21] while some private equity firms are treading over the line onto the hedge fund side, such as the Carlyle Group[22] and TPG.[23]

Traditionally, hedge funds invested short term, used hedging strategies, dealt in publicly traded securities, and did not get involved with the management of companies. Private equity firms, however, invested longer term, took companies private, and often got deeply involved in the running of the companies in which they invested, including taking control.

But hedge funds have grown enormously, both in the number of funds created and in the capital they have available to them. This makes earning the large returns that their investors have come to expect increasingly difficult to achieve. As a result, at least some hedge fund managers are expanding their universe of investment opportunities. These include buying stakes in private companies that are not very liquid and getting involved with the running of these companies.

Sound familiar? Yes, this sounds suspiciously like what private equity firms do.

At the same time, there are aspects of the hedge fund game that are highly desirable to private equity firms. For example, hedge fund investors have fairly ready access to their assets, while private equity investors must endure longer lock-up periods—sometimes for many years—when they can't touch their money. Put another way, hedge fund investments are more liquid than private equity investments.[24]

Access to hedge funds also gives the private equity investor the opportunity to diversify his or her holdings. If the private equity firm has hedge funds to offer its investors when they do liquidate their private equity investments, the private equity firm can keep their money, rather than seeing it go across the street to someone else's hedge fund. This allows the private equity firm to hold on to more of its clients' money, and gives the clients, who are looking for a more liquid investment, the opportunity to stay with a firm that they like and trust.

Simply put, client stickiness.

There may also be synergies within the hedge fund or private equity firm. These firms compete for investors' money and for managerial talent, and having both forms of investing under one roof can give them a competitive advantage for both money and talent.

Another factor in the private equity world worth noting is the club deal. Historically, private equity firms made their investments alone. But in recent years, private equity firms have joined together—into "clubs"—to make purchases that each individually might not be able to finance, while also spreading the risk. We saw this club mentality surrounding the purchase of SunGard. Two of the leading lights in the private equity world—Blackstone and KKR—teamed together to pull this deal off.[25] Interestingly, this development is in sharp contrast to what one sees on the sell side. Goldman Sachs and JPMorgan don't team up when pursuing sell-side acquisitions, for example.

It's ironic how convergence can take on multiple meanings. Two examples come to mind. One, as I mentioned earlier in the chapter, involved the sell-side meeting with a fair amount of resistance from private equity to the allure of financial service opportunities. Well, currently, we have successful private equity firms whose sole strategy is what these folks once strenuously avoided—financial services. A prime example is J. C. Flowers.

To the outside world, Chris Flowers is a well-known, savvy investor whose track record includes the takeover and makeover of Shinsei Bank.[26] Insiders, though, know we can add Chris Flowers to the list of sell-side talent migration to the buy side. Flowers was a product of Goldman Sachs's farm system.

Fund of Funds

"A mutual fund that invests in other mutual funds. Just as a mutual fund invests in a number of different securities, a fund of funds holds shares of many different mutual funds. These funds were designed to achieve even greater diversification than traditional mutual funds."

Source: InvestorWords.com, Web Finance, Inc., www.investorwords.com/2129/fund_of_funds.html.

The second example involves a variation of the hedge fund world entering private equity space. The concept of a fund of funds, which found its way to hedge funds, has now taken root in the private equity arena and is called private equity fund of funds.[27]

Simply put, if you have an investor, such as a public pension, contemplating a capital commitment of, say, $3 billion to the private equity market, now there's an intermediary, a fund of funds, that steps in and slices and dices the pension's monies. It could take the $3 billion and divide it up among three private equity firms, giving each $1 billion. I would suspect this makes private equity more appealing to a broader range of investors.

Bottom Line

Investment opportunities for private equity firms are expanding as they move into the hedge fund world. They are also expanding as private equity firms band together into clubs to make joint investments. The plan of going vertical into other businesses is adding fuel to private equity's growth engine.

The Lehman Incubator

As we discussed in Chapter 4, the sell side served as a farm system for the hedge funds. Bankers, traders, and research analysts developed their skill base before moving over to the buy side. And the sell-siders who migrated to the buy side were not just heading to the hedge funds, but to the private equity firms as well.

A popular route originated from Lehman Brothers. You could say it was one of the largest sell-side farm systems for private equity talent. I was a member of the team of associates at Lehman Brothers Kuhn Loeb, before the firm was sold to American Express. Until then, Lehman was a private partnership.

Over time, I watched my teammates move to private equity firms. One example was Matt Barger, who went on to become the managing general partner of Hellman-Friedman, which is one of the oldest and most successful private equity firms.[28] In fact, one of Hellman-Friedman's cofounders was from Lehman Brothers.

Serendipitously, when I was at Lehman, my office was directly opposite the investment banking analyst pool. This pool was composed of recent college graduates who spent a two-year tour of duty at Lehman before going off for something else, such as graduate school. From my office's vantage point, I saw analysts make their way to successful careers in private equity firms, including Jim Coulter, cofounder of the third-largest private equity firm, TPG.[29]

It wasn't just the junior ranks leaving Lehman. I watched senior managing directors exiting stage left, only to reenter stage right to form their own private equity firms like Cypress Group[30] or to head private equity firms like AEA.[31]

One more point: Lehman and BlackRock, sell- and buy-side companies, share an interesting past. Two notable Lehman alums—Ralph Schlosstein and Sue Wagner—were part of the original BlackRock team. The battleground for Wall Street is smaller than you may think.

Bottom Line

In its battle with the buy side, the sell side is fighting a talent exodus on two fronts. It's not just the hedge funds but the private equity firms that are penetrating deep into the sell side for talent. I suspect this talent migration, unfolding on two fronts, is somewhat uneven. The switching of uniforms from the sell side to the buy side is probably greater with hedge funds than with private equity funds.

Case Study: Blackstone—From Sell-Side M&A to Private Equity

The most notable Lehman alumni to make their way to the private equity world were Pete Peterson and Steve Schwarzman, who formed the Blackstone Group in 1985.

In early 2007, *Fortune* magazine ranked today's top private equity firms, and leading the pack was Blackstone Group.[32] The Blackstone story is a spectacular one. The firm opened its doors with $400,000, and today has tens of billions of dollars under management.[33] This isn't just a story about a giant in the private equity industry, but one of a company that went vertical into a number of highly successful ventures.

Blackstone started as a merger-and-acquisition (M&A) advisory business and a private equity firm. It could well have opened its doors with the motto "Senior-level advice on an unconflicted basis." One of Blackstone's first deals was advising E. F. Hutton on its sale to Shearson Lehman, a return of sorts to their old firm, Lehman. As an offshoot of their traditional private equity firm, they started a real estate private equity business. Today, it is one of the very biggest, including an investment in Hilton Hotels, with a transaction value of about $20 billion.[34]

And let's not forget their $39 billion real estate play, Equity Office Partners Trust.[35] In the course of the deal, they simultaneously unloaded $13 billion.[36] Clever guys. They also branched out into a restructuring practice and into debt products, namely mezzanine financing (a hybrid of debt and equity financing that is typically used to finance the expansion of existing companies), while also moving into hedge funds.

Blackstone was one of the first U.S. firms to go to Asia looking for outside investors, and teamed up with Nikko Securities.[37] The new capital was used to invest in Blackstone's own hedge funds for its own account, eventually growing this internal hedge fund business into one of the world's largest fund-of-fund complexes.[38] Clever guys.

Blackstone was also good at identifying entrepreneurs able to run start-up businesses.[39] Its vision was to provide seed money to smart guys with good business plans. One of its ventures was Blackstone Financial, which had Larry Fink at its helm. As I said in Chapter 1, Blackstone Financial is now the legendary BlackRock.

In 2008, the investor pool is deep and wide, as there are plenty of pension funds and endowments, but when Blackstone started in the 1980s, all it had to work with, I suspect, was its advisory M&A Rolodex, and, for the most part, all it could call on to raise money were the corporate pension funds (pension funds set up for the employees of corporations). The public pension funds, like CalPERS, weren't really playing in this space. Nonetheless, Blackstone raised the largest first-time private equity fund.[40]

In a further intentional move, we have seen Blackstone team up with an other Asian investor, this time the Chinese government, which invested $3 billion in the firm.[41] I guess you could say the Chinese government likes the Blackstone story. Another way to look at it is that the Chinese government gets a $3 billion peek inside the workings of Blackstone's investment strategies.[42]

A bit of irony: While Blackstone is a wonderful success story, it has become its own fertile ground for those who passed through there and then set off on their own. This includes Glenn Hutchins at Silver Lake Partners,[43] whose investors include Michael Dell, Bill Gates, and Larry Ellison. Another example: Roger Altman, former Deputy Secretary of the Treasury, who founded the successful boutique, Evercore Partners.[44]

Case Study: Fortress Investment Group— From Sell-Side Traders to Private Equity

Smart folks, those guys at Fortress. We could say they built a business around the concept that risk comes in all shapes and sizes. It appears they maintain a laser-like focus on monitoring risk by considering risk from an overall business construct.

The origin of their thinking may come from the mortgage, fixed-income side of the business, which is where the top guys came from. The CEO, Wesley Edens, long ago was a senior member of the Lehman mortgage trading area.[45] And he shares a sell-side background at UBS and buy-side experience at BlackRock with his two founding partners, Robert Kauffman[46] and Randal Nardone.[47]

Two other noteworthy members of the senior management team who joined Fortress after its founding are Peter Briger Jr. and Michael Novogratz, who were Goldman Sachs alumni.[48] It looks like our sell-side farm team, that great Wall Street incubator, was working overtime for Fortress.

What did this team build? A diversified model—part hedge fund, part private equity firm, part real estate, and part real estate debt instruments. The private equity business involved control-oriented management buyouts.[49] The hedge fund business looked at undervalued and distressed assets, while also looking to capitalize on market inefficiencies in the fixed-income and equity markets.[50]

They truly understood the importance of permanent, outside capital and tapped into two sources. In late 2006, Fortress orchestrated a capital investment from Nomura Holdings, Japan's largest securities firm, which resulted in Nomura's holding a 15 percent interest in Fortress.[51] A few months later, Fortress brought in more money by being the first U.S. hedge fund to go public.[52] And a few months after that, Blackstone went down the same initial public offering (IPO) path.

Speaking of pools of capital, it's my understanding that the folks at Fortress don't allocate capital based on business lines (like retail banking or investment banking). Instead, it appears that they allocate it across their entire portfolio and move the capital to where the opportunities are. This is in contrast to a number of other firms that designate capital for specific types of businesses. Wise move.

Not surprisingly, given the clubby nature of Wall Street, the underwriters of Fortress's IPO were none other than Goldman Sachs and Lehman Brothers, the incubators of those in Fortress's senior management suites.[53]

A piece of news: One of the early Democratic presidential contenders of the 2008 election was John Edwards. As write this, Edwards has an association with a hedge fund—none other than Fortress.

I also find it interesting that Fortress was reported to have taken a look at buying Bear Stearns, or at least part of it, a few months prior to Bear's collapse.[54] Though the linkup never occurred, it is noteworthy that it was even considered. Here was a buy-side fixed-income player potentially looking to acquire a sell-side fixed-income player, or selected fixed-income businesses.

Five years ago, that would have been inconceivable.

Question: Why was Fortress even looking at Bear Stearns? A place like Fortress lives on information, particularly in the fixed income market. So why wouldn't it look at Bear and see what there is to learn?

In a situation like that, Fortress could have gained information just by taking a close look at Bear, much as home buyers do by looking at homes in the neighborhood where they want to live, even if they're not interested in buying most of the homes they see. Fortress may have thought that it could buy pools of assets or select businesses from Bear Stearns at attractive levels. As I note elsewhere, Bear's collapse was not a standard situation, and I don't think Fortress expected a run on Bear's bank, or for it to implode as quickly as it did. Fortress probably has benefited from Bear's collapse anyway, as I suspect a few Bear alumni resumes have made their way to Fortress. This is one more example of the migration of talent from the sell to buy side.

The Fortress guys are pretty good at assembling information and putting it to work. Where do they find it? They have access to great pools of information. In some ways, they are like the sell side. Fortress has established strong working relationships with everybody, and is able to tap into this network, much like sell-side firms have done for a long time.

No question, though, that Fortress hit a bump in the road with the subprime crisis. It got hurt and its stock plummeted. Hopefully, better days ahead. You have to like their sell side's understanding of information and their buy side's culture of nimbleness and entrepreneurship.

Implications

This chapter provokes three questions to think about:

1. Will the private equity firms disintermediate the sell side from its need for financing?

I'm hearing private equity firms talk about disintermediating from the sell side, but I think the answer is—as always—size. On a small scale, maybe, but on a large scale, no. For a $300 million financing, maybe. But for a $5 billion one, no. They can't create money. They need the sell side.

2. Will we see civil war, with major casualties and blowups, among the major private equity firms?

It's a timely question. As I write this, the sell-side foundation is experiencing a major break in the collapses of Bear Stearns, Lehman Brothers, and Washington Mutual, while the hedge fund foundation is experiencing a number of cracks. A few of the smaller funds are falling. A few of the larger funds are suffering first-time losses.

However, the private equity foundation is being supported by two beams, duration and diversification. By definition, private equity firms see the world through a long-range lens. They are long-term players who can weather market volatility like that seen in the credit crunch of 2007–2008.

These firms may own 20, 30, even 100 companies. This diversifies their risk. They are clever and will continue to diversify into other businesses, further spreading their risk. Therefore, the private equity foundation is not breaking like the sell side or experiencing a series of shocks like the hedge funds—it is holding its own.

3. What will the private equity landscape look like in 2008 and beyond?

As I write this, the private equity firms are singing the small-deal-size blues. It wasn't that long ago that we were seeing headlines about $100 billion private equity deals hovering just over the horizon. Well, that horizon is further in the distance. What do I see in the near term? Private equity firms hoping for $1 billion deals.

Now is a tough time for the big private equity funds, namely the $20 billion–plus funds. Let's say that the fund is leveraged 5 to 1. That equates to $100 billion, which means it has to do $100 billion worth of deals. The problem: You cannot do $100 billion worth of deals in 2008. The arithmetic just doesn't work.

Guess what? You're not the only $20 billion private equity fund out there. There may be four other guys like you. With a total of five, we now have $500 billion worth of deals to do. Well, how's this for arithmetic: If you couldn't do $100 billion worth of deals, good luck with $500 billion worth.

While the private equity deal size is decreasing, the strategic industry players' ability to compete against the private equity firms is increasing. The low-cost, high-amount of leverage financing for the private equity players has disappeared in 2008, and with that has disappeared the private equity firms' prime advantage over the industry players when buying companies.

Also working against a number of the private equity firms is their performance going forward. Let's put into the blender the possibility that they have to review the market value of their positions.

What comes out of the blender? These firms may have to revisit their historical performance numbers, which could lead to restating their numbers downward. And as investment performance starts to lag or is not what it was thought to be, it could be more difficult for a number of these firms to raise new investor money.

Common sense says the private equity machine has to slow down. If anyone has a problem, everyone has a problem, so the private equity firms and the sell-side firms are scrambling as I write this book.

What about going forward? The sell-side institutions should not hold their breath for a return of the glory days of high leverage and big private equity fees.

The private equity firms may not see a return to the glory days of high leverage and big deals, but they will see what I call a return to the good days, thanks to hoards of uninvested capital and the opportunity to acquire undervalued assets or businesses into the aftermath of the 2007–2008 credit crisis.

Battle Victorious: Buy side.

Chapter 6

Entrepreneurs to Endowments: Buy-Side Catalysts

M ention the names Seth Merrin and Liquidnet to someone on Wall Street, and if you see a smile, chances are you are talking to a buy-sider; a frown indicates that you're probably speaking to a member of the sell side.

Merrin is a notable member of a fraternity that I refer to as Wall Street entrepreneurs. This group is made up of innovative folks who have helped transform Wall Street by building trading services and creating execution platforms used by both the buy and sell sides.

Think of people like Merrin as being Wall Street's equivalent of Thomas Edison. Edison invented the light bulb; Merrin helped reinvent Wall Street's landscape.

On Wall Street, the technology-maker entrepreneurs, while willing to sell to either side, were mostly interested in the buy side. The entrepreneurs' sales pitch to the buy side could have been quite simple: "You're lacking the research and development capabilities and the information technology infrastructure of the sell side."

What these entrepreneurs offered the buy side, notably hedge funds, was access to cheaper, faster, broader technology and alternative trading channels. These entrepreneurs allowed the buy side to break away from the sell side—to be more independent and self-sufficient, to stand on their own two feet. Is it any surprise the buy side asked where it could sign up?

This led to a shift in the balance of power on Wall Street.

Only the Buy Side Need Apply

Seth Merrin is the story of Liquidnet.[1] Historically, if you were a buy-side player and you had a large block of shares to trade, you would call a sell-side player to execute your order. But you did the trade under a cloud of fear that the market would get wind of what you were trying to do, which, in turn, could hurt the price you received or paid. You sweated the whole time.

As discussed in Chapter 2, algorithmic trading is a tool for handling this challenge. Briefly, algorithmic trading uses technology to "spread" the trades. Such tactics camouflage what the buy-side trader is doing, while increasing the opportunities to find parties to trade with, all of which helps to trade large blocks of shares without having the market move against the trader.

Traditionally, the large buy-side trader was virtually dependent on the sell side. With the advent of computers and sophisticated software, algorithmic trading became a second option. Merrin provided the buy side with a third way: He created a network whose only members were from the buy side. Sell-side firms were not admitted into the club. The network he created is called Liquidnet.[2]

Let's look at a hypothetical example of how Liquidnet works. Imagine a buy-side player, say a hedge fund trader, sitting at his desk.

A manager in his organization sends him a message telling him to sell 1 million shares of Company A at $50 per share. The trader contacts a permissioned member of Liquidnet, also a hedge fund, and asks if he'd like to buy the shares at $50. The Liquidnet player pings back the trader and says, "I'll buy them at $49." The first trader counters with, "How about 250,000 shares at $49?" The buyer says, "Done," clicks on his computer to confirm the trade, and the deal is completed.

Why would this be so revolutionary? Because this trade was done totally between buy-side players; there were no sell-side firms involved. In addition, no one learned the identities of the trading partners until after it was done, because there was no widespread dissemination of news about the trade before it was completed.[3] It is a whole new face for the trading space.

One benefit of this new face is the inherent value of the price not moving against you. To demonstrate this, my understanding is that Merrin looked at studies that showed the average cost of doing a block trade was high, and the high cost was not just because of exchange fees and broker fees.[4] The big cost was the market itself being in front of the trade, figuring out what was going on, and then moving the price against the trader.

According to industry observers, Liquidnet's sales pitch could have been as simple as: "We can save you money. And if we don't, you can go back to what you always did—using the services of the sell side. You've got nothing to lose."

The first investors who helped finance Liquidnet were venture capitalists, followed by a handful of private equity firms.[5] It's not surprising that they footed the bill, since the sell side had no incentive to do so. You're probably thinking that when Merrin went out with his Liquidnet story and told the buy side that he could achieve better pricing, the buy side hugged him and asked where he had been all this time.

But, according to industry observers, the buy side's reaction back then was more like, "No thanks." The buy side could have said: "Excuse me, but you want to take my super secret order and put it on your network where all my competitors are? That's crazy. Why would I want to share my secrets with my competitors?" This would have been a new twist on the Battle for Wall Street, with the buy side fighting the buy side.

The buy side might very well have figured that by using the sell side, trading would be a bit pricier, but that was better than trading on a network with its closest competitors. Imagine mutual fund giants Fidelity Investments and Vanguard sharing such information.

To such an argument, Liquidnet, according to industry observers, could have responded with something like: "First, you already trust your sell-side brokers with your block trades. That's a lot of trust. Second, our network is anonymous—no one will know it's you. And third, our network is voluntary.[6] If it doesn't work, you haven't lost anything. It's an opportunity to execute orders before you pick up a phone and call the sell side. The only cost with Liquidnet is seconds."[7]

Liquidnet and Merrin's vision have become one of Wall Street's wonderful entrepreneurial stories.

Bottom Line

It took the buy side time to realize the value that Seth Merrin and all the other Wall Street entrepreneurs brought to the table. Today, they're quite happy that these entrepreneurs knocked on their doors. They ask of the Seth Merrins, "Where have you been all my life?"

As I write this, Liquidnet has filed registration to go public at a multibillion-dollar valuation.[8] Of course, the underwriters of such an offering would be sell side firms. Yes, you could say the sell side finally has a role with Seth Merrin.

If this happens, the sell side can now smile, not frown.

Here Comes the Cavalry—The Entrepreneurs

For the longest time, the buy side relied on the sell side for market price, for market color, for market execution. What the sell side offered, for the most part, was more commodity-like than a customized service. Over time, the buy side began to look for less expensive, more independent ways to trade. It was looking for an advantage.

That's when Wall Street's entrepreneurs came along and asked the buy-side traders what tools they wanted, what they needed to do their jobs better. They asked, "What is your wish list?"

In addition to Seth Merrin's revolutionary weapon, let me give you two other examples of where entrepreneurs filled buy-side needs—where Christmas came early.

One was by providing comprehensive market information. The market is fragmented. There may be three different places that provide quotes on a stock. Would the buy side like to see all three quotes or just the quote from, say, the New York Stock Exchange (NYSE)? Of course, seeing all three quotes is preferred.

In response to this need, the entrepreneur builds a computer system that provides the buy-side trader with data from all sources who are providing quotes on a stock. By doing so, he or she has effectively given the buy-side trader the ability to see the whole market on one computer display. The buy side today has one less reason to call the sell-side broker for market information. When the two sides are not talking to one another, it's one less chance for the sell side to make a sale—less money in their pockets. No surprise: advantage, buy side.

Another example of the role of entrepreneurs in the Battle for Wall Street relates to fair value pricing (FPV). Think of this as something you can't read in newspapers or on your Yahoo! screen. You go to your Yahoo! screen and type, "XYZ 2010 bonds yielding 10 percent." It's easy to find a quote for IBM, but it tends to be much more difficult for such XYZ bonds. Quite simply, how can you know the fair value price of the bonds if you cannot locate them?

Fair Value Pricing

"Fair value pricing (FVP) can be defined as an application of a Manager's best estimate of the amount an investment fund might receive on a sale, or expect to pay on a purchase, of one or more securities, or even an entire portfolio of securities, at the time of the fund's valuation point, with the intention of producing a 'fairer' dealing price thereby protecting ongoing, incoming and outgoing investors."

Source: "Pricing Guidance for Investment Firms: Fair Value Pricing." Investment Management Association, September 2004; www.investmentfunds.org.uk/press/2004/20041006-01.pdf.

Let me give you another take on FVP. The buy side wants to sell an exotic derivative for, say, $100. The trader calls up a sell-side broker, who offers $95. Another broker offers $96. That broker wins because he has offered the best price. But thanks to the tools created by our fraternity of entrepreneurs, the buy side can now get a better picture of the market and find that the fair value price of that exotic derivative is, in fact, $100.

Mark to Market

"Recording the price or value of a security, portfolio, or account on a daily basis, to calculate profits and losses or to confirm that margin requirements are being met."

Source: InvestorWords.com, Web Finance, Inc., www.investorwords.com/2996/mark_to_market.html.

The trader now has access to much of the same information as the sell side, so he now knows what the fair price is. Until then, the sell side had no reason to give away pricing information. It could make money on the spread—the difference between what it paid or sold a security for and what its customer received. But if the buy side knew the real fair value price, it would go to another source and the sell-side broker would lose his fees. No surprise: advantage, buy side.

There's a related issue worth mentioning. There are many exotic contracts, like over-the-counter interest rate swaps. Issues regarding such contracts have been dealt with deftly by Wall Street's entrepreneurs. For example, suppose you're a hedge fund and want to mark to market your portfolio. You have a limited partner, an outside auditor or whomever, who comes to you and asks what your portfolio is worth.

The trader responds by saying, "My system tells me it's worth $1 billion."

The partner responds by saying, "That's your valuation, but I need an independent third party to tell me the value."

The partner is, in effect, looking for a Good Housekeeping–type seal of approval.

The challenge: It's hard to understand the true value of a portfolio of exotic securities because their market is limited and hard to find, and therefore their prices are difficult to pin down.

Coming up with an independent appraisal of exotic investments isn't easy. Enter a number of entrepreneurs, who saw this problem and decided they would develop software to independently price whatever is inside an investor's portfolio, no matter how exotic it is. These entrepreneurs have produced a third-party mark-to-market software product. The hedge fund can buy it off the shelf and run the models. Such mark-to-market valuations are becoming more popular and may even become required as people look for external confirmation.

Overlay the safety net of external portfolio confirmation with a hedge fund producing high returns and what do you get? A win–win for hedge funds and advantage for the buy side.

From market information and pricing to market execution, we've witnessed another breed of entrepreneurs who have developed DMA—direct market access.[9] These entrepreneurs were aware of the fact that hedge fund traders traditionally call sell-side brokers to put through trades, and that hedge fund traders may not want to do that for fear of tipping their hand to the sell side.

So this breed of entrepreneurs went out and obtained broker/dealer licenses.[10] We'll call one of them Acme Broker/Dealer. These Acme folks put an Acme screen on a hedge fund desktop. The hedge fund trader clicks on the computer to confirm the trade and the order does not go through the sell-side system, but rather through Acme and straight on to an exchange like the NYSE or Nasdaq, bypassing the sell side.[11]

Acme can't provide any other services for the buy side. It's a single-purpose entity, a conduit; with no research capabilities, no prime brokerage.[12] It can't even take you to lunch.

It is simply a connection—the way you might connect to the Internet. As a result, it doesn't provide a lot of value. But if you're a cynic, you might think it's good

Direct Market Access

"The buy side is taking more control of its trading decisions while looking for faster, lower-cost and anonymous executions. Direct market access (DMA) tools permit buy-side traders to access liquidity pools and multiple execution venues directly, without intervention from a broker's trading desk. . . . With DMA, they [the buy side] are renting a broker's infrastructure and clearing via the broker, but they are controlling the order. The real motivation for aggressive DMA trading on the buy side is cheaper commissions—DMA commissions are about one cent a share, while program trades cost roughly two cents a share and block trades cost four cents to five cents per share."

Source: Ivy Schmerken, "Direct Market Access Trading," *Wall Street & Technology,* February 4, 2005; www.wallstreetandtech.com/features/showArticle.jhtml?articleID=59301336.

that they're a single-oriented entity, because if you're the buy side, how do you know what happens when your order goes through the sell-side system?

These sell-side guys are pretty clever and they could take advantage of the buy side. A little bit of paranoia on the buy side's part played right into Acme's hand.

The irony is that, as I write this, a number of the DMAs have been acquired by other broker/dealers.[13] When an independent broker like Knight Capital makes this type of acquisition, I understand.[14] What's hard for me to understand is when sell-side firms buy DMAs. But buying them, they are.

Merrill bought a DMA called Wave Securities.[15] I understand the logic of the sell side's wanting to reconnect to the buy side and capture hedge fund trading flows. But I would think that the perception of a conflict of interest with the DMA no longer being an independent entity may come into play with the hedge fund. I suspect the sell side's view regarding ownership of a DMA is that it will position DMAs in a nonconflicting light and will offer its buy-side clientele an alternative electronic platform providing faster, cheaper execution.[16]

Bottom Line

There was a time, 10 or 15 years ago, when you would call a sell-side broker for something as simple as price information. There's no reason to do that today. The buy side can effectively see the whole market. It has access to good information on pricing and can trade electronically.

The entrepreneur is filling the needs of the buy side at the expense of the sell side. As this happens, the Battle for Wall Street shifts slightly in favor of the buy side.

Entrepreneurs Are Created, Not Born

Where can one find the products and services produced by these entrepreneurs? One place to look is the front end—something you put on the desktop that collects all the price quotes in the market. Let's say you're a trader and you want to look at the price of X relative to the price of Y and relative to the price of Z. There's a good chance that the traditional sources of a trader's information don't provide this kind of comparison. It's just too specific, too limited.

But an entrepreneur looking for market niches will say to the trader that he will create a screen just the way the trader wants it. He'll jump in and cater to the trader's needs.

Taking the time, trouble, and risk to provide this kind of a service requires a certain type of personality.

Who are such entrepreneurs? The majority of the time I would suspect that they're ex-traders. Makes sense, right? They know what traders are looking for, and they can talk with all the advantages of an insider.

Another type of entrepreneur is the person from the sell side's information technology (IT) department. IT departments can, in fact, become their own farm systems: places where smart folks hone their skills, learn the workings of Wall Street, and then are creative enough to see where there are market niches they can exploit. They raise a little money; develop a product or service that is cheaper, faster, and broader than anything available; and then offer it to buy-side traders, as well as their old sell-side colleagues.

Is the buy side thinking of sending flowers to our entrepreneurs for making their lives somewhat easier? In fact, they may want to extend their goodwill by sending chocolates to their fellow private-equity colleagues as well as venture capital firms. (As I discussed earlier, a number of private equity firms, as one example, have assisted entrepreneurs with funding.) The private equity firms that have stepped up are not, for the most part, household names like Blackstone or Carlyle. Instead, they're Summit Partners, which invested in Liquidnet,[17] and TA Associates, which invested in Lava Trading, just to name two.[18]

I'd be remiss if I didn't mention the important role venture capital firms played in the growth of financial entrepreneurial companies. Sequoia Capital is one.[19] It's best known for its technology investments in Apple, Yahoo!, Google, and YouTube, among others. Sequoia then crossed over into financial technology by also investing in such Wall Street companies as Merlin Securities, which links prime brokerage services to the buy side.

You may recall that we discussed prime brokerage in an earlier chapter. That it comes up again is indicative of how many aspects of the Battle for Wall Street are interrelated.

Another firm worth mentioning is GTCR Golder Rauner. They took the concept of financing entrepreneurs one step further by teaming up with a financial institution, Bank of New York, and an entrepreneur, Eze Castle. Together, they formed a new venture called BNY ConvergEx Group.[20]

Order Management Systems

"Systems that receive customer order information and inventory availability from the warehouse management system and then group orders by customer and priority, allocate inventory by warehouse site, and establish delivery dates."

Source: Bitpipe.com, www.bitpipe.com/tlist/Order-Management-Systems.html.

In the true spirit of this chapter on entrepreneurs, all three partners in this venture, along with company management, were equity owners in the new company. This new enterprise will play on the cross-selling theme of offering a suite of services to buy-side traders and sell-side brokers alike, ranging from DMAs to order management systems (OMSs). Convergence of buy-side solutions is alive and well.

Bottom Line

The sell side is losing ground to the buy side thanks to the advancing entrepreneurial network supplied by private equity and venture capital firms. The entrepreneurs are arming the buy side with independent information and execution. Private equity and venture capital firms are financing and accelerating entrepreneurial growth. A winning combination for the buy side.

Case Study: Lava Trading—Comprehensive Market Information

One of my favorite stories is about Lava Trading, a company of entrepreneurs who developed a front-end comprehensive market information screen. The folks at Lava watched the Securities and Exchange Commission (SEC) change the rules and created matching engines, where for the first time, traders were free to send an equity order to locales like an electronic communication network (ECN).[21] Previously, they were limited to destinations like Nasdaq or the NYSE. The Lava folks saw an opportunity.

What if the trader wants a quote from, say, an ECN or electronic exchange? (I will discuss both in the next chapter.) Nasdaq has no reason to build that into its screen. It wants you trading on its exchange, not someone else's.

Lava took another tack. It offered traders quotes from multiple sources, and placed the best quotes at the top of the screen.[22] All the trader needed to do was click on the desired quote, and the order was executed on the exchange originating the quote. A simple idea, but a great one. The Lava folks are clever.

Lava ended up affecting not only buy-side players like hedge funds and institutional investors, but the sell side as well, who fell in love with the product. As I write this, Lava and other Lava-type direct market technology providers, which directly hook up the trader with the exchange, have been acquired by the sell side. Lava was bought by Citigroup.[23] Goldman Sachs jumped into this arena as well when it bought Spear Leeds & Kellogg, which had an attractive asset in the direct access technology space called REDIPlus.[24]

Of course, the Lavas of the world are supposed to be broker neutral. I'm assuming that Citigroup will have Lava continue as a separate, brokerage-neutral platform. I am sure, though, that these conflict-of-interest questions will continue to come up and make for interesting conversations that I suspect the sell side is only too happy to have with the buy side.[25]

Throughout the 2000s, the sell side steadily lost its information advantage and those almighty fees to the buy side. Acquisitions of entrepreneurs like Lava allow the sell side to restock its arsenal and reengage with the buy side. The sell side can only hope that by taking out independent providers like Lava, allied to the buy side, the fee pendulum swings back to its side of the line.

Case Study: Markit Group—Fair Value Pricing

This is a story of entrepreneurs who built on the concept of independent pricing. If you want a stock or bond quote, open the newspaper or look at your desktop terminal. But what if you want to price or trade, say, credit derivatives, which are not easy to find?

To fill this niche came credit derivative traders (as I mentioned earlier, many Wall Street entrepreneurs came from the traders' ranks). They realized that there's no reference price for credit derivatives. Historically, if you wanted to trade credit derivatives, you would have to call the sell

Credit Derivatives

"A contract between two parties that allows for the use of a derivative instrument to transfer credit risk from one party to another. The party transferring risk away has to pay a fee to the party that will take the risk."

Source: InvestorWords.com, Web Finance, Inc., www.investorwords.com/1200/credit_derivative.html.

side and ask the price. In general, the sell side had no interest and no incentive to provide a public price.[26] (The sell side likes the fact that you have to call and ask them.)

Well, the Markit guys came along and decided they would go to all of the sell-side dealers to get their prices. They would then average the prices, create a reference price, and publish it.[27] This wasn't that easy, though, since the Markit guys needed the sell side to give up the market information.

We can surmise from industry observers say that the Markit folks went to the sell-side dealers and discussed two possibilities: (1) that they wanted the information for free, and (2) that they would charge the buy side for the information.

At first, one could imagine, the sell-side dealers said no. They may have wondered why they should give away market information that would lessen opacity in the market. That lack of transparency worked to the sell side's advantage. The Markit guys were brilliant. They could have proposed the following sell-side discussion: "It's going to happen anyway—would you like to own and control it or let someone else do it?" They let the sell side become owners. It worked. Very clever.[28]

With the sell side in the fold—no surprise—the Markit folks turned their attention to the other side of the battlefield. According to industry observers, it is possible that their proposal to the buy side (after all, they wanted the buy side to pay for the information) went something like: "Now, if you want to trade, say, an insurance product, you have to call the sell side and ask what the quote is on $100 of protection. To which they say, 'X cents.' But with the information we will provide you, you'll have a reference price. Now, if they say X cents, you can counter with a reference price that says Y cents."[29]

Providing such a wealth of information to the buy side gave them a pricing advantage. And, like the sell side, the buy-side guys said, "Sign me up."

The Markit team turned a simple concept into a valuable asset whose value today is speculated to be multibillions of dollars.[30]

Markit is a great example of profiting from the Battle for Wall Street. Markit is letting both sides win. Markit is feeding the buy-side appetite for independent pricing information, while it is feeding the sell side's desire to stay in the game and have a piece of the buy-side action or, should I say, a piece of the buy-side fees.

Case Study: G-Trade—Electronic Execution

The battle lines between the sell side and the buy side blurred when two colorful characters who hailed from the sell side recognized the importance of the ascending buy side. Both characters were part of CLSA Emerging Markets, an innovative brokerage house for the Asia-Pacific Markets, and its subsidiary, G-Trade, one of the global leaders in wholesale electronic trade execution services. Their names are Gary Coull and Jonathan Slone.

Gary Coull began his career as a business journalist in Hong Kong. After six years, he left journalism for the business world, eventually cofounding CLSA in 1996. Everyone who met him loved him because he was a forward thinker with great people skills and commercial judgment. Everyone went to the CLSA Emerging Markets Asian conferences, not so much to mingle with each other as to spend an hour or two with Coull.

Coull was a classic entrepreneur, and his mind was always working on new ideas. One of those novel concepts was to hire journalists as researchers for CLSA.[31] He believed they would give the reader the "angle" on a story and the essentials, and not get bogged down in unimportant details. He would tell his research analysts to "stick the story at the front and leave the numbers at the back." He was after the big story, not the micro facts.

One of his most powerful ideas was that the buy side needed independent research in general and Asian research in particular. It was a combination that locked the buy side into his side of the Street at a time when the buy side relied on the sell side for information and research.

Interestingly enough, now that information and research are more readily available, the buy side is still knocking on CLSA's doors due to its unique combination of independence, innovations, and insight into the emerging markets of Asia. How many sell-side firms can make that claim in 2008?

Coull's partner, Jonathan Slone, is another true visionary. You could spend hour after hour talking with Slone—about wine, China, investing, whatever—and he could speak intelligently about the topic. He has very eclectic tastes.

Slone and others foresaw the commercial value of electronic trade execution versus the traditional human trade execution. Then he took it one step further. He orchestrated a winning formula that connected the dots between a brand name front-end portal and his back-end electronic execution platform. That front-end portal was none other than Bloomberg Tradebook.

Wait a minute. One of your first thoughts has to be that the name Bloomberg conjures up an information screen. Well, it is. In addition, there is Bloomberg Tradebook (a global agency broker and subsidiary of Bloomberg L.P.) went on to establish a partnership with G-Trade.

How does the G-Trade/Bloomberg Tradebook partnership work? G-Trade is the executing and clearing broker for non–U.S. equities for Bloomberg Tradebook and provides an electronic link between the Hong Kong exchange and Bloomberg Tradebook.[32] I'm not sure a joint venture gets any better than that.

These G-Trade guys, led by Slone in New York City and Coull in Asia, were clever. They "got it" on several levels. They understood the importance of the interface with the customer (the buy side and, to a lesser extent, the sell side) through the front end, in this case Bloomberg Tradebook. Second, they understood the importance of staying with the customer right through the back end by clearing and settling the trade. Third, they understood the increasing importance to the customer of the international markets and the international exchanges, and are applying technological solutions to global trades.

Once again, Coull, Slone and their team found a way to keep the buy side on their side of the Street.

In 2001, the sell-sider Bank of New York, also recognizing the value of servicing and connecting to the buy side, acquired G-Trade. They also appreciated the significance of G-Trade's partnership with Bloomberg Tradebook. As I write this, G-Trade is separating from Bank of New York and jumping into the bank's new venture, BNY ConvergEx Group. And as this happens, the Bloomberg Tradebook joint venture is coming to an end.[33]

Being the entrepreneur that he is, Jonathan Slone, as I write this, is off and running on a new venture (with a major service provider). And the investment banker who represented CLSA and G-Trade with its sale to Bank of New York? He's writing a book.

The Battle for Wall Street does not stop there. Entrepreneurs like Slone will keep dreaming and scheming, and the buy side will keep welcoming their allies with open arms. The sell side, like Bank of New York, will continue to acquire or form joint ventures or partnerships with these entrepreneurs in order to retake positions that were once theirs—proprietary information, pricing, and execution. Never a dull moment on Wall Street.

More Reinforcements—The Endowments

While entrepreneurs have been fueling the growth of the buy side, including hedge funds, and becoming a major factor in the Battle for Wall Street, endowments, such as those at universities, have become important players as well.

If I were writing this book 20 years ago, I doubt I would have mentioned endowments, even in passing. These endowments simply were not players on Wall Street. If a Battle for Wall Street were occurring in, say, the 1980s, endowments would have been off on the sidelines, observing.

Endowments historically invested in things that were safe, unexciting, and had low returns, such as high-quality fixed-income investments like government bonds. Such investors do not engage the passions of Wall Street's traders, investors, or movers and shakers. Also, while university endowments weren't tiny, they were small by today's standards, and hardly large enough to generate great interest on the Street.

Today, this has all changed, thanks to a few players who have shifted from Wall Street to the campus quad.

Yale University and David Swensen

The man arguably most responsible for the transformation of endowments from nonentities to major players is David Swensen, Yale University's chief investment officer and the man in charge of the university's endowment.

As has been widely reported in the press, when Swensen took over the endowment's management in 1985, it had $1.1 billion. Today, it has more than $22 billion, and has garnered an annual rate of return just north of 16 percent, the highest of any major university endowment.[34] In fact, in the 10 years between 1997 and 2007, the Yale Endowment earned a 17.8 percent average annual return.[35] This is impressive for any time period, but particularly so given the bear market of the early 2000s.

When Swensen took over the running of the Yale Endowment, it was investing in the traditional types of investments that endowments invested in. In the early 1980s, reports *Yale Alumni Magazine*, the university's endowment held more than three-quarters of its money in U.S. stocks, bonds, and cash.

Swensen knew there were plenty of other asset classes that could be put to work for the endowment, and he quickly started moving into them, turning over the endowment's investment strategy and turbo-charging its returns.

"What Swensen taught everyone to do was not to get the preferred return on bonds because it was too low and to control risk by diversification and by careful selection of managers," Bruce Greenwald, professor of finance at Columbia Business School, told the *New York Times*.[36]

So why is David Swensen a major player in the Battle for Wall Street? Simple: Swensen's basic strategy was to diversify.

He took endowment money out of stocks and bonds and started investing it in such places like private equity firms and hedge funds.

Today, those hedge funds and private equity firms are getting more than 33 percent of Yale's money.[37] Is that a significant piece of the pie? Absolutely. And in absolute dollars, it is very significant because of the sterling growth in the endowment over the years. Yale alone will be investing billions of dollars in these buy-side investments.

But Swensen's influence on the Battle for Wall Street goes way beyond Yale's $22 billion. During his more than two decades at the helm of the Yale Endowment, Swensen has arguably transformed endowment investing across the entire country. Though a pioneer in the mid- to late 1980s, today his approach has become mainstream. Many endowments now incorporate some of his thinking, which means many hedge funds and private equity firms are attracting more and more money from many other university endowments. His impact on the Battle for Wall Street has a multiplier effect.

According to the National Association of College & University Business Officers, schools with endowments of $1 billion or more had, on average, 21.7 percent of their funds invested in hedge funds.[38]

In fact, these endowments were a major source of fuel behind the entire hedge fund industry. "For years endowments plowed ever bigger amounts of money into alternative investments, making them largely responsible for helping hedge fund assets double to $2 trillion in roughly three years," writes Svea Herbst-Bayliss.[39]

I talk elsewhere in this book about new players who have become a significant presence on Wall Street, such as sovereign wealth funds. I think we can say here that David Swensen has—perhaps not single-handedly, but certainly with great influence—helped bring endowments to the attention of Wall Street, to the jubilation of the buy side.

An additional note: Remember our earlier discussion of private equity, and how Lehman Brothers has been an incubator of buy-side talent? Well, add David Swensen to Lehman's list of successful alumni.

Harvard University and Jack Meyer

Let me tell you about one more notable endowment leader, namely, Jack Meyer, who, for 15 years starting in 1990, led Harvard Management Company, which oversees Harvard University's endowment. Today, it has about $35 billion in assets (it is the largest among university endowments, while Yale's is number two).[40] Meyer's track record at Harvard was similar to Swensen's, and the difference was perhaps a couple of tenths of a percentage point.[41]

Like Swensen, Meyer was held in very high esteem by the endowment and university communities. He used an investment strategy that, as far as I can tell, was a mirror image of Swensen's. And because this strategy includes private equity and hedge funds, it, like Yale's, has made Harvard a player in the Battle for Wall Street. In many respects, Swensen's and Meyer's stories are the same.

But in at least one important respect, they differ. Swensen, as I write this, is still at Yale. The last published figure that I saw concerning his pay was that he earned $2.7 million.[42] Meyer earned millions more (one figure I saw was $7.2 million in his last year at Harvard), and at least one of his managers earned over $25 million.[43]

In fact, the compensation for some of Meyer's team was so high that it became a major public relations issue for the university.[44] What did Meyer eventually do? Remember my refrain about the migration of talent to the buy-side hedge funds?

Well, in 2005, Meyer left Harvard, took 30 of his people with him, and started, yes, a hedge fund. Called Convexity Capital Management, it began life with $6 billion in the kitty, the most money ever raised at the time by a new hedge fund.[45]

It was speculated and reported that Meyer got tired of having to explain and justify the compensation program he had at Harvard (even though hedge fund managers who earned his returns would have earned far more money than Meyer and his team).

Meyer didn't just like the world of buy-side hedge funds—he crossed over to it. He is a classic example of how the buy side attracts very talented people, in part because it is willing to compensate folks based on what they produce. As I've mentioned before, on the buy side, you eat what you kill. You earn based on what you produce. It's a pure formula, and one that appeals for obvious reasons—especially when you're talented enough to write your ticket anywhere.

The endowment community is not just a player in the Battle for Wall Street because of the size of its wallet and its willingness to invest in the buy side, but also because it has become a training ground for some of the buy side's management talent.

In fact, Meyer is not the only endowment leader to head over to the other side. Michael McCaffery, head of Stanford University's endowment, started a money management firm called Makena Capital, and one of his partners was Microsoft cofounder Paul Allen.[46]

Bottom Line

Endowments have been important contributors to the growth of the buy side. But there are indications that with so much endowment money invested in alternative investments like hedge funds, the peak may be near.

In 2007, endowments had about 42 percent of their money in hedge funds and other alternatives, up from 27 percent in 2000.[47] It's hard to imagine that much more money would be allocated to such investments, given the need to diversify. Of course, as long as these alternative investments continue to perform well and post sizable gains, they will attract plenty of endowment money. It's just that the growth of the buy side coming from endowments may very well moderate them.

Implications

The entrepreneurial genie is out of the bottle. The entrepreneurs are smart guys. They'll continue to design and rework trading products and trading services. They'll continue to embrace the buy side, and continue to offer new trading toys.

Likewise, the buy side will be only too happy to welcome this ally of entrepreneurs. An endless cycle forms, and it's a cycle that I can't imagine the sell side is happy about. Like their buy-side counterparts, the sell side will welcome entrepreneurs with open arms for no other reason than to regain the home court advantage: to reconnect to the buy side. This is one reason why they acquired Lava, Wave, and others.

Stepping back, there will always be menu items the sell side can provide the buy side with, such as capital markets. They can always fine-tune external hedge fund services and add new features through prime brokerage.

The bigger issue is that the sell side is witnessing the separation between itself and the buy side—it has to be asking itself what value it provides the buy side. From where I sit, it seems like that's less and less.

This will force the sell side to be more innovative, more inventive, when it comes to new enterprises.

A more innovative approach for the sell side is trying to create new forms of connectivity to the buy side. As an example, the sell side is building up its execution venues with brand-name partners, such as a fixed-income trading platform that was initially owned by Thomson, and later evolved into a sell-side Thomson partnership. The deal they struck was twofold: For fixed-income products, Thomson owned the majority and the sell side owned the minority. Going forward, for all new products, Thomson gets 20 percent and the sell side 80 percent.[48] Hats off to the sell side.

In a second example, the sell side has begun adapting its own form of exchanges. As I write this, there is a new exchange (for both the buy side and the sell side), ELX Electronic Liquidity Exchange, a futures exchange designed to compete with the Chicago Mercantile Exchange.

The sell side here is bypassing traditional exchanges and hoping hedge funds will use them. The sell side is doing now to the exchanges what the entrepreneurs did to the sell side. Entrepreneurs were providing efficient, cheaper tools and services, and the buy side bought these services from the entrepreneurs instead of from the sell side.

Well, the sell side took a page from the entrepreneur's playbook—and they can point out to the buy side that their prototype exchanges may very well provide a service more efficient and less expensive than, say, the traditional exchanges. They can claim added value—always a good thing. A clever offensive approach to reconnect with the buy side: score one, sell side.

Turning our attention to endowments, although they may not increase the percentage of their assets allocated to alternative investments by much, they'll continue to be major factors to the buy side. And as total endowment monies grow, the absolute amount they place with hedge funds will grow, too. There will be a spillover effect.

From the sell side's perspective, endowments will continue to seek yield from buy-side hedge fund products, until there is a substitute, suitable alpha (high-yielding) product. But don't feel too badly for the sell side. It's in a pretty good position to capture its fair share of the endowment pot of gold.

Specifically, the sell side gets two bites of the endowment apple. First, sell-side firms like Goldman Sachs have in-house, captive hedge funds that are attracting endowment allocations. Second, let's not forget the sell side's prime brokerage operations. These operations cater to hedge funds, and the more trading hedge funds do, the more business—and commissions—they produce for the sell side's prime brokers.

The sell side will have to continue to reinvent itself, coming up with new services to offer the buy side, like ELX. Otherwise, the buy side will continue to disaggregate itself from the sell side and wider the power gap between them.

Battle Victorious: Buy side.

Chapter 7

Exchanges: Sell-Side Voice, Buy-Side Electronics

D id you buy this book at a bookstore? If so, you probably drove there in a car that had an internal combustion engine. This technology has improved over time, but it's essentially the same one that's been used in cars since the late nineteenth century.

If you're sitting indoors, the light you're using to read this book probably comes from an incandescent or fluorescent bulb. Both technologies are also products of the nineteenth century.

Things we use today that are so common we don't give them a second thought often date back decades, even centuries. We think we live in an era of unparalleled technological change, but the truth is that we're surrounded by newer versions of older things. We still teach the Pythagorean theorem, which originated thousands of years ago, and Newton's universal laws of motion, which are over 300 years old.

With so much of our society and lifestyle based on old ideas, it should be no surprise that aspects of our financial system also have relatively ancient origins. In fact, in this chapter, I'll talk about one financial institution—the exchange—that dates back hundreds of years and is still in use today.

What's interesting is that the exchange will continue to undergo a transformation that may make it almost unrecognizable during the next few years and, consequently, have an effect on the buy and sell sides.

When I landed on Wall Street in the early 1980s, exchanges like the New York Stock Exchange (NYSE) were in their heyday. Institutions like the NYSE were fondly referred to as open outcry auctions, where buyers and sellers gathered on a boisterous trading floor and shouted out their buy and sell orders.[1] The NYSE still has a trading floor where traders interact, but it's probably destined to become a dinosaur—a place some industry observers would guess isn't long for this world.[2]

Today, a major method of trading communication is electronic, and I suspect that machines talk to machines far more often than people talk to people.

Buy-Side Ally

A recurring theme in this book is the increasingly important role of financial technology to the investment community, and the exchanges are a prime example of how technology has changed the battlefield for this important corner of Wall Street. Technology created the electronic trading venues, which have become such strong competitors to the traditional exchanges.

Historically, exchanges were closely aligned with the sell side. The buy-side community, including hedge funds, traded on traditional exchanges like the NYSE because they were the only places available to them.[3]

The exchanges, in turn, provided considerable value, bringing together buyers and sellers, thereby creating liquidity. Score one for the exchanges.

But to access the exchanges' market, the buy side had to go through the sell side, namely the sell side's brokers.[4] One could not just go on the NYSE trading floor and place a buy or sell order. Such orders had to be entered by an intermediary, a sell-side brokerage firm. Score one for the sell side.

The buy-side community understood the value of traditional exchanges. But over time this community could have asked itself a few questions, particularly about how well its trades were executed.

When the buy side places an order with a traditional exchange, the specialists match up the buyer and seller. Let's say there is a better quote on a regional exchange. Does the buy side get the benefit of that?

What about when the buy side sends an order to the trading floor, which is received by the sell-side floor broker. Do floor brokers ever trade against these buy side orders?

The buy side could very well ask itself, "Why do I need a specialist? Maybe I need one for a large block of stock, or when I'm trading a thinly traded stock, but if I'm trad-ing Microsoft or Wal-Mart, why do I want to expose my trade to special-ists, who are intermediaries and creatures of a traditional exchange?"

Specialist

"A specialist is a dealer representing a NYSE specialist firm—one of the main facilitators of trade on the exchange. Each specialist deals with specific stocks and is obligated to buy or sell these stocks as a last resort, to assure there is always a market for them."

Source: InvestorWords.com, WebFinance, Inc., www.investorwords.com/4634/specialist.html.

Electronic versions of exchanges popped up in response, and offered an alternative to the traditional exchanges. One such alternative is an electronic communication network (ECN).[5]

Think of ECNs as computer networks that match both sides of the order, which is placed faster and cheaper than on a traditional exchange, to the delight of the buy side. Plus, the buy-side trader, in particular, has more anonymity when using a computer network than with the face-to-face trading found on an exchange floor.

Bottom Line

Is it any wonder that today, significant buy-side trading volume lands at the doorstep of electronic version of exchanges and away from the hand-held doors of the sell-side brokers and traditional voice exchanges?

One Man's Vision of Exchanges

How did all of this come about? One of the key players was a vision-ary named Gerald Putnam, the driving force behind the creation of Archipelago Holdings, which operated the ArcaEx stock exchange.

ArcaEx was one of the four original ECNs that came into being in January 1997,[6] when new Securities and Exchange Commission (SEC)-mandated regulations encouraged the development of alterna-tive venues, like ECNs.

Remember the fraternity of Wall Street entrepreneurs from the last chapter—those visionary technology dealers? Putnam became the new-est member of that fraternity with the debut of ArcaEx. This new player made life easier for buy-side and sell-side traders in part because of its compelling value proposition: speed is the name of the game.

Let's break down the importance of faster trading. Electronic trad-ing offered the potential for faster trading. A typical trade on the NYSE took 22 seconds, while on a fully automated system like an ECN, this type of trade took less than a second.[7] Putnam has been quoted as say-ing the difference in time between a traditional floor trade and an elec-tronic trade was a "lifetime" in an active market.[8]

Markets can move blindingly fast, and seconds can make large dif-ferences in what price a trader receives. Putnam and his team recog-nized the importance of time to the buy side, and addressing this issue helped them attract a client roster of large buy-side firms, hedge funds, and the like.

Putnam and his team took it one step farther and built a best price execution model. Using this model, they first tried to get the investor the best price on ArcaEx. When that was not possible, ArcaEx initiated a search—a sweep—of other venues to assure the investor got the best price.[9] Compare this to Nasdaq, which was a closed system that didn't route orders outside its own system.[10]

The technology behind the best execution model is based on a word I toss around a lot in this book, algorithms, which search for best prices inside and outside a system.[11] No question, ArcaEx's best execu-tion model was an innovation and distinguished it from other ECNs. Not to mention the fact that this model strengthened ArcaEx's rela-tionships with the buy side.

With its best execution model handling equities, ArcaEx moved into a new asset class—options.[12] Putnam and his team were clever enough to see that their platform should handle multiple asset classes—an asset menu for the buy side and the sell side.

ArcaEx continued to evolve. In a transaction with the Pacific Stock Exchange, Putnam and his team created the first ECN that would become a fully regulated stock exchange.[13] The Pacific Stock Exchange deal could be characterized as a win–win on two fronts: (1) it provided the ArcaEx investor base with more liquidity; and (2) it linked the investor base of the Pacific Stock Exchange with ArcaEx's execution model.

In his final act with Archipelago, Putnam merged his baby with the NYSE, which created a giant, publicly traded exchange, now called the New York Stock Exchange Euronext, which I'll elaborate on in a case study later on in the chapter.

Two days following the NYSE-Archipelago combination, Nasdaq acquired the ECN Instinet.[14] That was a busy week on Wall Street and a transformational time for the exchanges.

Hookups like NYSE-Archipelago and Nasdaq-Instinet highlight the importance of financial technology and specifically electronic trading, as well as the value of capturing the exploding buy-side trading volume.

In a bit of irony, Putnam was a son of an Army officer[15] (in fact, the NYSE-Archipelago deal was code-named Army-Navy).[16] In the spirit of the Battle for Wall Street, he took aim at the NYSE, Nasdaq, and other members of the exchange establishment.[17] His shot was heard around the buy-side and sell-side worlds. He let loose with a double blast, which were the twin promises of "fairness" and "transparent order execution."[18]

Bottom Line

ECNs were the outgrowth of the regulators. These are the same regulators the hedge funds try to shy away from, but in this case, the hedge funds are quietly clapping for the regulators. After all, one could surmise that the ECNs as well as the electronic exchanges were to the buy side what the traditional auction exchanges were to the sell side.

Electronic Version of Exchanges

There's no question that the buy side has been a beneficiary of the electronic version of exchanges, but it took a while for these venues to take hold. Time was needed for financial technology and liquidity to intersect. It's important to remember that for a long time, the traditional exchanges—not the electronic exchanges or the ECNs—had the liquidity. The traditional exchanges had the participants because everyone traded there.

Take a traditional exchange like the New York Mercantile Exchange (NYMEX). Investment banks and energy companies have seats there. Buyers and sellers trade there in large quantities.

The same couldn't be said for electronic venues at first. Let me walk you through how it may have worked. They offer really great screens with transparent trading and all the information the buy side wants. Since the exchange is electronic, it's fast and efficient. But when the buy side went to trade, there were only a handful of other guys on the screen. This situation doesn't do the buy side any good, since the market lacked liquidity and players.

Think about it this way: Suppose I open xBay, an eBay spin-off, only with lower fees. You want to list your lawn mower there for sale. If no one shows up at xBay to buy the lawn mower, you won't be happy, no matter what I charge. You might as well advertise that lawn mower in outer space.

The point is that these electronic venues had to find people willing to trade. It wasn't easy and it took time. Liquidity is fluid, though, so eventually the sellers and buyers gravitated toward the winning combination of lower fees and faster execution. Yes, the sell side, like the buy side, recognized the benefit of utilizing these electronic venues.

I've been referring to two types of venues, which have more similarities than differences: ECNs and electronic exchanges. The main difference between them is regulatory, in that electronic exchanges are regulated like traditional exchanges.[19]

But there's a more practical difference, too: namely, that electronic exchanges have market makers, so there's always liquidity. ECNs don't have those makers, which means there may be times when liquidity is lacking.[20]

A trader wanting to sell an illiquid security on ECN might wait a second, a minute, a day or more before a buyer shows up. In fact, a buyer may never show up.[21] But that same order sent to an electronic exchange would find an immediate counterparty because there's a market maker at the exchange who has to buy or sell the asset at some price. Granted, it may not be the best price, but he or she will buy it, and there will be liquidity.

When discussing ECNs, it's worth pointing out their origins. They were born out of the Nasdaq scandals of the mid-1990s, where market makers were taking advantage of the system.[22] These guys practiced a form of price fixing. A new regulation came into effect called NMS that introduced transparency and competition into what had been the opaque world of traditional exchanges.

Score one for the buy side.

When I talk about ECNs as well as electronic exchanges, I remember an old retail investor story. The retail investor looks at a Yahoo! screen and sees that Company X's price is $100, and wants to buy at that price. A market order is placed, and the next thing he knows, he owns it at $105. "Wait a minute," the retail investor says, "the price is $100." The broker's response is, "the market moved."

How many times has the retail investor heard that? How many times has the buy side heard it? This scenario is a likely concern for retail investors as well as buy-side firms, and could apply to all

Market Maker

"A broker-dealer firm that accepts the risk of holding a certain number of shares of a particular security in order to facilitate trading in that security. Each market maker competes for customer order flow by displaying buy and sell quotations for a guaranteed number of shares. Once an order is received, the market maker immediately sells from its own inventory or seeks an offsetting order."

The Nasdaq is the prime example of an operation of market makers. There are more than 500 member firms that act as Nasdaq market makers, keeping the financial markets running efficiently because they are willing to quote both bid and offer prices for an asset.

Source: Investopedia, www.investopedia.com/terms/m/marketmaker.asp.

Regulation NMS

"National Market System (NMS) is a set of rules passed by the SEC, which looks to improve the U.S. exchanges through improved fairness in price execution as well as improve the displaying of quotes and amount and access to market data."

Source: Investopedia, www.investopedia.com/terms/r/regulation-NMS.asp.

exchanges. Investors may not be seeing the best execution with a trade put through the traditional exchanges.

The folks involved with electronic exchanges were well aware of these concerns, and that could have been behind their thinking in creating an electronic exchange. Three great stories come to mind regarding these exchanges.

The first story is about International Securities Exchange (ISE), which began in May 2000.[23] When I think of options as an asset class, I go back to a time when the Chicago Board Options Exchange (CBOE) was the biggest options exchange.[24] The American and Philadelphia Exchanges were also important players. A few entrepreneurial folks got together and may have asked themselves, "What if we build an options exchange that is, effectively, the first fully electronic U.S. options exchange?" Such an exchange would introduce the efficiencies of purely electronic trading to the options industry.[25] And that is the ISE story.

ISE went from a little start-up company to one approximately the same size as the CBOE in a few years. In early 2007, approximately seven years after its launch, the ISE traded its two billionth options contract.[26] Not bad. And it ended the year by becoming part of Eurex, which is part of Deutsche Boerse.[27] The sales price for ISE: about $2.8 billion.[28] Guess you could say an impressive seven-year run that is still working well. Hats off to ISE.

The second story is about IntercontinentalExchange (ICE), which began in May 2000.[29] It's my understanding that ICE first marketed itself as a business-to-business market for power companies. This business model, according to industry observers, never gained much traction. At some point, ICE rethought its business plan to attract traders to its business-to-business model. The traders loved it because they had something to trade—energy—that was fast moving and liquid.[30]

This business model worked, and ICE ended up as a big-time energy exchange and, through a series of clever synergistic transactions, ICE has become a major exchange.

A telling fact about the new guard exchange, ICE, is how they went toe to toe with the old-guard exchange, the Chicago Mercantile Exchange (CME).[31] In a 2008 skirmish, ICE took on the CME in a battle to win over the exchange, the Chicago Board of Trade (CBOT), which at the time was in discussions to merge with CME. The outcome: the veteran was victorious—in merging with the CBOT—over the youngster.

As I write this, ICE's market value is north of $6.5 billion.[32] Like ISE, it earned a multibillion-dollar valuation in a relatively short period of time.

In the Battle for Wall Street, organizations like ISE and ICE played a significant role. The buy side experienced real value from these exchanges. Specifically, the buy side had a venue—liquidity—to trade high-growth asset classes like options and energy with the benefit of electronic execution and without the cost of exposing their trade.

Fast-forward from the early 2000s of ISE and ICE to 2008. Our third story is about one of the newest electronic exchanges. As I write this, a new player is joining the exchange battle. Like ISE and ICE, it is focusing on an exploding asset class, embracing financial technology and taking on an old-guard exchange.

This new player is an electronic futures exchange, designed to compete with the CME, called the ELX (Electronic Liquidity Exchange).[33] The media reports that it plans to compete on price, by being a lower-cost venue than the competition.

It's too soon to tell if ELX will succeed. Others, including Eurex, have tried to take on the CME, only to stumble.[34] As I noted above, players like ELX have a chance against the establishment only if they can provide investors with liquidity, and how much liquidity ELX will have, how many traders it will attract, is still unknown.

What is known is that ELX is backed by an impressive lineup of sell-side commercial banks like Barclays and JPMorgan, and sell-side investment banks like Credit Suisse and Merrill Lynch.[35] But the significance of ELX's creation goes beyond the fact that it has a very impressive list of backers and is aimed at the CME; it also helps validate electronic trading as the exchange type of the future.

Let's look at the future of electronic trading from a European perspective. As I write this, an electronic competitor to Europe's traditional exchanges, code-named Project Turquoise, has been proposed, though it's not yet up and running. It has the backing of such heavyweights as Citigroup, Credit Suisse, Deutsche Bank, Goldman Sachs, Merrill Lynch, Morgan Stanley, and UBS—another impressive group.[36] Project Turquoise will reportedly offer not just a trading platform but dark pools, where the trading of large blocks of stock can be done beyond the glare of the public spotlight.[37]

We've seen many power struggles between the sell and buy side. Now we're seeing those struggles between exchanges. Project Turquoise is expected to compete with the traditional European exchanges, and ELX and ICE have taken on the CME in different skirmishes.

Bottom Line

There are four words worth noting here: *electronic version of exchanges.* The buy side must rejoice over those four words, which helped fuel its growth. With those four words came an additional two to delight the buy side: autonomy and price. These helped bring about the creation of the electronic version of exchanges, and help explain why these exchanges have so quickly put traditional exchanges on the run.

I must say that all these players crossing paths has made Wall Street more interesting.

Case Study: New York Stock Exchange— Voice, Domestic to Electronic, International

I think it's remarkable how little things have changed on the NYSE and other exchanges over their first 200 or so years. Back then, traders gathered in a room and called out to one another what they wanted and for how much. And to an extent, they still do.

The pace of change at the NYSE went from glacial to rocket-like when John Thain left Goldman Sachs to become CEO of the exchange in 2003. By the time he left to take a comparable position at Merrill Lynch in 2007, he had moved the NYSE onto an almost entirely new road.[38]

The new NYSE road could have been designed around a two-part vision of what an exchange should look like today and tomorrow. One part of that vision: The trading world was going electronic since this technology brought speed, low cost, and transparency to trading. Another aspect of that vision: the financial markets were going global.

With that game plan in mind, how did the NYSE go about adding a meaningful electronic component to its offerings as well as positioning itself as a global player?

This electronic trading gambit came in the context of merging the NYSE, a private, not-for-profit company, with Archipelago Holdings Inc., a public, for-profit electronic exchange, in March 2006.[39]

Yes, Gerry Putnam and his ArcaEx, which took on the established exchanges like the NYSE, became such a formidable competitor that the NYSE, then over 200 years old, decided that it made commercial sense to join forces with this competitor barely old enough to enter elementary school. Archipelago may have been the new kid in school, but it allowed the NYSE to significantly capture that lightning in a bottle called electronic trading.

The global positioning gambit played out in at least two transactions. In 2006 the NYSE also purchased the Marco Polo Network, an electronic trading platform for global investors.[40] This opened up the NYSE to emerging markets.

About a year after the Archipelago partnership, in April 2007, the NYSE merged with Euronext, which itself was the result of several mergers or acquisitions involving the local exchanges of Amsterdam, Brussels, Paris, and Portugal, and the London-based derivatives market, London International Financial Futures Exchange (LIFFE). This transaction not only linked the NYSE to the European markets, it added another arrow—derivatives—to its quiver of asset offerings.[41]

These type of transformational moves provided the NYSE with a greater geographical reach, a wider range of products, and a stronger hybrid of electronic and voice trading. This allowed the exchange to span the battlefield and more effectively embrace the needs of both the sell side and the buy side.

Let's circle back for a moment to Thain's days at Goldman Sachs, which many believe is the most successful hybrid of sell-side and buy-side activities to date. It's no surprise that Thain (at the helm of the NYSE) recognized the importance of having both sides of the Street trading on the NYSE.

Implications

Today's exchanges are significantly different from yesterday's—not just the exchanges of the 1980s and 1990s, but those of the first years of the twenty-first century. And tomorrow's exchange will not be like today's.

The transformational journey by these exchanges reaches across both sides of the Battle for Wall Street and provokes these questions:

1. Will the exchanges disintermediate the sell side—do an end run around the sell side?

I've asked a similar question before: Will private-equity firms and hedge funds bring sell-side services, such as capital raising or prime brokerage, in-house? I think the exchanges ask themselves this same question.

The exchanges could say to themselves, "We understand the market—why don't we offer even more market and trading tools? We have the infrastructure—why not go one step further than these analytical services and offer prime brokerage?

It just so happens that these are sell-side services.

This disintermediation, to a degree, puts the exchanges in direct competition with the sell side. The sell side is, after all, the exchanges' traditional customer. Will the exchanges want to compete directly with its customer?

Yet, step back a moment and ask, "Who is the real client of the exchanges? Is it actually the sell side?" I would say no.

I would say the real client is the buy side, because in general, it's the buy side that's doing the trading, and the sell side, in part, is just an intermediary. That might suggest that it's worth it to the exchanges to go head to head with the sell side by disintermediation. But that would be a mistake. At this time, though, the risks are too great. Nor do I think the exchanges are inclined to begin such a drastic process.

In the short term, I foresee the exchanges looking for weaknesses to see where they might profitably encroach on the sell side without incurring too high a cost. ICE is an example of one such foray. It recently bought a company called YellowJacket Software, a pre-trade communication platform, which one could suspect is competing with sell-side brokers to some extent.[42]

While exchanges like ICE are potentially nibbling on the sell-side turf, I would say the sell side is encroaching on exchange turf. For example, the sell side is offering an alternative to exchanges through a vehicle called dark pools. Think of dark pools as venues where traders talk to traders and bypass the exchange, thus preventing third parties from gaining information.[43]

We now have a third front to the Battle for Wall Street. The sell side is battling the buy side on one front, and exchanges are battling each other on another. The sell side is also skirmishing with the exchanges, as they both appear to be encroaching on opposing turf.

Therefore, in the short term, I expect exchanges to continue little firefights with the sell side. However, it is unlikely that the exchanges will fully disintermediate from the sell side.

2. How have the exchanges changed with the times and subsequently impacted the sell and buy sides?

There are four ways to view how the exchanges have evolved:

- First, all exchanges, like sell- and buy-side players, have embraced financial technology today. Before, people actually communicated on the floor of places like the American Stock Exchange with hand signals. Traders learned prices from a ticker tape running across a screen in a trading room. Now all traders have desktop computer screens and handheld devices. In my view, exchanges today are all very similar, benefiting both sides of the Street with faster information. The old adage "time is money" is particularly true in the world of trading.

- Second, no exchange today is quite traditional. The old, auction-type-only, voice-method exchanges of yesterday are a thing of the past. They've morphed into hybrids, using both voice and electronic execution. Take the NYSE. It might very well claim its electronic execution is as good as the other guy's. In fact, it might say: "We're better than the other guy in terms of size; we have a bigger sandbox to play in, and therefore more liquidity than the other guy. We offer the best of both worlds—electronic and liquidity." These two words benefit the buy side. Liquidity helps get the trades done, while the electronics move the trades along with less cost and more autonomy. These two words equate to one less phone call from the buy side to the sell side intermediary broker.

- Third, the number of different asset classes traded today on individual exchanges has increased. The NYSE was historically an equity player, for example. But by purchasing Euronext, NYSE also has become a derivatives player. Deutsche Boerse was also primarily an equity player.[44] It has now added options by buying ISE. At some point, exchanges will not be just an NYSE stock exchange or a CME futures exchange. They will morph into exchanges that list virtually all asset classes that trade. Think of this as a convergence of different asset classes on one execution platform. It's no surprise that having a menu of tradeable assets on one screen makes life easier for the sell-side and buy-side traders.

- Fourth, there is a new player in the mix today, to the delight of the exchanges and the sell and buy sides. Sovereign wealth funds, which I discuss in detail in the next chapter, have attracted the interest of exchanges. On one hand, sovereign wealth funds have been investors in exchanges, including Dubai taking a minority stake in Nasdaq. On the other hand, exchanges are pursuing sovereign wealth funds because these funds have more money than ever and are therefore trading more, and the exchanges want some of this action. I wonder if the sovereign wealth funds will be to the hybrid exchanges today what the buy side, particularly the hedge funds, was to the electronic exchanges of yesterday. They are new entrants that are expected to pump up the trading volume for the exchanges. This means more fees for the exchanges over time. With this expanding scale, I suspect there will also be lower execution costs for the sell and the buy sides. I guess you could say in the latter half of the 2000s, through 2008, we have witnessed exchanges adapt to the times and needs of the buy side and sell side, while welcoming a new player to the lineup of sellers and buyers, sovereign wealth funds.

3. How will exchanges evolve in the future and influence the sell side and the buy side?

Stepping back, we have witnessed massive consolidation of exchanges from 2005.

Not long ago, we had plenty of regional exchanges, such as the Philadelphia and Boston stock exchanges. Today, these regional exchanges are, for the most part, a thing of the past. The Boston and Philadelphia exchanges are now part of Nasdaq, for example.

Just as there used to be many regional exchanges, there was a time when we had a number of futures exchanges, including the CBOT and the NYMEX. Today the CBOT is part of the CME family,[45] and as I write this, the CME is in the process of buying the NYMEX as well.[46] Once this purchase is complete, I suspect the CME will be offering just about every futures contract you can imagine.

Some observers were surprised the CME was allowed to buy the CBOT because of monopoly concerns. But the government approved this takeover.

Why has the CME been allowed to concentrate futures trading to such a degree? One could only speculate. Perhaps the CME said to thegovernment, "The combined scale of CME/CBOT will benefit the U.S. investor." And/or "If we don't buy the CBOT, maybe the Deutsche Boerse will buy it, and that will hurt the U.S. financial community's competitive position."

In any case, where does all this lead? I think it invariably leads to a handful of global exchanges. It's not just that there will be hybrid exchanges which encompass voice and electronic trading. And it's not just that many asset classes will be traded on each exchange.

What I see happening is the establishment of three possible global giants, with everyone around the world connected to them. There could be the New York group (NYSE, perhaps merged with Nasdaq), the Chicago group (CME), and the Frankfurt group (Deutsche Boerse).

A question that has to be on the minds of the sell side and the buy side is whether only three global exchanges will lead to unfair competition. I suspect this handful of exchanges will stay extremely competitive. The auto industry in the United States, after all, was for many years dominated by three players, and it remained competitive.

New York, Chicago, and Frankfurt groups could, for the foreseeable future, be our international financial supermarkets. Three worldwide giants bring global positioning and global change agents to the Battle for Wall Street.

Battle Victorious: Buy side.

Chapter 8

Sovereign Wealth Funds: Sell Side Today, Buy Side Tomorrow

There's a new participant in the Battle for Wall Street—one that has emerged from the sidelines in recent years. Flush with cash and quick to react, sovereign wealth funds are playing a major role on the global financial scene.

Their capital infusions of U.S. companies like Citigroup during the 2007–2008 credit crunch proved that they were forces to be reckoned with, and their power and influence seem to be increasing on a daily basis. Just what their role will be, though, remains to be seen: They're still too new on the scene for us to confidently predict their ultimate influence.

Though sovereign wealth funds have been around for some time, it was not until the turn of the new millennium that they started their ascent towards financial power. These financial institutions, which few even on Wall Street had heard of five years ago, are fast becoming a major force on both the buy side and sell side. They are proving themselves to be savvy investors.

And, today, sovereign wealth funds can take a seat alongside our supporting cast of aforementioned players in the Battle for Wall Street. The exchanges, for instance, have played the role of facilitator between the buy and sell sides. Technology is another example, playing catalyst to the change in the balance of power between the sell and buy sides.

My take on the sovereign wealth fund role is that they are international capital dealers—open for business, open to all takers. For sell-side takers, sovereign wealth funds stepped up with capital on both sides of the Atlantic, including Citigroup and Merrill Lynch in the United States and Barclays and HSBC in the United Kingdom.[1]

For buy-side takers, sovereign wealth funds opened up the capital window to private equity firms like Carlyle Group and hedge funds like Och-Ziff. If you were the sell side or the buy side and you needed capital relief, who did you call? The international capital dealers.

A Powerhouse Player

If there is one person in the United States who is indelibly linked to sovereign wealth funds and global financial institutions, it is H. Rodgin (Rodge) Cohen. Cohen is chairman of Sullivan & Cromwell, a leading Wall Street law firm and a key participant in the Battle for Wall Street.[2]

Since the start of the credit crisis of 2007, Cohen and team have been sitting at tables filled with bankers and sovereign wealth fund managers as frequently as blackjack players sit at Vegas power tables. (In the old days, Cohen could actually be seen at the bridge tables.[3]) Whenever he sits down, impressive names circle him.

At the sell-side investment banking table was Temasek Holdings' investment in Merrill Lynch; and China Investment Corporation's investment in Morgan Stanley.[4]

At the sell-side commercial banking table, there was Abu Dhabi Investment Authority's (ADIA) investment in Citigroup[5] and Singapore's Government Investment Corporation's investment in UBS.[6]

Am I surprised that Rodge Cohen and Sullivan & Cromwell have a good seat around the sovereign wealth table? Not really. Cohen and team have cut a wide and impressive path across both the sell-side and buy-side landscape. They played a major role in a number of sell-side transactions, including the UBS and Paine Webber merger. Goldman Sachs appointed Cohen and his firm as its legal counsel time and time again, almost to the point where it had them on speed dial.

And it wasn't just the investment banks—it was the commercial banks, too. A number of these banks looked to Cohen as one of their top go-to guys when it came to putting together their deals. Lock-step with the times, Cohen and Sullivan & Cromwell jumped over to the buy side and played legal shotgun to a wide range of buy-side players, including hedge funds like Citadel, the private equity firm Carlyle Group, and exchanges like ICE.[7]

Cohen and Sullivan & Cromwell not only worked both sides of the sell-buy aisle, they actually found themselves in the middle of the Street—advising sell-sider Merrill Lynch in its transaction with buy-sider BlackRock.[8] So to say that they left their stamp on both the sell side and buy side would be an understatement: they are key players in the Battle for Wall Street.

If anyone can provide the American perspective on sovereign wealth funds, it's Rodge Cohen.

While critics worry about sovereign wealth funds accumulating too large a stake in U.S. financial interests, Cohen has said that he's not too concerned, and believes that these funds are looking for investments, not control. He likens them to private equity funds in terms of their investment strategy: both kinds of funds invest relatively large amounts of money in a relatively small number of opportunities.[9]

This strategy is why, he says, private equity firms earn returns far in excess of mutual funds, and why he thinks sovereign wealth funds will be content making sizable investments in American financial institutions, without seeking to control them.[10]

Bottom Line

Whether Cohen is right remains to be seen, but given his experience with sovereign wealth funds, as well as global financial institutions, his opinion carries a good deal of weight.

Financial Institutions: Have Needs, Will Travel

Historically, sovereign wealth funds have tended to play it safe: They've stuck to investments in low-risk assets like sovereign bonds, especially U.S. Treasuries. Well, those days are coming to an end—and fast.

Larger sovereign wealth funds have radically shifted strategies from "stabilization (savings) funds" to "wealth (accumulation) funds."[11] Over the next three years, sovereign wealth funds are expected to double or even triple their investments in riskier global assets, especially equities and nonsovereign bonds.[12]

These funds have also become increasingly aggressive in purchasing stakes in companies, including those in the financial services industry. My sell-side home team happened to be the opportunistic target of these funds in 2007 and 2008.

Reeling under the losses they incurred from the subprime mortgage credit crisis, these companies were open to the advances of new liquidity players. For example, Singapore-owned Temasek Holdings has approximately 38 percent of its portfolio in financial assets.[13] A quick look inside their portfolio reveals a surprising amount of household names—Barclays, Merrill Lynch, and so on.

Who would have guessed, a few years back, that household names like these would be inside the portfolio of a sovereign wealth fund? Someday, the subprime mortgage credit market crisis will pass, but sovereign wealth funds' financial imprint promises to be with us for a long, long time.

Just open up the financial pages of any newspaper in 2007–2008: These funds were making headlines on a regular basis. Sell-side firm Morgan Stanley sold a chunk of itself to the China Investment Corporation.[14] Private equity firm Blackstone Group sold nearly 10 percent of itself to the China's state investment company.[15] Perhaps in the most telling show of their increasing appetite, two funds from the Middle East now own nearly 50 percent of the London Stock Exchange,[16] while another owns nearly 20 percent of Nasdaq.[17] Morgan Stanley, London Stock Exchange, Blackstone, Nasdaq—these funds are getting their hands into the very heart of the global financial world.

Okay, so sovereign wealth funds like the financial services sector. They must think it will offer the best returns, right? Maybe, but not necessarily. A former Merrill Lynch economist was recently quoted as saying that the funds are not interested in shoring up cash-poor U.S. financial companies hit by the subprime mortgage crisis.[18] Instead, he argued, sovereign wealth funds—especially China's—are looking for a bargain, as well as some banking expertise: "What we have, then, are sovereign wealth funds using their financial muscle to not just gain ownership of foreign assets, but to gain expertise that foreigners have but they, the developing countries, do not."

Of course, we can't paint all sovereign wealth funds with the same brush. True, they're all pots of government money created by trade imbalances and high commodity prices, but in the same way that governments don't all have identical policies, their funds differ in a number of ways, from size to transparency to willingness to take on risk.

Bottom Line

The overall significance of sovereign wealth funds to Wall Street may not be known for some time. But what we do know in 2008 is that U.S. financial institutions were finding their way to the sovereign wealth fund ATMs.

The sell side was going when balance sheet cash was warranted, the buy side when liquidity was there for the taking.

> **Sovereign Wealth Funds—Big and Rich**
> While a number of these funds, including those of the United Arab Emirates, Singapore, and Canada, date back to the 1970s and 1980s,[19] these funds were largely under the financial world's radar screen because of their relatively small size and the fact that they usually operated within a cloud of considerable secrecy.
>
> They still are secret about their operations and their wealth, but they are no longer small. The largest is ADIA, whose size is estimated by Reuters to be between $250 billion and $875 billion.[20] This broad range is an indication of just how secretive these funds can be.

(continued)

Norway's Government Pension Fund, Global, is one of the most open about its assets, and it is ranked by Reuters as the second-largest sovereign wealth fund, with assets of $350 billion.[21] Kuwait's and Singapore's funds are in the range of $250 to $330 billion.[22]

The size of some of these funds is remarkable, given their home countries. Norway's fund is estimated to represent more than $70,000 for every person in the country.[23] ADIA is estimated at the top end of the range to have as much as $875 billion, though its home country has only 5.2 million people.[24] This works out to nearly $170,000 dollars per person.

As I write this, the overall size of sovereign wealth funds is estimated at around $2.5 trillion. That's a lot of money, though on a global scale, it's a small percentage. There are $167 trillion in global financial assets,[25] while institutional investors control $53 trillion.[26] Looked at from another perspective, the United States' gross domestic product is estimated at nearly $14 trillion a year.[27]

What's striking is that sovereign wealth funds are estimated to have more money than hedge funds and private equity firms combined.

At their current level, sovereign wealth funds control 4.7 percent of the amount of assets of institutional investors and 2 percent of total global financial assets. While these percentages may seem small when considering the total of global financial assets in existence, the funds themselves have enough money now to be important players on Wall Street and overseas—and their growth is expected to be dramatic over the next several years. In 2006 alone, they grew by $1.2 trillion.[28]

But don't just take my word for it. Morgan Stanley says these funds will probably have $12 trillion under management by 2015, while the International Monetary Fund says they could have $10 trillion by 2012.[29]

Hopefully, the sell-side firms, post the credit crisis of 2007–2008, won't say, "Let's indulge more, take on riskier assets, and if need be, cover our balance sheet miscues with the big and rich sovereign wealth funds."

Sovereign Wealth Funds: Have Advantages, Will Travel

Over the past few decades, there's been a real revolution in financial technology. And just like everyone else, sovereign wealth funds are benefiting from this revolution.

They are acting in the same way that buy-side firms did when they used advances in financial technology to reduce the information asymmetry between them and sell-side firms.

There is nothing backward or unsophisticated about these funds. Portfolio managers at Norway's Government Pension Fund, for example, one of the few transparent sovereign wealth funds, have many if not all of the financial tools, trading techniques, and market information that buy-siders have used to level the playing field in the Battle for Wall Street. Is it fair to assume that other, less transparent funds use the same methods? Absolutely.

Indeed, sovereign wealth funds have a lot to smile about. In addition to the benefits they're seeing from incorporating cutting-edge financial technology, they have three built-in advantages over Wall Street firms.

First, they have broader investment strategies, which might include noneconomic considerations like politics or foreign policy. Any fund with that kind of mandate has the ability to acquire assets—including companies—at higher prices than profit-maximizing firms would be willing to pay.

Second, these funds can offer preferential treatment in their home markets in exchange for assets—making them very attractive to foreign companies. In fact, this may have been a motive in Blackstone's decision to sell a 10 percent stake of itself to China, while it tries to invest in the Chinese market.

Third, a lack of transparency requirements allows sovereign wealth funds to shield their investment strategies in ways that other financial firms just can't. This protective cloak prevents prying eyes from seeing—and judging—their strategic moves.

Bottom Line

The sovereign wealth funds' arsenal is not just about pots of gold at the end of the rainbow—they have strategic weapons at their disposal, including financial technology, the home court advantage, open-ended investment philosophy, and closed-ended transparency. They're in an enviable position, and they know it. Going forward, this should make for an interesting conversation with our Wall Street players.

Case Study: Citigroup—Can You Spare a Few Dollars?

Time after time, it seems that all roads lead to sovereign wealth funds.

It's no secret that in the midst of the subprime mortgage crisis, Citigroup traveled east for outside capital—twice. In November 2007, it picked up $7.5 billion from ADIA;[30] in January 2008, it received another $12.5 billion from the governments of Singapore, Kuwait, and a group of investors.[31] And it has been down this road before. In 1991, strapped for cash in the middle of a U.S. property downturn, Citigroup went to a Gulf investor, Saudi Arabia's Prince Walid bin Talal, who stepped up with cash in hand.

While Citigroup was traveling on the yellow brick road to sovereign wealth funds, its home front faced significant financial hits in 2007–2008. Citigroup began 2008 by reporting a nearly $10 billion loss from the fourth quarter of 2007—the largest loss in its history, thanks to an $18 billion write-down of loans.[32] And just a few months later, the financial picture still bleak, Citigroup reported its second loss. The good news? It was only $5 billion this time—progress!—after writing down $12 billion of loans for the first quarter of 2008.[33] Not the best of times for Citigroup.

In the middle of its financial crisis, Citigroup brought in a new CEO, Vikram Pandit. No surprise. What some observers found surprising was his whopping compensation package: according to the press, in addition to the usual salary, stock, and other options, Pandit picked up $165 million from the sale of his hedge fund, a company called Old Lane, to Citigroup.[34]

Citigroup intimated that it bought Old Lane to recruit Pandit and his team.[35] Guess you could say that the purchase was akin to flowers and candy leading up to a relationship: a wooing technique. And at $165 million plus other goodies, believed to be close to a quarter of a billion dollars (including salary and stock paid out over time) is it any surprise that Pandit let himself be wooed?[36]

Well, here's a bit of irony for you: Eleven months after it brought Pandit on board, Old Lane fell apart. Citigroup wrote down part of its investment in Old Lane, and outside investors in the fund headed to the exits.[37]

Amazing. And it's even more amazing that just prior to Citigroup's purchase of Old Lane, it shut down its own hedge fund, Tribeca Capital.[38]

There's a lesson to be learned here. If the sell side, like Citigroup, wants to offer buy-side services like hedge funds, one could argue it should grow them internally rather than buy them. Those acquisitions can be a costly move. Play in the space you know.

To the credit of Pandit and his team, they are making some clever moves at Citigroup. First, given the importance of sovereign wealth funds and the resources of the Far East, they have moved one of their senior bankers to that part of the world.[39] Second, Pandit and team disbanded the existing management committee and replaced it with a management structure that's regionally oriented.[40] In other words, they dialed up the decision making and dialed down the bureaucracy. (Gee, sounds more like a nimble buy-side firm to me.)

A third smart move on Pandit's part is one that plays off one of our book's principal themes, the migration of talent from the sell side to the buy side. He is going back to the sell-side incubator—mainly, his old haunt, Morgan Stanley—to recruit old allies, including John Havens, by way of Old Lane.

So what's the sovereign wealth fund take on investing in Citigroup today? Well, Tony Tan, the deputy chairman of Singapore's Government Investment Corporation, said that "financial contagion has now spread beyond the U.S. shores, increasing the likelihood of a global financial crisis." Investments in Citigroup and other U.S. giants, he said, will be "long-term investments which will give us good returns when markets stabilize and economic conditions return to more normal levels."[41]

Time will tell.

Implications

What are the consequences of having sovereign wealth funds enter the Battle for Wall Street? In 2008, without a crystal ball, it's just too early to tell. They're still too new, too untested, too little understood.

What I suspect, though, is that sovereign wealth funds will play more of a supporting role than anything else. And that role will be played out against the backdrop of three macro considerations:

1. On a policy level, regulators in developed countries are able to resist protectionist pressure and don't enact regulations that substantially limit sovereign wealth fund investment.
2. On an investment level, sovereign wealth funds are able to maintain their healthy appetite for high-yielding, riskier assets.
3. On a strategic level, the funds tell the world, "Relax a little. We're only thinking about noncontrolling, conventional investments. We're not the sell-side firms, thinking 'proprietary trading.' We're not the exchanges, thinking 'consolidation.' We're not the private equity firms, thinking 'management control.' And we're not the hedge funds, thinking 'leverage.'"

If all these macro considerations are there, I think the sovereign wealth funds' supporting role will develop on two fronts:

- On the first front, I foresee the funds investing significant portions of their portfolios through external asset managers. No surprise: This type of shift will produce a surge of business for the asset management industry. If such an event were to occur, Merrill Lynch predicts that it will add $8 billion of annual revenue for global asset managers by 2011.[42]

  This is very good news for the buy side, and to a lesser extent, good news for the sell side's in-house asset management. And watch both sides, with big smiles on their faces, race to the innovation window to introduce new products that fit the needs of the sovereign wealth fund guys.
- On the second front, the funds will be active investors in the financial services industry. As we've seen, the funds have minority stakes in both commercial and investment banks as well as investments in

hedge funds and private equity firms. In a sense, they were historically promoting the growth of both the sell side and buy side.

Going forward, I suspect sovereign wealth funds will be thinking less about investments in the sell side. In the latter half of 2008, sell-side firms are falling more and more under the knife of the subprime crisis. A major sell-side investment bank, Lehman, and a top depository institution, Washington Mutual, fell on the battlefield.

Consequently, sovereign wealth funds should be more interested in buy-side investments. This shift in focus will not be lost on the buy side.

A number of the buy-side firms will start hanging the liquidity sign in the window; sovereign wealth fund investments in private equity and hedge funds and in traditional asset managers could well be on the upswing. The buy-side players will monetize their holdings, and the sovereign wealth funds will leverage and bring home the buy-side expertise. No question, a good trade for both sides.

Sovereign wealth funds have found their way to the Battle for Wall Street. And one thing both the buy side and the sell side can agree on is six words on the Scrabble board: SOVEREIGN WEALTH FUNDS WORK FOR US.

Battle Victorious: Sell side, for the moment.

Part Three

IMPLICATIONS
OF CHANGE

Chapter 9

Sell-Side Casualties, Buy-Side Implications

W hat will you remember about March 17, 2008? Will it be Saint Patrick's Day? Or will it be the day that shocked the financial markets; sell side and buy side alike? That shock, of course, was the sudden collapse of Bear Stearns, the Wall Street powerhouse. We'll be discussing the story of that shock in this chapter.

But first, let's step back in history, to the subprime mortgage crisis and credit crunch that began in 2007. That crisis had an inauspicious beginning, and one early name was New Century.

From Main Street to Wall Street

If you don't remember New Century Financial, you're not alone. New Century was one of the largest U.S. subprime mortgage lenders until the time of its collapse in March 2007.[1] Its demise got a little bit of press time—but not much. After a few days, coverage trickled off. This company's fall from grace hardly seemed noteworthy at the time, but it proved to be a harbinger of the turmoil that was to come in just a few months. New Century would turn out to be a black cat crossing our path.

Another notable casualty was Countrywide, the top residential mortgage lender in the United States.[2] Its troubles became publicly known in the summer of 2007. By January 2008, right before Bank of America bought it for a deep discount, there was speculation that it was on the verge of collapse. Countrywide, bigger and more well known than New Century, made headlines for a bit longer—a few weeks. Then it, too, was forgotten about.

Both Countrywide and New Century were far removed from the saga of the Battle for Wall Street's clash between the buy and sell sides. Not for long, though.

The effects of the 2007–2008 credit crunch soon found their way to a player right in the thick of Wall Street: Bear Stearns. In early 2008, Bear was one of this country's five principal investment banks, and the smallest of the group (the others being Goldman Sachs, Lehman Brothers, Merrill Lynch, and Morgan Stanley).

On Friday, March 14, 2008, Bear suffered what has been described as a run on the bank, though instead of retail customers lining up outside its doors demanding their money as is typical of bank runs (investment bankers don't have hordes of retail—individual—customers), it was Bear's institutional customers, such as hedge funds, that headed for the exits, creating a liquidity crisis so thick that Bear unfortunately suffocated from a lack of the air it breathed: money.

With the demise of Bear, the sell side lost one of its own. The Bear story is unfolding as I write this, but unlike New Century and Countrywide, the Bear story will, I believe, be in the news for months and be remembered for a long time.

Why the intense interest in Bear, which was hardly a household name outside of Wall Street? One reason was that its fall was so rapid and spectacular. Also, its problems conjured up images of other corporate titans who quickly went from king to beheaded monarch, like Drexel Burnham Lambert, which crashed and burned over junk bonds in the 1980s; Enron; and Long-Term Capital Management, a hedge fund that failed spectacularly in the late 1990s. In fact, Bear's story has more than a few similarities with these other infamous defeats.

Bear and Drexel, for example, were smaller and scrappier than traditional investment banks. Both were hit by unexpected downturns: Bear, with the subprime meltdown/credit crunch, and Drexel with junk bonds.

And there are other similarities, too: Both were the subjects of the rumor mill, which hurt their financial staying power. Colorful characters—Jimmy Cayne of Bear[3] and Michael Milken of Drexel[4]—led both firms. And both were affected by what one could call "bad market karma"[5]—both were not the most popular Wall Street players.

A big—and important—difference between Bear and Drexel, though, was Drexel's having to pay huge government fines (and Milken spending time behind bars) for its wrongdoings, while, as I write this, there's no suggestion of any wrongdoing at Bear.

Enron and Bear also had similarities. I think they'll long be linked in the public's mind because of the effects of their collapse on their employees. When Enron imploded, about $2 billion in employee pension funds were wiped out: a terrible blow to its workers and their families.[6]

Similarly, Bear had a culture that encouraged employees to have skin in the game (a term coined by another colorful character, Warren Buffett) and when it tanked, employees lost billions, since they owned about one third of the bank.

Bear and Long-Term Capital Management share an unfortunate spotlight, as well, since Bear was, at the time, the biggest financial blowup since Long-Term Capital's disintegration in 1998.[7] Also, both cases required Federal Reserve (Fed) intervention.

There's another connection, too: When the Fed rallied Wall Street banks to bail out Long-Term Capital, 14 firms signed on to avoid a forced sale.[8] There was a notable holdout: Bear.[9]

Did Bear's peers and the Fed have a long memory? When Bear got into trouble, were its problems compounded by a lingering memory of 1998? Either way, talk about bad karma. . . .

The truth is, I've always been a fan of Bear. Many of Wall Street's hard-driving leaders worked there, including Sandy Weill of Citigroup;[10] Ace Greenberg of Bear;[11] Sy Lewis of Bear;[12] Jerome Kohlberg Jr. and Henry Kravis of Kohlberg Kravis Roberts;[13] Herb Sandler[14] of Sandler O'Neill (which lost approximately one third of its employees in the 9/11 attack, and which was successfully rebuilt by another Bear alumnus, Jimmy Dunne[15]) and plenty of others.

Historically, Bear was very good at understanding how to balance risk and reward. It was judicious at building new businesses, since it tended to stick to what it knew best. Its compensation was very results driven: If you produced, you reaped the rewards.

But Bear got caught up in being Bear. Too big to fail is one thing. Too small to survive is another.

Was Bear large enough; did it have the liquidity to survive in a world of big players and big bets? No.

Was Bear taking significant internal and external hedge fund risks in too small a sandbox of liquidity? Yes.

Bottom Line

Liquidity and hedge funds both played a role in Bear's demise. The firm got caught up in many of the very things we've been talking about. By understanding how the Battle for Wall Street plays out, you can understand how a firm as well established as Bear could wither and die so quickly.

Three-Act Demise: Bear Stearns

The saga of Bear Stearns's collapse played out in three acts.

Act I: The Beginning of the End

We have to look back only eight months before its fatal day to see the origins of Bear's slide into oblivion: its troubles with its buy-side products, hedge funds.

On July 18, 2007, the *New York Times* reported that Bear Stearns had, the previous day, told its clients that two of its hedge funds (one started three years earlier, and the second the previous summer) were virtually worthless. The estimated losses were about $1.5 billion.[16] On July 17, 2007, the last day of trading before this announcement hit the press, Bear's stock closed at $139.[17] (The stock's high was $170 on January 12, 2007.) On March 16, 2008, two days short of eight months later, Bear collapsed. It was purchased by JPMorgan for $10 per share.[18]

Bear's hedge funds were invested in securities linked to the sub-prime real estate market, and their collapse helped make clear to the public that something was very wrong in the financial world. Sell-side Bear's love affair with the buy side—starting its own hedge funds—contributed to its downfall.

Chasing returns as so many others were doing on the sell side, Bear was relatively late to the hedge fund party. Other sell-side banks were already intoxicated on high hedge fund profits before Bear even showed up, but one could suspect that Bear was anxious to make a financial splash.

In doing so, it pursued risky assets (subprime mortgages) and stretched—overleveraged—its balance sheet for its hedge funds. Overplaying your hand on risk and leverage in a strong financial market is one thing. In the credit crunch of 2007–2008, it's another thing. With the credit crisis raging, Bear's hedge funds were experiencing huge losses and losing value.

It's no surprise that investors and lenders in Bear's hedge funds were uneasy. One such lender, Merrill Lynch, stopped worrying and started acting. Merrill actually seized their collateral—assets that backed their loans to the hedge funds.

Following Merrill's withdrawal from Bear's hedge funds, Bear used its own money to pledge up to $3.2 billion in loans to protect its failing hedge funds.[19]

As a result, Bear was weakened, both internally, as it took a hit to its capital base, and externally, as it took a hit to its public perception.

Ironically, Merrill's withdrawal from Bear's hedge funds was a dress rehearsal: a mini-run on Bear, eight months before the run that contributed to its demise. Less noted, but also significant, was a third Bear hedge fund that went down in January 2008.[20] In total, the failures of these three funds cost their investors over $2 billion.[21]

Hedge funds were Bear's femme fatale, an enticing object of affection and one of the factors leading it to a tragic end.

Act II: Confidence Unraveling

Not surprisingly, Bear's hedge fund failures started to unravel investor confidence. I can envision two investor-type questions being tossed around at the time. From a financial perspective, did Bear have the liquidity to support its entire franchise? From a managerial perspective, did Bear truly understand the value of the mortgage-based assets it held? (The irony here is that Bear's largest business was mortgages; it was a major mortgage trader.)

Bear, likely hearing similar questions, knew it needed to respond, to restore investor confidence by shoring up its financial position and dialing up its managerial leadership. On the financial front, Bear attracted the interest of at least two reported parties.

The first interested party was British billionaire currency speculator Joe Lewis, a friend of Bear's then-CEO, James (Jimmy) Cayne.

Lewis, in fact, bought seven percent of Bear in September 2007. According to the *New York Times*,[22] Lewis—over a period of a year prior to Bear's collapse—invested $1.26 billion in Bear at an average share price of $104 (a period when Bear's shares tended down), and became Bear's largest shareholder. Lewis was not a household name on this side of the Atlantic, and his involvement appeared to have little consolation to those concerned with Bear's overall capital position.

Around the time of Lewis's investment, there were rumors that noted investor Warren Buffett was interested in taking over Bear (remember, he once took control of Salomon Brothers), and Bear's stock jumped up as a result.[23] Nothing came of it, though, and I suspect it was just rumors.

The second interested player was a foreign financial institution. Like its sell-side peers, Bear looked to Asia for a financial partner who could strengthen its balance sheet. Unlike its peers (who sold parts of themselves in return for billions of dollars), Bear came away with a very different deal.

In October 2007, Bear announced a joint venture with Citic Securities, China's largest investment bank.[24] For a firm that needed money, this deal seemed peculiar, since Bear said that it would invest the same amount of money as Citic invested in it. Wall Street was not impressed.

The *New York Times* reported: "Investor reaction [to the deal] was muted; shares ended up 1.2 percent. The quiet response, analysts said, was partly a realization that a larger investment in Bear will still be needed."[25]

That larger investment never happened. In fact, the Citic deal never happened either. Bear went to the well to improve its liquidity, but the well proved dry.

Bear's above-mentioned actions to effectively shore up its capital base could not have helped with investor confidence. In this context, the firm's collapse in March 2008 is not really a total surprise. Nothing seemed to work: not rumors of Buffett's interest, not money from Lewis, not the deal announced with Citic.

And to the lack of meaningful third-party financial support, we can add management turmoil. Instead of dialing up, Bear appeared to have dialed down its managerial position with two actions open to debate. The first move in question took place in August 2007, when co-president Warren Spector, a bond trader, was forced out. Taking over as sole president was investment banker Alan Schwartz, who had been co-president.

An article from Bloomberg.com had the following quote:

> "Spector is the person most associated with making decisions in the mortgage and fixed-income business at Bear Stearns, and that's where the problems are," said Richard Bove, an analyst at Punk, Ziegel & Co. in Lutz, Florida, who has a "sell" rating on the company's stock. By removing Spector, the management is acting as if it "didn't know what was going on, and that is just totally unsupportable. If there is no oversight system, people should be looking at Jimmy Cayne."[26]

The second management miscue involved Jimmy Cayne. What was Cayne thinking? While Bear was struggling, he was missing in action. In November 2007, *The Wall Street Journal* reported that he had been playing bridge in Tennessee during the firm's hedge fund collapse in July.[27]

Where's the investor confidence when you're in a mortgage crisis, your stock is rapidly declining, and the credit agencies decide to lower your corporate ratings?

I guess you could say that Bear's financial and managerial moves weren't the answers investors were looking for, and thus their confidence continued to unravel.

Act III: The Last Days of an 85-Year History

Bear succumbed to JPMorgan on Sunday, March 16, 2008. The previous Wednesday, Schwartz appeared on CNBC and told the world that all was well. That day, Bear announced that it would move its quarterly earnings call up to the following Monday, which was ahead of schedule. This was no doubt another move to allay market fears that Bear was facing financial difficulties. That earnings call never took place, though: by Monday, Bear was no more.

Counterparty

"The other party that participates in a financial transaction.
Every transaction must have a counterparty in order for the transaction to go through. More specifically, every buyer of an asset must be paired up with a seller that is willing to sell and vice versa."

In Bear Stearns's case, the counterparties were the creditors to its hedge funds.

Source: Investopedia, www.investopedia .com/terms/c/counterparty.asp.

Repo Market

"Investment banks like Bear Stearns and other financial players often use short-term (including overnight) borrowing to finance their operations. Every night, they sell a security, called a repo or repurchase agreement, for which they receive cash. In return, they promise to buy back the security the next day for what they paid for it, plus a little something extra. This extra is the interest they pay on this short-term loan. The repo market is huge—$4.5 trillion."[29]

Source: www.finance-glossary.com/ terms/repo-market.htm?ginPtrCode=00 000&id=12401&Popup Mode=false

Several days prior to the Bear collapse, according to industry observers, rumors began to circulate that the firm was trying to unload its debt at a discount, and that it was losing the support of its major trading counterparties. Also circulating were rumors that Bear was heavily dependent on overnight funding—the repo market—and that it was having trouble raising cash to pay back these repo loans. As a result, it was effectively being shut out of this market.[28]

This put a major crimp in the firm's short-term liquidity.

Bear's issues with the repo market were really twofold.[30] First, it couldn't get loans because people were worried that it couldn't pay them back. Second, Bear—like the other Wall Street firms—not only bought repo loans, but also sold them to others to earn interest. Bear looked in its lockbox to see if it had enough repo loans to call in sufficient cash to cover its cash needs—and found that it didn't. It therefore couldn't get additional loans or sell enough existing loans to raise sufficient cash to cover its short-term needs: double jeopardy at the wrong time.

With rumors circulating that Bear was losing the faith of counterparties, banks, and other funding sources, clients started to withdraw and demand their cash balances. This was a classic run on the bank—only it was institutional customers on the run, not the more common retail customers seen in the past.

Interestingly, the majority of the clients who wanted their money back were hedge funds, clients of Bear's prime brokerage business. This business, which seemed so wonderful for so long, came back to bite Bear, as these hedge funds made an important contribution to Bear's demise by withdrawing what was reported to be $17 billion from it within a two-day period.[31] Not a winning combination.

Three acts in eight months and Bear was no longer Bear. It's hard to understand in the context of a firm with an 85-year history that survived the Depression and every financial downturn since.

But it's easy to understand what happened to Bear in the context of the factors we've been talking about—liquidity, hedge funds—which all managed to converge at one place at one time and create a perfect storm, thus throwing Bear to the brink of potential bankruptcy.[32]

Bottom Line

The only thing preventing Bear from going over the cliff—potential bankruptcy—were the efforts of the Fed—and a forced walk down the matrimonial aisle with JPMorgan—a shotgun wedding if ever there was one.

Shotgun Wedding

With Bear falling into what looked like a financial black hole, its stock dropped dramatically. Opening on the week of the firm's demise at about $70, it closed the week on Friday at $30. The Fed stepped in, along with JPMorgan, on an emergency funding rescue mission at the beginning of the weekend. By Sunday, Bear was sold to JPMorgan for one third the price it had closed at only days earlier. Its days as an independent sell-side firm were forever over.

Some folks at Bear felt the Fed forced the sale to prove a point. It wanted to pin the housing meltdown on Wall Street, not Main Street. Others think the sale was necessary at the time to protect the overall integrity of the financial system and protect the sell side and buy side alike.

Fueling speculation that this was a Fed-forced sale was the decision by the Fed two days after the JPMorgan purchase to provide investment banks access to the Fed's discount window. Now the Fed was directly lending to sell-side investment banks. The discount window, historically reserved for commercial banks, was providing, for the first time, investment banks with a lender of last resort.

Federal Reserve Bank Discount Window

"This is where banks can borrow money from the Fed at the current discount rate. Historically, the discount window was available only to commercial banks, which are regulated by the Fed. In response to the credit crisis that began in 2007 and its threat to the financial system, the Fed now allows other financial institutions, so-called primary dealers, which include investment banks, to borrow at the discount window."

Source: "The Federal Reserve Discount Window"; www.frbdiscountwindow .org/discountwindowbook .cfm?hdrID=14&dtlID=43

If you were sitting at Bear and watching this, you had to think: If we had access to the discount window, would we have had a run on the bank? Who knows? Bear's balance sheet was covered with relatively high counterparty and balance sheet risk and low liquidity—a combination that did not bode well for survivability in the credit crisis of 2007–2008.

In the 1980s, Continental Illinois, a major commercial bank, failed, despite having access to the discount window, so credit from the Fed is no guarantee a financial institution will always have enough liquidity. And in September 2008, we can add Lehman's name to failed institutions with access to the Fed's discount window.

Circling back to Bear, was the Fed frustrated that Bear was not working hard enough to shore up its capital base? What were Bear's peers doing? They were tapping into sovereign wealth funds and using the capital markets as best they could. But then again, it's possible that Bear did go down the sovereign wealth fund road, only to come up empty-handed. (The Citic Securities deal, if it had been consummated, was not a capital infusion but a swapping of interests.)

I wouldn't be surprised to learn that Bear may have also been interested in selling all of itself to someone else, like a sell-side bank.

If Bear was looking for a blank sell-side partner, one could speculate that no one was home to take the call.

To many observers, JPMorgan's purchase of Bear was as if Christmas had come early for the sell-side commercial bank. JPMorgan was buying Bear at an 88 percent discount to book value.[33] Earlier,

I mentioned that Countrywide sold for a 67 percent discount, and that looked mighty steep.[34] Well, Bear went for even less.

Bear, in fact, had a number of valuable assets. Its building in midtown Manhattan, according to various reports, was worth more than JPMorgan's offering price for Bear's stock. Bear also had valuable clearing and prime brokerage businesses. In fact, one of the first things JPMorgan did after announcing the Bear purchase was to court those same Bear hedge fund clients who had abandoned ship. It even announced that it was looking forward to retaining Bear's prime brokerage operation.[35]

Some believe that, if Bear went down, JPMorgan stood to lose millions, if not billions of dollars, because it was a counterparty to Bear's derivative trades. As of December 30, 2007, JPMorgan had the most credit derivative exposure of any investment or commercial bank,[36] including twice that of its archrival, Citigroup.

Another point: JPMorgan was Bear's clearing bank, which meant it had a good sense of Bear's inner workings. This allowed it to move its due diligence along very quickly, a fact I'm sure was not lost on the Fed.

A little irony: As part of the JPMorgan–Bear deal, the Fed set up a special financing facility to house Bear's toxic mortgage assets in order to liquidate them in a timely and opportunistic fashion, not unlike the original Fed bailout package that captured headlines in September and October 2008. BlackRock, the buy-side powerhouse, was chosen by the Fed to manage this facility and wind down the portfolio. It was the buy side that ended up being among the last major beneficiaries of a sell-side demise.

Bottom Line

There's one thing we can all agree on: The market liked the JPMorgan takeover of Bear. JPMorgan's stock went from its close on Friday, March 14, at $37, to its close the following Monday at $40, increasing the bank's market value by nearly $13 billion or 10 percent.[37]

Case Study: JPMorgan—Winning on the Battlefield

One way to look at Bear's real value was in JPMorgan's gain after the Bear announcement: $13 billion appears to be higher than JPMorgan's transaction costs (such as the purchase of Bear's equity, potential losses on its mortgage portfolio, integration, and severance expenses) associated with buying Bear. Time will tell.

The more we talk about Bear's collapse, the more we sing the praises of JPMorgan, which looks like the king of Wall Street in the spring of 2008. There is much to like about this bank.

It appears that JPMorgan has surpassed Citigroup as the nation's premiere financial conglomerate, with JPMorgan's market cap exceeding that of Citigroup as I write this. JPMorgan's CEO Jamie Dimon must be smiling, since, while he looked like the probable successor to his long-time mentor, Sandy Weill, he was ousted before he could take the reins at Citigroup. Dimon played a key role, while working alongside Weill, in transforming Citigroup into a financial giant, with a diverse mix of products and geographic markets.[38]

JPMorgan, with approximately $1.5 trillion in assets, has the scale to be a dominant financial player. In the credit crunch of 2007–2008, with banks having lax lending standards, it fared much better than most. It took its blows, but those blows were substantially less than its peers. For example, between the summer of 2007 and February 2008, JPMorgan had about $3 billion in mortgage and leverage lending write-downs; Citigroup during this time had write-downs exceeding $20 billion.[39]

Thumbs up, JPMorgan; thumbs down, Citigroup.

Another good point about JPMorgan was that while its peers faced liquidity issues and ran to the sovereign wealth funds, it stayed put. It didn't need to sell pieces of itself to raise capital.[40]

But not everything about JPMorgan is positive. Like Bear, it holds counterparty risks that are a concern. Bear had about $2.5 trillion in notional exposure with others. JPMorgan is the largest player in the credit derivative space, and its notional exposure is approximately $77 trillion.[41] Now, that's a number that makes me pause. That is a number to keep an eye on.

As I think about Jamie Dimon, I'm reminded of Ace Greenberg, Bear's legendary CEO, who ruled the roost before Jimmy Cayne. Another banking titan he reminds me of is Hugh McColl, who, through acquisitions, transformed a small North Carolina bank into NationsBank and, eventually, Bank of America. Greenberg and McColl believed in rational management. They were about making statements and having people think about things in a particular way. It appears that Dimon is like that, too. He takes a sensible management approach to business.

Speaking of sensible management, JPMorgan announced an acquisition of the sell-side depository institution Washington Mutual (WaMu) in September 2008. This acquisition makes commercial sense from two perspectives.

First, the WaMu transaction provides meaningful upside with geographically strategic branches and consumer deposits.

Second, the WaMu transaction is balanced with limited downside as JPMorgan is acquiring the banking operation only, and leaving behind, in the hands of the U.S. government, WaMu's holding company of assets and liabilities.

I wonder if Jamie Dimon and his team will continue to be highly be successful at sell-side investment banking. I'm not talking about today, but down the road, the long term. It's not possible to be a global, powerful bank without investment banking, as corporate customers look for investment banking services.

Notional Counterparty Exposure

"Think of notional counterparty exposure as a seller, such as Bear, guaranteeing the face value of its derivative contracts. If a firm sold $2.5 trillion of derivative contracts, that's its notional counterparty exposure. It would, in theory, be on the hook for this amount of money if the derivatives fell to zero. Practically speaking, the likelihood of these contracts falling to zero is just about nil, but with exposure of $2.5 trillion, the contracts do not have to fall very far before Bear's obligations start to add up to significant amounts of money."

Source: Eduardo Canabarro and Darrell Duffie, "Measuring and Marking Counterparty Risk"; www.stanford .edu/~duffie/Chapter_09.pdf.

Does JPMorgan have the mind-set continue to build a strong team of investment bankers? It is, in part, succeeding now, because the market is working in its favor. The market volatility of 2008 does not provide investment bankers with much leverage.

When things change, will JPMorgan be willing to pay investment bankers the big bucks they expect? Granted, investment banking compensation levels post the credit crisis of 2007–2008 will be lower than in the past. This will not stop investment bankers from asking for millions on top of millions in compensation. I'm guessing that providing such huge payouts across the board is not JPMorgan's mentality, and a number of investment bankers could well drift away to the buy side.

That said, I expect JPMorgan's investment banking bench to remain deep and talented. The successful investment banking franchise JPMorgan has today should be the one it has tomorrow.

Case Study: Lehman Brothers—Falling on the Battlefield

Time after time, when a financial crisis struck Wall Street, Lehman found itself on the unhappy end of the liquidity rumor mill. Through the years, the liquidity judges have doubted Lehman, wondering whether it could survive.

Like its sell-side colleagues, Lehman was tossed around in the turbulence of the credit crunch of 1990, the Russian debt crisis of 1998, and the Bear Stearns collapse of 2008.

Lehman stood firm.

Lehman's survivability did not come easy—and there were other factors at play aside from liquidity concerns. First, there were the classic investment banking and trading wars in 1983 that nearly imploded the firm. And then there was September 11, 2001, which left the firm homeless, spread across 40 temporary locations.

Lehman's nine lives of survivability came to an end in a subsequent September—seven years after 9/11. No question, Lehman, like other sell-side firms, was caught in the credit crisis storm of 2007–2008. But let's take it one step further and examine what appears to be Lehman's flawed business model.

Lehman's business strategy, I suspect, can be seen through several lenses:

1. It overplayed its balance-sheet leverage and reliance on short-term funding.
2. It underplayed its control of balance-sheet risk.
3. Similar to AIG and Merrill Lynch, it was severely wounded by the tip of spear coming at it from one overly concentrated product area.

In the case of Lehman, that product was real estate. (For AIG, you might remember, it was credit default swaps; for Merrill Lynch it was collateralized debt obligations.)

I'm reminded of Lehman's long-reigning CEO, Dick Fuld. Lehman's survivability in the previously mentioned liquidity and credit crises can be traced directly to Fuld's hands-on, tough mind-set.

In this crisis, though, did Fuld lose sight of being the tough guy on controlling balance sheet risk?

As Lehman kept loading up its balance sheet with real estate assets, its cash register was ringing up more and more profits. This in turn led to tremendous compensation benefits for those in a position to say no.

Talk about the possibility of lips sealed and eyes wide shut.

Well, the public markets and investors were eyes wide open. As the Lehman gang was thumbs up on leverage, short-term funding, risk, and real estate, the markets and investors were thumbs down—way down— on value and confidence in Lehman. And Lehman was finding this lack of support across the board.

In its fateful final weeks, Lehman was looking for a safe haven. Its journey took it to the public arena—U.S. government bailout—and the private arena—a strategic or financial partner. But they found both ports of call closed. Lehman finally landed at the port of last resort— bankruptcy court.

As I write this, the bankruptcy courts are working diligently in scattering a 158-year-old franchise across the battlefield, with the sell side (Barclays and Nomura Securities) and the buy side (Bain Capital and Hellman & Friedman) picking up the business pieces at attractive prices.

It appears that Lehman's signature Jumbotron, at its headquarters in the New York theater district, will no longer glow with the Lehman name over the Battle for Wall Street.

Implications

In thinking about the Bear Stearns fall from grace, the Fed opening the discount window, and Lehman and WaMu going down, two questions arise.

1. Why did the Fed's actions on opening the discount window to investment banks fail?

Let's start with the Fed and Bear Stearns crisis.

The Fed's announcement of opening the discount window at exactly the same time as the Bear–JPMorgan deal was not entirely a coincidence.

Nor was it a knee-jerk reaction to the crisis of the moment. I would speculate the Fed had been thinking about this for a long time. I would also speculate that the Fed did not want to do this because it was outside its ordinary course of business; it did not come with normal checks and balances because the Fed has no oversight over investment banks.

But the Fed was facing a problem, and it was not just Bear. No one was lending against anything. Even for creditworthy companies, getting credit was tough. So the Fed, watching this from afar, went into its funding toolkit. The plan could have been: funding from an open discount window would in turn open the credit window.

However, one new avenue of funding could not stop a systemic financial crisis. The Fed's opening the discount window to provide more borrowing capacity generated only a temporary spike in the financial markets.

A familiar theme in this book is that when one person has a problem, everyone has a problem. As the credit crisis raged on and on, and the sell-side balance-sheet issues grew larger and larger, we were not just talking about investment banking collapses like Bear Stearns, but also depository institution collapses like WaMu.

As we have painfully seen, this action was only a band-aid to the financial soldier on the battlefield, who was actually a hemophiliac.

2. Who's next to fail?

The credit crisis blaze that took down Bear and Lehman and led Merrill Lynch into the waiting hands of Bank of America, will continue to burn through the sell-side landscape similar to the forest fires in California that jumped the line. I will address the future implications of the sell side in a later chapter.

At this juncture, let's look at a sample of future implications for the buy side, namely hedge funds.

If we take the position that failure is tied to a lack of liquidity, then it's likely that we'll witness a number of hedge funds going down. Why? Well, thanks to the sell-side banks facing their own survivability issues, they will continue to put the brakes on borrowing capacity. And hedge funds will be in a weaker financial position.

Not all hedge funds are likely to be equally affected, though. Sell-side banks with prime brokerage operations will want to protect this valuable cash cow, which provides financing to hedge funds. No surprise: Sell-side banks, looking to curtail credit, will most likely not pick up the phone for their smaller hedge fund clients.

This ripple effect won't just be a size-related issue, but a strategy-related one. Not only will small funds be among the first starved for credit, but so will those funds which use strategies people have less confidence in. Hedge funds may suffer if the sell-side banks do not like their underlying collateral. And it doesn't matter how well known the fund is. The sell-side banks will be out of town that day.

There's no question that the sell side has suffered large and notable casualties in the 2007–2008 credit crunch. Sorry, buy side; that's only part of it. Quite simply, at the gaming tables, where the stakes are liquidity, the sell side will be holding onto—not dealing—its liquidity hand for a while.

Battle Victorious: Sell side, buy side—a draw.

Chapter 10

Buy-Side Casualties, Sell-Side Implications

Months after the fateful weekend when the story of Bear Stearns's collapse became known, I find that most of my conversations with friends and colleagues still center around what happened. It seems like everyone I know is consumed with the drama.

I try to find places of respite, moments of quiet time, such as on my commute on the Metro North trains into New York's Grand Central Terminal, when I can hide behind my newspapers. But it's not easy, as I almost always run into someone who worked at Bear or someone who knows someone who did. Bear's story will long be told on Wall Street.

Bear Stearns's story is not the only one I associate with train travel. About a year before Bear's demise, I took another train ride, this time on Amtrak, headed to Boston. That trip was to a prominent private-equity firm, where I was prepared to talk about a number of opportunities in the financial technology space. But before I could begin, everyone wanted to talk about something else. Only later was I able to get back to the topic at hand.

The hot news of the day was the buy-side firm Fortress Investment Group, which is involved with both hedge funds and private equity.[1] Founded in 1998, it was going public on the day of my meeting. The stock was initially priced at $18.50 per share, which was at the top end of the range the sell-side underwriters had projected it would price its stock.[2] At that price, the firm had a market capitalization of $7 billion.[3] And that was only the half of it.

It didn't take long for Fortress's offering price to seem mighty cheap. In fact, the stock opened at $35, nearly twice its initial public offering (IPO) price.[4] This gave the firm a market cap of nearly $14 billion. True, the Fortress lineup was filled with impressive folks. But, still, that appeared to be a "rich" evaluation for a hybrid hedge fund, private-equity shop with a track record less than 10 years old.

You could say this caught people's attention, and not just the few of us meeting in Boston that day—I suspect that a few Wall Street types, sell and buy side alike, were adjusting their mental calculations about their own net worth. It seemed that virtually everyone on the Street was asking himself, "If Fortress is worth that much, what am I worth?"

That was then, this is now. If I were to go back on that train and travel to meet those private-equity guys in Boston, and Fortress were to come up in conversation, it would no doubt be to marvel at how fast one can stumble. As I write this, Fortress's stock trades at one-third its 52-week high, though in fairness, I need to point out that the entire financial services sector, not just Fortress, has taken its lumps in the public markets.

Fortress is not alone in watching its fortunes decline between 2007 and 2008. Other multibillion-dollar buy-side firms, particularly hedge funds, have stumbled. One noteworthy hedge fund that hit a speed bump is Renaissance Technology, which was long at the forefront of quantitative strategies. After 20 years in business, it reported its first fund loss in 2008.[5]

AQR, another technology leader and one of the fastest-growing hedge funds (with a founder who passed through the Goldman Sachs farm system), reported in 2008 that one of its funds had back-to-back monthly losses.[6] It was the first time any AQR fund had such losses. In both the Renaissance and AQR cases, the funds with the losses just happened to have been the firm's flagship funds, Renaissance's Medallion Fund and AQR's Absolute Return Fund.[7] Two brand name hedge fund players, two brand name funds—no one is immune.

Bottom Line

We have witnessed some spectacular sell-side casualties, including the collapse of Bear Stearns and Lehman Brothers. I discussed these stories and the possible implications of these casualties in Chapter 9. Are we now witnessing the beginnings of the same thing happening on the buy side? Is the buy side likely to see a prominent hedge fund falling on the battlefield? Or are the cracks we are seeing in the buy side dam just aberrations, relatively minor to moderate glitches caused by the credit crunch of 2007–2008?

Cracks in the Buy-Side Dam

The ongoing turmoil in the financial world, namely, the implosion of the subprime market and the resulting credit crunch, is triggering rumors up and down Wall Street regarding hedge fund failures. The buy-side dam (the part of the buy side that I refer to as the "buy-side dam" throughout this chapter is primarily hedge funds), seemingly so solid and invincible, is showing signs of cracking. Some funds are faltering, others failing.

Achieving the high investment returns commonly seen in the past will be very tough to achieve in the 2007–2008 credit squeeze. The old days of the bull market of the 2000s are behind us. Then, it was relatively easy to make leveraged bets. Liquidity was plentiful and the market was rising. In that type of market, leverage makes everyone look like an investment star.

In 2008, such returns are no longer so easy. I recently had lunch with a buy-sider, a man who, no matter what was happening, seemed implacable. He was late, which was unusual for him. As I was waiting, I noticed him pacing back and forth in front of the restaurant, talking intently on his cell phone. When he finally came into the restaurant and sat down, the first thing he said was, "It's tough times out there." For him, this was as strong a show of concern as I had ever seen. Everyone is feeling the pressure, both buy and sell side alike.

The buy-side dam is showing its vulnerabilities in two ways. First, some big players have made news in 2008—and not in a good way. Atticus Capital,[8] Maverick Capital,[9] and even Goldman Sachs's[10] hedge funds are looking at month-over-month losses. This is in strong contrast to days of the past, when double-digit returns were commonplace. Second, there have been a number of smaller, well-branded funds that have been casualties of the 2007–2008 credit market crisis. One example was Sailfish Capital, which was founded by two savvy veterans. One of these guys was from well-regarded SAC Capital, while the other was a long-standing global fixed income professional at UBS Securities. Despite this kind of pedigree, Sailfish is gone, a victim of current market conditions.[11]

Another goner is Sowood Capital Management. It, too, had an experienced pilot at its helm, a veteran of Harvard University's endowment.[12] I find it ironic that as the Sowood fund liquidates its assets, it's another hedge fund, Citadel, who is picking up the pieces.[13]

These failures are not limited to the popular hedge fund beltway that runs from Boston to Connecticut to New York. We can look across the pond and also see the effects of the credit crunch. One of the most successful buy-side players in London, Peloton Partners, just liquidated its largest fund.[14]

Let me go from naming names to citing numbers. You need to look no farther than the longevity of the players in the hedge fund world to see why the buy side dam is sprouting leaks. Of the approximately 10,000 existing hedge funds, fewer than 3 percent have been in existence for 15 years or more.[15] At the same time, those that are no more than a year old constitute around 10 percent of all hedge funds.

There's a correlation between more players with shorter histories and the health of an industry—any industry. When an industry is filled with companies that lack significant track records, that industry is in a precarious position. Young, untested firms are, of course, more likely to fail than larger, richer, more battle-tested firms. Again, approximately 3 percent of all hedge funds are 15 years old or more, and around 10 percent are one year or younger.[16] I must admit that I'm more taken aback by these numbers than the famous hedge fund fee structure of 2 and 20, which we discussed previously.

Bottom Line

In 2008 and, I suspect, 2009, we'll see more bad news coming from hedge funds. The seemingly impervious dam made up of successful hedge funds will likely show more and more cracks. But I suspect the casualties will be confined to the smaller funds. It's been a while since we've seen a large fund fail, such as Amaranth Advisors, a $9 billion fund that bet the wrong way in the energy sector.[17]

Future of the Buy-Side Dam

When I look at the cracks in the buy-side dam—weaknesses in the buy side—I take a slightly different view than most. I see these cracks from more of a positive perspective. When I think of approximately 10,000 hedge funds that now exist, with about 35 starting up every month as of July 2008,[18] I have to wonder if there's enough good managerial talent available to oversee this many funds. My guess is that there is not. A culling in the number of hedge funds would be a good thing because the remaining funds would have access to a better group of managers. The excess wood would be gone, and the remaining leaders should be more successful with the surviving funds.

Second, consider all the volatility that existed in the marketplace. That was a function, at least of part, of the amount of liquidity—money—that was sloshing around in the reservoir. In fact, I think there was too much money, which was one reason the buy-side dam sprung leaks. Because of all this money, there were too many practitioners chasing too few good ideas.

A number of hedge funds have a strategy based on one great high-octane idea. This idea looks for differences in the market to exploit, and it tries not to be correlated to the market. It's hard for me to believe 10,000 hedge fund managers each have a unique idea not correlated to the market. I just don't know how that can happen. Again, fewer hedge funds will be good because there will be fewer funds chasing good ideas—fewer cracks in the future dam.

There are some hedge funds, of course, that are doing well despite the subprime crisis—they've proven that they can navigate the turbulent credit markets of 2007–2008. Paulson & Co. is just one example. The market will separate those that have it from those that don't. I would say that this is a good development for the buy-side dam.

Another benefit is that the hedge funds—at least some of them—are seeing more capital scrutiny from investors. These hedge funds can no longer take the easy way out. They can't continue to do a trade, make some money, and then lever up. Then they make some more money and then, of course, lever up again. In no time, they're highly leveraged. I would suspect that corporate pensions, for example, opening their capital wallets to these hedge funds, are not thrilled with this strategy.

These corporate folks may very well look more closely at the hedge funds and want them to move away from the one great idea, the arbitrage philosophy. This, too, could be a good development because it will force the hedge funds to be more creative, more diversified, and less reliant on one strategy.

All of this will be for the good. The current situation for hedge funds will prompt them to be more careful, to do more due diligence. Who knows? They may even go out and buy more risk management software. In fact, the sell side will be doing much of the same thing— be more careful, check each other out, use better tools like risk management software.

Circling back to the first section of this chapter, I primarily talked about quantitative strategy fund losses in 2008. We are in a global credit crisis and the possibility exists of a disconnect between the quantitative shop's financial models and the reality of the times as I write this. The fact that this scenario is playing out is not surprising. I say that because we've been down this road before, with the financial models saying one thing and the market saying something else.

In 1998, we had a global credit squeeze as well,[19] which began with Russia's credit defaults.[20] And there was a famous Bear Stearns, Lehman Brothers–type casualty, namely Long-Term Capital.[21] And as happened before, Wall Street, specifically the quantitative shops, are filled with smart guys who will recalibrate; wait out the storm of 2007–2008.

Who knows? They might even go vertical and continue to add new hedge fund strategies. And they may even find their way into new realms of computational finance.

On a broader scale, the hedge fund world in general is being tossed around in the turbulence of the 2007–2008 credit crunch like a tiny plane in a storm. Some hedge funds will find a way to navigate through the turbulence, some won't.

One question on everyone's mind is, will these cracks in the dam spill over and take down a Bear Stearns–like buy-side player?

Well, as I write this book, I can't imagine that happening.

Computational Finance

"Computational finance as a discipline emerged in the 1980s. It is also sometimes referred to as 'financial engineering,' 'financial mathematics,' 'mathematical finance,' or 'quantitative finance.' It uses the tools of mathematics, statistics, and computing to solve problems in finance. Computational methods and the mathematics behind them have become an indispensable part of the finance industry."

Source: www.math.cmu.edu/~bscf/ informationframe.html.

Of course, you never know: 10 years ago we said that Long-Term Capital was too big and smart to fail, and fail it did. It was reported that there was a one in a billion chance the fund would lose 50 percent of its net asset value.[22] And we saw what happened. There's no question that markets can panic and things can go wrong. Hedge funds can bet wrong. Big hedge funds can leverage up big time, making their fall, if it happens, all the more spectacular. Big-time failures are always a possibility, and as the credit crisis of 2007–2008 rages on, that possibility becomes even greater.

Bottom Line

There will be a shake-out. Some buy-side hedge fund firms will fail, some hedge funds will sustain losses, and cracks in the dam will continue, but the dam should hold. That's good news for the buy side, less than good news for the sell side.

No more nonsense about how we shouldn't worry about excess leverage or that this or that event cannot happen. When I hear that the buy side or sell side has stress-tested or back-tested their portfolio, and all is well, I respond with the hurricane story: The real estate folks in southeast

Leverage—Stretching and Breaking the Band

As I write this, sell side and buy side alike are pushing the envelope on leverage.

A leverage-to-equity ratio in single digits is, to my mind, reasonable and reasonably conservative. When both sides of the Street are moving the ratio into the 20s and 30s, it creates a risky situation. I call this "super-sized leverage." I consider those who rely on super-sized leverage to achieve desirable results to be more like investment plumbers than investment architects.

The problem? With high leverage, you'll make excellent profits about 80 percent of the time. Not bad. However, with this kind of leverage, the other 20 percent of the time will catch up with you, and you're guaranteed to blow up at some point. When using super-sized leverage, a very small price movement can wipe you out. Using super-sized leverage as a basic business strategy is as dangerous as riding a motorbike without a helmet. And yet in recent years, such risk taking has become somewhat commonplace.

These risks have actually contributed to both sell and buy side casualties in 2008. Two such fatalities come to mind: the sell-side Bear Stearns and the private equity Carlyle Group's publicly traded mortgage bond fund.[23]

Specifically, they both took a small spread and leveraged it, say, 25 or 30 times—whatever. When you do that, trust me, you're playing with dynamite. How much dynamite? Just ask Bear Stearns or Carlyle. Not a smart way to operate. Other players that super-sized their leverage also put themselves in a delicate position.

And such behavior does not just affect those overplaying their leverage hand. Markets are interdependent. If anybody has a problem, everybody has a problem. And if there is a problem, it goes first to the weakest link. Who's going to suffer? The guy who's the weakest. Who's the weakest? The buy-side hedge fund or the sell-side firm leveraged 25 times or more.

Florida always say that a devastating hurricane is a once-in-a-100-year event. Well, tell that to the people whose homes were destroyed twice in five years.

If you want to take the risk of supersized leverage, be aware you're also taking on the greater risk of failure. Everyone likes leverage. Everyone likes liquidity.

Be careful for what you wish for—whether you're sell side or buy side.

> **Back Testing**
>
> "The process of testing a trading strategy on prior time periods."
>
> *Source:* Investopedia, www.investopedia .com/terms/b/backtesting.asp.

Case Study: Morgan Stanley—A Believer in the Buy Side

You have to like John Mack and his vision of Morgan Stanley in 2008. In his first stint at Morgan Stanley in the 1970s, 1980s and 1990s, he was a product of the traditional sell-side model.[24]

In his second tour of duty, which began in 2005, John Mack and his team have been revamping a number of Morgan Stanley businesses. In particular, Morgan Stanley has spun off the unsexy Discover Card division and has moved more to the buy-side world of alternative asset management, namely, hedge funds.

Embracing hedge funds at Morgan Stanley today is very different from the old Morgan Stanley model. Prior to John Mack's return, Morgan Stanley's asset management focus was considered to be old-fashioned mutual fund sales. It sold proprietary Morgan Stanley–originated in-house mutual funds via Morgan Stanley brokers.[25] But a number of clients wanted a choice of funds, not to be limited only to Morgan Stanley's.

As I discussed in a previous chapter, if a buy-side hedge fund provided clients with better results—namely, higher returns than in-house products—sell-side clients are quick to say no and quick to shop elsewhere. Clients shop for performance. Morgan Stanley, like other sell-side firms, saw a number of its clients become buy-side clients.

Such asset management services are good counters to the sell side's capital market operation, which is an inherently volatile revenue stream. In a good market, you get great returns and great revenues. But in a poor market, the opposite happens. (Look no further than the credit crisis of 2007–2008). So asset management provides a valuable balance.

This fact was not lost on Morgan Stanley. Since Mack's return, senior management has been emphasizing asset management revenues. Morgan Stanley has gone even farther by orchestrating major moves in the hedge fund world. Morgan Stanley even looked at merging with BlackRock, a premiere buy-side firm. Speculation is that price and control were insolvable issues that caused it to walk away from the deal.[26]

As I write this, Morgan Stanley, wanting to pump up the asset management volume, has new managers and new products. It has announced seven new hedge fund alliances.[27] Nearly all of these ventures take the form of minority investments, where Morgan Stanley invests its capital as well as contributes its distribution channel to the venture, and the hedge fund contributes its products and expertise.

These hedge fund transactions include U.S. players like Avenue Capital[28] (which is a prominent player in distressed assets[29]), and Traxis Partners[30] (which reunites John Mack with Barton Briggs, who was Morgan Stanley's chief strategist[31]). These transactions also include the London players, Hawker Capital (commodities strategies)[32] and Lansdowne Partners[33] (global strategies[34]). Morgan Stanley didn't just stop with minority investments.

It acquired FrontPoint Partners,[35] which is an incubator holding company of sorts for hedge funds. It raises money for hedge funds, monitors risk for hedge funds and processes trades for hedge funds.[36] FrontPoint provides a sell-side firm like Morgan Stanley a larger window in the buy-side hedge fund space.

Interestingly, Morgan Stanley took someone from FrontPoint, a guy by the name of Stu Bohart, and made him co-head of Morgan Stanley's asset management business.[37] The Battle for Wall Street, unlike military battles, is fought by generals who one day are on the sell side and the next day on the buy side, or vice versa.

It looks like Morgan Stanley sees those cracks in the buy-side dam as aberrations. It appears they see a bright future for hedge funds, judging from how the firm is working to restructure its asset management business.[38]

Case Study: D. E. Shaw—A Believer in the Sell Side

A quick take on D. E. Shaw: It is a buy-side believer in the sell side. When David Shaw opened for business as a quantitative shop in 1988, computerized trading was just a few dots on the radar screen. Shaw and his original investors (the Tisch family, Paloma Partners), began with $28 million in assets under management, and envisioned a future where they could use quantitative strategies to create a real business.[39] And in 2008 those strategies are the basis of a $225 billion industry.[40]

Shaw's world was a blend of academia and the sell side. He was a Columbia professor with a PhD in artificial intelligence.[41] He also went through the Morgan Stanley farm system, and was one of the alumni who jumped to the buy side.

And over time, D. E. Shaw became a farm system, too. It was the spawning ground for a group of amazingly talented people who have migrated to a wide range of successful ventures, including Jeff Bezos, the creator of Amazon.com.

Shaw prides itself on being a highly secretive firm that searches for the highest level of human talent. I personally know how secretive it is. When it was selling selected businesses, I was its investment banker.

People trust their investment banker because we bankers are dealing with valuable assets and sensitive information. When I go to a client's offices, I generally see what they're up to. Not at D. E. Shaw. Over an approximately six-month period, I was in D. E. Shaw's offices two or three times a week. Yet, during this time, my contact was limited to a handful of selected folks in primarily the same conference room. I can't imagine the CIA being any more secretive than D. E. Shaw.

If *U.S. News & World Report* was ranking the difficulty of being hired by D. E. Shaw like it ranks the difficulty of getting admitted to colleges, it would characterize the firm as extremely selective, every bit as selective as Harvard and Princeton.

When my students ask about job possibilities at D. E. Shaw, my response is: Are you a chess champion? Are you a life master bridge player?

Did you take first prize at the math Olympiad? Are you a *Jeopardy!* winner? Were you a U.S. Treasury secretary (it hired Larry Summers, former U.S. Treasury secretary and former president of Harvard University[42])? These are the kinds of folks D. E. Shaw looks for.

In recent years, D. E. Shaw has gone vertical by diversifying into a variety of buy-side activities, such as private equity. Yet, admittedly, life at the company has not always been smooth sailing. At the halfway point of the firm's history, in 1997, it formed a strategic alliance with Bank of America.[43] Bank of America made a $1.4 billion bank loan to a D. E. Shaw fund. This was a creative way to bring to bear the best of both worlds— D. E. Shaw's world-class quantitative analytical abilities and Bank of America's world-class distribution capabilities and balance sheet prowess.

A year or so later, D. E. Shaw, like others, found itself mired in the Russian bond default, which led to a global credit crunch. One casualty: the D. E. Shaw–Bank of America fund. This forced Bank of America to write down $372 million of its investment, and there was speculation on the Street that this episode cost Bank of America's CEO, David Coulter, his job.[44] In that year, Bank of America merged with NationsBank, led by Hugh McColl. The irony is that David Coulter rebounded nicely by jumping to the buy side, where he's a partner at Warburg Pincus.[45]

Ten years later, in 2007, the firm entered into a new alliance with another sell-side firm. This time, D. E. Shaw sold 20 percent of the company to the classic sell-side firm of Lehman Brothers. In spite of Lehman's demise in 2008, the concept of a buy-side partnership with sell-side distribution was a clever move then, and still is today.

Speaking of Lehman Brothers, our recurring theme of talent migration from the sell side to the buy side continues with Lehman and D. E. Shaw. In September 2008, Richard McKinney, senior executive at Lehman, left just prior to its collapse to lead a new group at D. E. Shaw that will invest in asset-backed securities.

This talent move has a second significance. Specifically, this action suggests an opportunity for hedge funds like D. E. Shaw, similar to the private equity firms discussed in Chapter 5, to invest in underperform-ing, underpriced securities today and sell those securities at a premium tomorrow.

I guess you could say David Shaw is a believer in the sell side, and 20 years after he left the sell side to jump over the fence, he has stepped back, at least with a few toes, onto sell-side territory.

In 2008, D. E. Shaw's original $28 million in assets has turned into one of the world's largest and most successful hedge funds, with over $30 billion in assets.[46]

Implications

As discussed in this chapter, the buy-side hedge funds are experiencing a series of cracks in the dam—fund performance is down, a number of funds are losing money, and some have even failed.

This series of buy-side events is not lost on the sell side. And I wonder if the sell side views this as an opportunity to strike back, go on the offensive.

For example, it could rebuild its own proprietary hedge fund complex.

But should the sell side invest capital in its own hedge fund business, I can see the shareholders screaming: "Not so fast! This is one way to get into trouble. If you're Goldman Sachs, you can show how you successfully navigated through the credit crunch." A firm like Goldman Sachs could say, "With the exception of several funds, we didn't do so bad, so trust us."

But what about the other guys who don't have the same Goldman Sachs reputation? Who will believe a sell-side firm when it says it will tie up the balance sheet to build up its hedge fund business?

The sell side could take another approach. It takes a run at the hedge funds by trying to attract buy-side talent, thus reversing the traditional farm system, with the sell side raiding the buy side. My speculation is that if they try this approach, the sell side will have a hard time.

The hedge fund folks will look at all the sell-side executives who were paid in stock in 2007–2008 and see that their options and stock holdings are doing poorly, or in some cases are worthless. If I'm a hedge fund manager, why would I want to join the sell side and get paid with that same weak currency? If I stay on the hedge fund side, I eat what I kill.

Where does this leave the sell-side firms? Well, they're not static, they're not standing still. In an attempt to increase their hedge fund capacity, a number of sell-side firms have embarked down the path of what I refer to as a modified offensive approach, where they acquire minority investments in hedge funds. This way, they have access to cash flow, and have product to distribute through their channels, and if the hedge fund blows up, it's off their balance sheet.

This sounds great, but a word of caution on this road to minority investments: How much control do they actually have? Does it immunize them from a hedge fund blowing up? If a hedge fund blows up, won't the shareholders go after the sell-side firm? They may nail the sell-side firm for lack of due diligence. The sell-side firm will tell its shareholders it is off balance sheet, but the shareholders could tell the sell side, "You picked these funds, and it's your problem—not the hedge fund's."

Compensation Ratio

"The compensation ratio is a ratio between a firm's revenues and its compensation. It indicates the percentage of a firm's revenues that goes to pay compensation to the firm's employees. It's not uncommon for the compensation ratio to be about 50 percent, where employees receive as compensation 50 percent of the revenue generated by the firm."

Source: www.exinfm.com/board/metrics_for_hr_management.htm.

Let's look at the implications of this minority investment strategy from a different perspective. How will these investments affect the ever-present compensation ratio? The compensation ratio is one of the most important valuation parameters of sell-side investment banks. Everyone looks at it and everyone wrestles with ways to lower it.

Just ask Lazard.[47] In its pre–initial public offering (IPO) discussions with its underwriters, I suspect the firm's compensation ratio was brought up. It was reported to be higher than the investment banking norm. Well, this isn't what investors want to hear when they consider buying a firm's stock. A sell-side firm with a high compensation ratio may have a harder time selling its stock to the public in an IPO. Did Lazard resist? No. Did Lazard lower its compensation ratio relative to industry standards? Yes.

Do the math. If a sell-side firm buys a hedge fund or hires a hedge fund team, it's adding to its cost basis because it's bringing aboard expensive talent. A minority investment leaves personnel expenses with the hedge fund, and it does not become a sell-side issue. Of course, there is a cost associated with investing in another company (namely, the cost of buying the equity), but the cost of a minority investment seems to be a less obvious valuation benchmark than the dreaded sell-side compensation ratio.

Where do I hope this leads for the sell side? Well, I hope they temper their buildup of hedge funds. Those sell-side firms that already have meaningful alternative investment operations such as hedge funds are perceived to look less and less like the traditional sell-side banks. Why add to that perception in the difficult financial times of 2008?

An appropriate direction would be to look inward, not outward, and a good place for the sell side to begin is to consider its shareholders. It needs their confidence. It needs to start thinking safety, not risk. It needs to reduce its dependence on leverage. The leverage game is a dangerous one. If you roll the dice on leverage, be prepared to get whacked at some point. Just ask Bear Stearns. Just ask Lehman Brothers.

As for the cracks in the buy-side dam, I would allow the hedge funds to find their own way to fill them. Going forward, I think that the sell side needs to strengthen its own dam with a fortress made up of capital, while lowering its leverage. I'd suspect that lower leverage and stronger capital ratios will bring higher investor confidence, which ultimately could move the all-important price-to-earnings needle in the right direction (up).

Unfortunately, as I write this, the credit crisis continues to rage. Sell-side casualties are mounting and it will be some time before we see that sell-side price-to-earnings multiple move in their favor.

Battle Victorious: Buy side.

Chapter 11

Regulatory Implications

As I write this book, the world is under a cloud. The subprime mortgage crisis of 2007–2008 is hanging over our heads, grabbing headlines and fueling anxiety. Everyone is worried—from Ben Bernanke to the Minnesota newlyweds looking to purchase their first home. Bring on the Pepto-Bismol.

Am I surprised by this turn of events? Well, no. Not really.

Over the course of my career on Wall Street, other financial crises have unfortunately crossed my path.

There was the savings-and-loan crisis in the 1980s and the Long-Term Capital Management collapse in the 1990s, to name just two.[1]

And now we're in the midst of this credit crunch, wondering how we ended up in this rocky, off-road terrain. Did the regulators miss the signals? Did the road have one too many untenable curves? Were we driving in the dark?

In this chapter, I'll take a look at how much heat the lenders, the sell side and the buy side, should—or should not—be taking for getting us here, so far off course.

The Blame Game

In this type of crisis, of course, fingers naturally start to point. And the regulators—the guys in charge of protecting us—come under fire.

In retrospect, some would say that it's pretty clear: The regulators should have foreseen the crisis. They should have known.

Others will say it's hard to blame the regulators. After all, they didn't have crystal balls. There's that old saying, "If you can't see the problem, you can't fix the problem." And credit risk, ironically enough, falls into that category. Why? Well, for starters, the risk was diffused throughout the system. One could argue that the regulators didn't even know where the poison was. In a sense, it was dispersed too widely to pinpoint.

Who, among the players in this game, was holding the risk? Who was holding the collateralized mortgage obligation (CMO) tranches that were behind the risk? Nobody knew.

And look at the subprime foreclosures. Can we blame the regulators for something that happens on an individual basis? After all, they can't follow risk down to the guy in Oklahoma who, for whatever reason, doesn't make his mortgage payment. In a sense, the regulators could argue, "There were too many moving risk pieces; too many probabilities for us to watch."

They could also argue that it's not their responsibility to stop the lenders from giving money to people who really shouldn't be borrowing. If Joe X doesn't have a job, and shows up at "Y" bank asking for $100,000, isn't it "Y" bank's fault if they approve him? Shouldn't they take the heat when Joe defaults on that loan?

There are those, of course, who don't agree with this line of thinking. They don't think the regulators deserve a "get out of jail free" card. They don't buy into the "if you can't see it, you can't fix it" defense. They don't accept the excuse that the problem was diffused throughout the system. They don't even look to the lenders—they look right back to the regulators. Why?

Well, they're thinking about a flashing red light, a danger signal that not only did the regulators see, but others should have seen, as well. And that danger signal was the leverage within the system.

The irony is, until late 2007, everything was working. People were making huge amounts of money. The economy was good. The response was clear, from the sell side and buy side alike: "If it ain't broke, why fix it?"

There was a mutually beneficial give and take. The sell side was feeding the buy side, and the buy side was enjoying what they were being fed. The candy in the system was making everyone happy—there was a real sugar high.

And then it stopped working. That sugar started bringing everyone down, and both the buy side and sell side began to kick themselves for indulging, by golly.

The truth is that the leverage was there. It was all out in the open—no one was trying to hide it; no rules were broken. When Bear Stearns went down, all you had to do was look at their balance sheet to see how much leverage they had. This, after all, is the old refrain of unregulated capitalism: "If you want to leverage, go leverage. If you choose to leverage, say, 30 to 1 and you roll up, well, that's just the price you pay in a free market."

"Sorry," unregulated capitalism says, "That's life. Next time we'll be smarter."

Well, that old song and dance doesn't really work for me. It's a fairytale calculus. In theory, if you leverage up the wazoo and then fall on your face, you may be able to pick yourself up—but, in reality, lives are destroyed. When you fall, you bring a lot of other people down with you.

And our society is simply not okay with that. We're not a society of people living on the streets or in the sewers. We're not a society waiting for the next revolution to come. We're a society that picks up the pieces. We're a society that expects the regulators to pick up the pieces for us. We have a certain amount of faith in the system—and when the system fails, we want answers.

Bottom Line

Battlefield casualties from the subprime crisis will not be limited to the risk takers on both sides of the Street. It will find its way to the risk protectors—those folks monitoring the Street. There's no question: There will be a regulatory fallout. Something will happen here, and it will be highly political.

The Fall of the Rating Agencies

I'm writing this book in 2008, in an election year. It's too early to predict where the cards will fall, and we'll see different results depending on whether a Democrat or a Republican ends up in the White House. Whoever wins the election, one thing that Democrats and Republicans can probably agree upon is that the rating agencies are going to take some hits. The idea that these agencies are one of our linchpins—one of our financial system's central features to complex, risky asset classes—is hard to fathom.

Internally, the hammer has already fallen at the rating agencies. As I am writing this, the presidents of both Moody's[2] and Standard & Poor's[3] (S&P) have been replaced. One could ask, "Too little, too late?"

And, of course, who pays the rating agencies? The sell side—the very people the agencies are supposed to be policing. No wonder things got a little sticky.

There's a whole host of problems here, not least of which is risk. Circling back to our earlier discussion, did the regulators know where the risk was concentrated? Some will say the rating agencies, like the regulators, could not isolate the problem. Why? They look at a CMO structure. If, on paper, it looks good, it is good. What the rating agencies don't look at is the actual paper within that structure.[4]

How could they? How could they go through every single tranche, every single CMO, and find every mortgage?

Not all tranches will fail, of course. We just don't know whether a majority will or won't—again, some would agree there are too many risk variables to consider.

So we know that there are problems. The question is: Is there a solution? Is there a way to protect the rating agencies and investors?

An easy fix would be to get the government involved. Uncle Sam could pay the rating agencies instead of the sell side. After all, that would prevent the agencies from being paid by the very people they're supposed to police.

That might very well be an easy fix, but I think it's a bad fix. Aside from the fact that involving Uncle Sam is a quasi-state solution, we'd be subjecting the government to headline risk. So do I believe that the government should step in and start regulating or paying the rating agencies? No. There's no question that what we need is a stand-alone rating agency, independent and free from influence.

Great, you might say. You want to have your cake and eat it, too. The government stays away—yet rating agencies are somehow perfect models of objectivity. How, exactly, will this work?

Well, let's look to New York's ex-governor, Eliot Spitzer. During his days as New York's attorney general, he helped fix a major problem on Wall Street: He found a way to solve the inherent conflict of interest between sell side's corporate and investment bankers and its research analysts.

That conflict could have gone something like this: an analyst at Sell Side "A" would research Company "B," say "I don't like this stock," and recommend selling it off.

And then the phone would ring.

On the other end of the line, an agitated member of the banking side of the company would remind the analyst (in no uncertain terms) that Company "B" had been writing them fat checks.

Whoops. There went that sell order. Despite that research analyst's diligence, the firm would continue to buy. For the writers of the fat checks, it was like Christmas and Hanukkah rolled into one. Remember Enron? Its stock went from high highs to low lows, but Wall Street kept on buying because Enron was lining sell-side pockets to the tune of big money year after year.[5]

And then Spitzer stepped in. He implemented what became known as the Global Settlement, which forced Wall Street firms to put money into a communal fund for the purpose of creating independent research bodies—"Chinese walls" aimed at preventing conflicts of interest.[6]

So, turning back to rating agencies, it's easy enough to imagine an independent body similar to the research firms created in the Global Settlement. Of course, I can only imagine going to the sell side and saying, "Guess what, guys? You're going to pay to keep the rating agencies independent!" Well, sorry, sell side: If the government comes after you for a second global settlement in order to fix the subprime mortgage crisis, I probably wouldn't answer the phone that day. Keep your heads down, guys.

And the buy side? Well, you keep your heads up. After all, you're the guys buying the securities—you don't exactly benefit from less-than-ideal rating agencies. If you want better oversight, you might be willing to pay for it. Maybe you can contribute half a base point or a base point into a pool, based on assets under management. Remember, buy side: You have more to lose here. So when the government starts knocking on doors, keep your heads up.

Here, of course, is where the buy side starts to scream at me about the money flowing out of their pockets. It's easy for me to say that they should pay, right?

Well, let's revisit our discussion of hedge funds from earlier chapters. Remember, there are just too many of them out there; too many guys chasing too few ideas. I'm not sure all of these funds have the tools or the sophistication for the sheer amount of products being sold on the sell side. So if I were the buy side, I might be a little gun-shy right now, when I'm buying from the sell side. Do these guys truly understand what they're selling me? Are they selling me something I really want?

And at the end of the day, isn't the buy side going through the same credit crunch we're all going through? So if I were in their shoes, I would fund the rating agencies. I would put in place a self-policing mechanism, knowing that I'd be better served down the road.

Bottom Line

The buy side should be thinking of ways to protect their turf. And if that means paying for independent rating agencies, I'd probably take that bet.

The Uneven Past

Remember that Bob Dylan song, "The Times They Are A-Changin'?" (If you're too young too remember, go out and buy the CD. It's a classic.)

Massive political and social changes were beginning to take hold of the United States back in 1964, and they only got more intense as the decade progressed—everywhere, that is, except on Wall Street.

In the 1960s, Wall Street was in a kind of time warp. It had been that way for about three decades. The shock of the Great Depression created government regulations that essentially put the financial markets in legal shackles.

Interest rates allowable on savings accounts were capped by the government,[7] and interest rates on checking accounts weren't allowed.[8] Forget about financial institutions competing for customers based on interest rates—it basically didn't happen.

Commercial banking and investment banking activities were strictly separated, resulting in the total separation of brokerage firms and their activities from the activities of banks. Banks couldn't even operate across state lines, while brokerage firms had limits placed on their commissions.[9] Banks and insurance were also kept apart. The foreign currency market, today a no-holds-barred free-for-all, didn't exist.[10]

Things began to change in the 1970s.

The goal of much of the regulation was transparency, whether in the full disclosure prospectuses accompanying initial public offerings (IPOs) or in quarterly and annual reports.

Interestingly, as regulations have been loosened over time, we've gone back to that murky time when less was known about companies and the financial system's sell side and buy side. Dark pools hide the presence of liquidity; algorithmic trading seeks to disguise who's doing what. Hedge funds are largely unregulated, and even major sell-side firms operate in ways that are not made public.

The changes in the regulatory climate have produced big changes in the financial community. Until recently, a lot of the money made on Wall Street was through relationships of long standing. Investment banks got clients for IPOs by establishing relationships with companies likely to go public. In fact, a lot of the rationale behind using an investment bank was the power of those relationships. The investment banks (at least in theory) understood the market. They knew those willing to make investments and they could help generate interest in a company's stock. It was a business that depended on who you knew—your Rolodex was a major asset.

And today? Well, partly due to deregulation, we're less relationship oriented and more transaction oriented. The money made by sell-side investment and commercial banks is increasingly being generated by trades they do themselves, rather than from commissions generated through relationships. Twenty years ago, there were only a few hedge funds; today, they're major players, and they're typically pure traders and arbitrageurs.

In a sense, private-equity firms are traders in companies. Banks and savings-and-loans used to lend money to home buyers, and then would hold the mortgages until they matured or the properties were sold. Well, the 2007–2008 credit crisis is due, in part, to the transformation of those mortgages into tradable securities. There's no longer a relationship between the lender and the homeowner.

Without much regulation, the market has created instruments that it doesn't fully understand. It may sound unlikely, but it's true. The *Wall Street Journal* recently wrote about the great Warren Buffett trying to untangle himself from some unregulated, opaque instruments. In 2002, he had his reinsurance subsidiary General Re Corporation pull back from dealing with credit-default swaps and other derivatives. It took General Re four years to reduce its portfolio of contracts from 23,218 to 197.

"Doing so involved tracking down hundreds of counterparties to General Re's trades, many of which Mr. Buffett and his colleagues had never heard of, he says, including a bank in Finland and a small loan company in Japan, to name just two. One contract, Mr. Buffett says, was designed to run for 100 years. 'We lost over $400 million on contracts that were supposedly' safe and properly priced, 'and we did it in a leisurely way in a benign market,' Mr. Buffett says. 'If we had to unwind it in one month [as might have happened during the credit crisis], who knows what would have happened?' "[11]

And in 2003, Buffett, in his annual letter to stockholders, referred to derivatives as "financial weapons of destruction."

Bottom Line

Government regulations have played a key role in the Battle for Wall Street. We can't fully understand what's currently happening on Wall Street if we ignore the regulatory climate the financial community operated under in the not-too-distant past—and, of course, what it's like today.

Times, once again, are a-changin'.

Long-Term Capital Management—Days of Yesterday

In 1998, the Greenwich, Connecticut–based hedge fund, Long-Term Capital Management (LTCM) caused a major stir. LTCM, while little known to the public, was in fact well known among those on Wall Street and a cadre of wealthy investors. It was filled with academic and trading superstars and raised an amount of money that was a record at the time. It subsequently flamed out in a spectacular collapse, saved by the Fed and a group of financial institutions who came to the rescue.

The following history is based on a report by Thayer Watkins, a professor in the economics department at San Jose State University and a case study published by Sunware BancWare ERisk. LTCM was founded in 1993. Its origins were in the Arbitrage Group created by John Meriwether at Salomon Brothers (now part of Citigroup). Meriwether was asked to resign from Salomon Brothers because of the unlawful conduct of one of his traders. He subsequently founded LTCM, which included $1.25 billion he was able to raise and a gilt-edged group of people that included many from his Salomon Brothers days.

These included a former vice chairman of the board of governors of the Federal Reserve, and Myron Scholes and Robert C. Merton; Scholes and Merton were to share the Nobel Prize in Economics in 1997. There were other academic and trading luminaries involved with LTCM.

Scholes is quoted as saying LTCM would function like a giant vacuum cleaner, sucking up nickels that everyone else had overlooked.

LTCM's strategy was finding securities that were mispriced from one another. They would buy the cheap ones and sell short the overpriced ones, and make their money on the difference. Such differences tended to be very small, hence Scholes's comment about vacuuming up nickels. In order to make real money with such small differences, the hedge fund had to do

(continued)

many, many such transactions, which required the use of leverage, and a lot of it.

At the beginning of 1998, the fund had equity of approximately $5 billion and had borrowed over $125 billion—a leverage factor of roughly 30 to 1. LTCM's partners believed, on the basis of their complex computer models, that the long and short positions were highly correlated and so the net risk was small.

Well, markets do not always work as computer models expect, as the partners and investors in LTCM found out in a costly bout of theory versus the real world. What triggered LTCM's demise was Russia's August 1998 default on its debt. This led investors to run from risky investments toward investments with far less risk such as government bonds—the so-called "flight to quality." The result was a liquidity crisis in the financial markets, which caused enormous problems for LTCM. On September 1, 1998, its equity had dropped to $2.3 billion, and three weeks later, on September 22, had fallen again, this time to $600 million.

At this point, the case study noted that "The portfolio has not shrunk significantly, and so its leverage is even higher. Banks begin to doubt the fund's ability to meet its margin calls but cannot move to liquidate for fear that it will precipitate a crisis that will cause huge losses among the fund's counterparties and potentially lead to a systemic crisis."

The next day, Warren Buffett, Goldman Sachs, and AIG offered to buy out the fund's partners and run it as part of Goldman's proprietary trading operation, but they were rebuffed. That day, the Federal Reserve Bank of New York began to organize a rescue.

About 14 banks each contributed $300 million or so to raise $3.65 billion. These major creditors took over management of the fund in exchange for 90 percent of the fund's equity. This pool of money, and what was left in LTCM, enabled the fund to hold on. Eventually, LTCM was reorganized, paid off its loans, and was liquidated by 2000.

Again, what does this crisis teach us about the Battle for Wall Street? In this case, the bailout was organized by the Fed and the money for the bailout came from Wall Street institutions. A major crisis had erupted on Wall Street, and the Street was able to finance the solution itself, with leadership from the Fed.

Isn't it refreshing when the public and private markets come together in a time of need?

Sources: Thayer Watkins, "Long-Term Capital Management," www.sjsu.edu/faculty/watkins/ltcm.htm; and "Case Study: LTCM—Long-Term Capital Management," www.erisk.com/Learning/CaseStudies/Long-TermCapitalManagemen.asp.

Undoing the Present

Did the U.S. government need a historic $700 billion bailout plan for the Street? I would say no.

Did the U.S. government need to rethink one accounting issue to restore confidence in the Street? I would say yes.

The accounting issue in question is commonly referred to as mark-to-market accounting. And mark-to-market accounting played a significant role with the sell side's financial woes in 2007–2008 and the Fed's $700 billion bailout (the bailout plan that I refer to throughout this section is the Fed's original version).

Let's step back. There was a practical reason behind the origin of mark-to-market accounting. Go back to the Enron days, a time when we questioned the financial reporting of public companies. There was mistrust across the board. No surprise, there was a backlash for tougher financial standards.

One such standard was that the value of an asset is not a financial model or theory. Rather, its value is what I can sell that asset at today. That standard is mark-to-market accounting.

Theoretically, how can you have anything other than mark-to-market accounting? If you're not going to have mark-to-market, what are you going to mark an asset at? The price of cheese? Or something else?

Of course, you're going to mark an asset to its market value. How can you defend anything other than the market? Well, there are certain circumstances when markets do not work. In 2008, we are in one of those situations.

In 2008, we are in a falling market. Consequently, mark-to-market accounting is caught in a death spiral. Simply put, if you have assets that are subject to mark-to-market accounting in an environment where no one wants the assets, and you sell the assets, the price heads south.

As the prices go down, you have more capital needs. You have to sell more assets to restore capital. The more you sell, the more the prices go down. The value of assets disappears. It becomes a self-fulfilling prophecy.

The government should have recognized that mark-to-market accounting doesn't work in failing markets and when you have really complicated assets. It doesn't work when the assets are not homogeneous and difficult to value.

Now enter, stage left, the Fed with its $700 billion bailout plan. The Fed is buying these failing assets under the theory that these assets are worth something. The Fed's take on the situation could well be: "People are overreacting in 2008. These assets—mortgages—are not as bad as people think. Not everyone in the United States is going to default on their homes.

"A good deal of these assets have intrinsic value and will ultimately have a higher value. We can afford, as the government, to hold these assets for a number of years, until people and markets become more rational."

If you follow the Fed's logic, that they will be holding undervalued assets today and selling them at a premium tomorrow, the government should have rescinded mark-to-market accounting in today's environment.

With no mark-to-market accounting, the sell side banks, in particular, could have carried these assets on their books and recognized higher value tomorrow without full balance-sheet impairment today.

And following that logic one step further, with no mark-to-market accounting and no devastating balance-sheet impairment issues, we could have been spared a $700 billion bailout plan that effectively moves assets from the sell side to the Fed.

Bottom Line

A lot of brain damage with this bailout plan, and all we had to do was suspend mark-to-market accounting, let the sell-side banks keep the spread on the assets and provide a financial subsidy at a value considerably less than $700 billion.

Those three actions alone, in my view, could have replaced the Fed bailout as a mechanism to restore investor confidence.

The Credit Crisis of 2007–2008—Days We Live In

As I write this in 2008, the credit crisis is still unfolding. I will not be able to provide you with a summary of the crisis gained from the vantage point of 20/20 hindsight.

But, as I've noted previously, financial credit crises have a nasty habit of rearing their heads over and over again. In this respect, the credit crisis of 2007–2008 is no different. But because it is so recent, and its ramifications already so significant that the Fed has had to get involved (i.e., the collapse of Bear Stearns and the sale of sizable percentages of major Wall Street firms to outside investors, including sovereign wealth funds), this is a crisis worth thinking about.

The origins of the crisis lie in the housing boom and bust of the first decade of the 2000s. Housing prices increased dramatically. At the same time, credit oversight of borrowers became lax. People were able to get mortgages without putting money down or even providing sufficient documentation of how much money they earn.

To this we can add the creation of complex mortgage-backed securities, which, for a while, largely removed the risk to the companies creating the mortgages.

These mortgage companies and banks provided home buyers with mortgages, only to turn around and repackage these

(continued)

mortgages into big bundles of mortgage-backed securities and collateralized debt obligations that had been sliced and diced to create different levels of risk. These securities were then sold to the public.

The mortgage companies and banks now had these securities off their books, allowing them to create even more. They had little incentive to make sure the borrowers would repay, since any defaults would fall on the backs of later investors who bought these repackaged securities.

All was well when housing prices were rising. Homeowners who could not pay their mortgages were able to sell their houses at a profit. But when home prices started to fall, which they did in 2006, stretched borrowers started to walk away from their homes.

This trend became even more pronounced when adjustable-rate mortgages started to readjust upward and homeowners found themselves facing significantly higher mortgage payments, at a time when the value of their homes was declining.

Defaults rose and banks and mortgage companies and hedge funds (which had invested in the securities) started to feel the pain. In the summer of 2007, two Bear Stearns hedge funds collapsed, in what was a precursor to the trouble that other financial institutions would face.

Since then, tens of billions of dollars have been written off from household names like Citigroup,[12] Merrill Lynch, UBS, and others.[13]

There is nothing new about financial crises. The current credit crisis will pass, and a new crisis will one day take its place—of this you can be sure. But what is worth remembering is that crises will always interrupt the ways of Wall Street.

It's unavoidable.

Implications

I'm going to play pundit here and throw my hat into the regulatory ring. Humor me for a second while I toss out a few potential implications that I think will make for a lively debate.

As we all sit around wondering what happened in 2007–2008, with the smoldering embers of the subprime crisis all around us, an interesting question to ponder is: "Where does the regulatory hammer fall? Will it land harder on the sell side or the buy side?"

In early 2008, it was intuitive to think that it was easier to regulate the smaller lineup of investment banks than thousands of hedge funds. Overlay that with the classic cause and effect—the cause being that investment banking had a real-time event in March 2008: the Bear Stearns collapse.

The effect was that there was a massive intervention by the regulators, who gallantly stepped up by opening the Fed discount window to the investment banks. Historically, the discount window was reserved for commercial banks, so in the first half of 2008, one could argue that by making it available to the investment banks, the government leveled the playing field between them—a nice little present for the investment banking guys at the time.

However, the playing field was not level when thinking about capital requirements in early 2008. See, the commercial guys have a thing called risk-based capital guidelines; investment banks didn't. That was a logical inconsistency.

Well, by September 2008, both that inconsistency and the four remaining U.S.-based independent investment banks were history.

Lehman disappeared into the night. Merrill Lynch disappeared into the hands of Bank of America. Goldman Sachs and Morgan Stanley disappeared into commercial banking holding companies, and begrudingly took on those risk-based capital guidelines.

Goldman Sachs and Morgan Stanley, caught in the winds of the credit crisis and an ongoing regulatory debate, could have said to themselves, "Let us, not someone else, choose our regulatory destiny. We know, at least, what a commercial bank holding company looks like. And let's have that discount window opened in perpetuity. Further, let's cement our viability in the financial uncertainty of 2008."

The irony of ironies is that if you approached those four investment banks with risk-based capital guidelines in early 2008, they may well have responded with: "New capital requirements would be too drastic a shock to our system."

From where I sit, the 2007–2008 credit crisis is really about the level of risk—and therefore, leverage—that was applied to businesses. Right now, there's just too much leverage: The financial system is positively bloated with it. Which leads us to the provocative question of whether there should be more financial requirements for the sell side and financial hurdles for the buy side.

I'm sure I have your attention now—but come on, guys. We've seen borrowing limits before. This isn't a completely unprecedented concept. Just think back to the margin requirements of 1929.[14]

Now, let's consider pumping up the volume of financial requirements to sell-side banks and buy-side firms. With respect to sell-side banks, I am okay with across-the-board risk-based capital requirements. What about risk-based capital requirements for the buy side, namely, hedge funds?

Philosophically, if you're going to regulate one entity, shouldn't you regulate all entities in the same fashion? Practically, the world does not really work that way.

Good news, hedge funds: I am not going to suggest the notion of risk-based capital requirements for you guys. Bad news: I'm going to knock on your door with a variation of leverage where, if you are going to trade in specific risky assets like credit defaults swaps (CDS) you need to put up "X" amount of collateral.

And before hedge funds come knocking, or should I say blowing down my door, I am not recommending across-the-board capital guidelines for every hedge fund, for every trade. I am just recommending containing specific tradable instruments, in particular derivative assets like CDS. The last thing we need is hedge funds damaging the whole financial system.

As I write this book, the market is actually *over*-correcting the financial system.

In a sense, the subprime mortgage crisis boils down to this: The market was not charging enough for the risk. We were living in a time where there were liquidity surpluses around the world, and they had to be redeployed. When that's the case, the markets aren't charging enough for liquidity or risk. They certainly weren't in the days leading up to the mortgage crisis—risk was being tossed around like popcorn. If risk in those days went for, say, five cents a pound, today's market is charging $1.25 a pound in an attempt to overcorrect itself.

Think of it this way: Risk is charged by widening or decreasing spreads. Take a bank loan in the collateralized loan obligation (CLO) market. In the old days, some guys would go out and buy a bunch of bank loans. And they would lever them up, of course.[15] Well, in the early half of 2007, the triple-A pieces of these securities were, say, 20 basis points over Treasury. In the early half of 2008, these spreads went up to approximately 180 basis points over Treasuries.[16] Wow—180 basis points versus 20? What's going on here? The market's swung too far to the other side, and the credit markets start to shut down.

And it's not just the CLO bank market. Spreads widened across the board. High-yield spreads, for example, went from approximately 250 basis points to 800 basis points over Treasuries.[17] Amazing how the pendulum shifts, isn't it?

Before the credit crisis, pricing to risk wasn't there; there was too much risk for the price. Now, pricing to risk is too expensive—it's gotten ahead of the risk. As a result, the risk creation business shuts down. We know that's not good for the economy—it has to open back up. The risk pendulum will have to swing back. And, over time, the market will find the right level of correlation between risk and price.

As I write this, the credit crisis rages on and the market is trying to find its correct balance. This is the time to rethink financial disclosure. Allow me to open the kimono on financial disclosure a little wider.

I don't want to hear more advocating for financial transparency tied to specifics. Rather, we should be thinking in terms of the total picture of risk exposures and positions.

Looking at the sell-side banks' balance sheets and income statements just isn't adequate anymore. Income statements look backward and balance sheets are guesstimates of what assets might be worth today. I would like a mechanism in place that is not related to GAAP (generally accepted accounting principles) and doesn't just rely on standard accounting practice.

For that matter, I do not want to rely on the regulators, either, to tell these guys what to do. We need to have a mechanism in place that tells us what could affect a sell-side bank's risk—economic—value.

This mechanism needs to look at the elements of risk throughout the sell-side institution. I'd like to know about the derivatives risk, about the counterparty risk. I want to look at all of their existing liabilities, both on and off the balance sheet—naked as a jaybird and with no place to hide. It's worth it, even if it adds another five pages to the annual report. Not that I am a fan of the paper world we live in, but I'd rather have a little more than a little less information when it comes to risk exposure, wouldn't you?

On the buy side, the hedge funds can say, "Hey, take a look at our investment strategies." Well, that's not sufficient—we need to look at their aggregate leverage positions. We need to have a sense of their risk exposures as well. Tell me how much you're taking on. Show me which cards are being dealt; I'll decide if I want to play.

Hedge funds could respond with, "Wait a minute. Since we are private, not public, entities, why is there a need for that type of disclosure?"

Normally, what people do in private is okay. Therefore, why do investors need to know what is going on behind closed doors? They need to be aware if hedge funds are overplaying their leverage and risk hand, which could ultimately blow up our financial system.

And, similarly, on the sell side, show me your risk profile. This is important stuff, guys. Without it, we're walking around blind in a minefield.

If the credit crisis has taught us anything, the political environment will be more realistic and, I suspect, more liberal when it comes to financial disclosure in the future.

Thus, the buy side and sell side alike should be more proactive and less reactive when it comes to individual company economic or risk disclosure. Guys, instead of waiting for the government to police you, police yourselves.

Now that I have you thinking of getting in front of the financial transparency question, let's take it one step farther than individual company reporting. How about creating a national clearinghouse that tracks everyone's high levels of derivatives/counterparty risk? As I write this, the government is contemplating a similar approach for CDS. This clearinghouse would identify the amounts of risky assets outstanding for every hand in every deal. This would provide a better sense of where the significant risks are in the entire financial system.

I could see approaching the sell side and buy side alike with this suggestion, and the welcome wagon would be out of service that day. Their resistance would not be cost-related, because the administrative expense for a national risk-tracking system is most likely minimal. Rather, their resistance would be more akin to wanting to keep their positions—on an individual or collective basis—private and proprietary. No shock here.

To those institutions that resist the notion of risk position reporting, I would say: Move to your own island. You can't make the theoretical argument that we live in a free market society. We don't. That is not how it works. Everything is regulated. We do not have patents on pharmaceuticals that last in perpetuity; they last 17 years. Companies cannot pollute wherever they want. Companies cannot fire people on a whim. We have rules for everything in the United States.

We shouldn't rely on the old disclosure requirements—just take a page from the medical playbook. Remember how we used to look at penicillin as an all-encompassing cure? Well, it worked for a while, and then we built up a resistance—other forms of bacteria popped up. But the medical world adjusted; they reworked the drugs. And if they can maneuver on the battlefield, so can we.

Let's bring financial disclosure into the twenty-first century—we'll be a lot healthier in the long run.

One could surmise that financial requirements and transparency in the twenty-first century will come with a cost. The sell side, most likely, will have to jump through more financial disclosure hoops than in the past, while the buy side, to a degree, will have to live in a brave new world of financial requirements and disclosure.

Battle Victorious: The investor.

Chapter 12

Future Implications

The subprime crisis of 2007–2008 caught virtually all of us by surprise. . . .

My take on the future implications for the financial system, the sell side and the buy side, may be just as surprising.

Financial System—Next Shoe to Drop

The falling knife of the credit crisis will stop. When it stops, is there a new blade waiting to slice and dice some more?

I'm afraid to say that is a possibility.

By 2018, we could have another financial meltdown. Once again, Wall Street could be wringing its hands and wiping sweat off its brow.

Here's how I would frame it.

Most of us reading this book are probably old enough (or should I say, old enough in financial-industry years) to remember the Bank of New England collapse.[1]

As you may recall, it had a swap exposure of approximately $7 billion.[2] Swaps, back in the 1980s, could only be done with triple-A counterparties—turbo-charged subsidiaries would go to the rating agencies and—bingo!—become triple A.

Where was the Fed? It was coming off, at the time, the peak of interest rates, and had finally gotten the credit market down to a point that was reasonable. Spotting a housing bubble on the horizon, the Fed could have said, "Wait a minute. We may be looking at a triple-A failing—the Bank of New England—with counterparty risk. That's too much for us to tolerate. The financial system just can't stomach it—drastic measures are in order." It realized that if Bank of New England went down, there was a strong possibility there would be no orderly way to liquidate its counterparty exposure.

So the Fed stepped in and arranged a shotgun marriage between Bank of New England and Fleet/Norstar Financial Group.[3]

Well, our institutional memory of the Bank of New England crisis lasted about nine years.

Then, in 1998, along came Long-Term Capital Management (LTCM). On the basis of approximately $5 billion worth of capital, LTCM had borrowings—trading positions—north of $100 billion.

Once again, the Fed concluded that the risk to the system was too great—$100 billion-plus of exposure, after all, isn't chump change. So it arranged an orderly liquidation of LTCM.

Fast-forward approximately a decade to the Bear Stearns downfall—and the scale of risk just keeps escalating. The Bank of New England crisis was child's play compared to what ended up happening to Bear Stearns and the others that followed.

Think about it. Bear Stearns had notional counterparty exposure of approximately $2.5 trillion. We went from $7 billion at Bank of New England, to $100 billion-plus at LTCM, to $2.5 trillion at Bear Stearns. Those are some pretty big leaps. However, to put it into context, the net counterparty exposure in the world was $45 trillion at the time of the Bear Stearns collapse.[4] Well, the Fed might have thought that was too great a risk to the financial system. So bye-bye, Bear Stearns. Welcome to your arranged marriage with JPMorgan.

Today, has the financial system shrunk its counterparty risk in response to Bear Stearns's falling like a house of cards? Ironically enough, no.

As I write this, the Bank for International Settlements, which serves as a bank for central banks, will tell you that net counterparty risk in the world is not $45 trillion anymore, but well beyond it. Where is this going?[5]

It can only go up—and it will. The only question is: Does the time period between financial crises shrink? Are we on a nine-year cycle, or will we be forced to face it even sooner? It's interesting to look at the timing of regulations: The regulators have actually gone from 10-year intervals to 5-year intervals in terms of substantive regulation. In a sense, they're trying to catch up to the markets—but the order of magnitude keeps growing.

So, going back to our gloomy prediction: Will the next financial crisis be in nine years, or sooner? And here's an even more interesting question: What's the flash point?

The flash point will be counterparty risk. Part of the reason why, in 2008, the counterparty risk—derivatives—is reported to be approximately $63 trillion, and growing, is that all sorts of assets qualify as derivatives because there aren't enough primary assets to make it worthwhile for the capital that's chasing it.[6]

I suspect no one buys or sells corporate debt on an unleveraged basis anymore.[7] Today, for the most part, people hold equity securities. And then, the music starts. You hold an equity security, and I come to you and say, "I can enhance your yield by 10 to 20 basis points if you let me write an option against it." Then I have to write another option to cancel that option because of the exposure. The beat goes on and on. Again, counterparty risk continues.

Today it appears there's no capital requirement put up against counterparty risk. There is no initial capital consequence—deduction to your capital base—for pulling the counterparty risk lever.

Before counterparty risk skids out of control, we need to bring it to a screeching halt.

Let's take the concept I put forward in Chapter 11—of hedge funds putting up collateral against risky assets—one step further. We need to force everyone to put up capital against their individual gross counterparty exposure. I know what you're thinking: That's just what the financial community wants to hear. Well, let me offer an approach that might be easier to digest: If you want to be a legitimate counterparty, put up "X" percent of your capital into a general fund that deals with systemic issues—a general fund for counterparty risk.

You want a chance to play in the casino? You have to be a dues-paying member. That's the price you pay—and it may very well be worth your while to pony up those dues.

The downside of counterparty exposure: What could actually happen? Look no further than 2008—nobody was doing business with anyone. The feeling on the Street was, "Who can you trust?" Nobody was sure of anything anymore. It all just stopped; one of the favorite financings of sell-side banks and buy-side private equity firms, which was the leveraged buyout, disappeared off the radar screen.[8]

2008 was a time when you shot first and asked questions later. A big question mark hung over Wall Street.

So, what will we remember about 2008? Maybe we'll remember it as a time when Bear Stearns and Lehman Brothers, among others, went down like the *Titanic,* when the markets came close to not working.

Or maybe we'll remember it as something else—the second time in recent memory that the market came close to shutting down.

The first day was October 20, 1987. Not the 19th of October, when the market was down 580 points—22 percent in one day.[9] In the first part of the day of October 20, none of the Dow Jones' 30 stocks opened.[10] Nobody would trade.

Then what happened? Goldman Sachs and Salomon Brothers each pledged tens of millions of dollars after a call from the Fed.[11] It took time to get the Dow Jones 30 going—and the rest, as you know, is history.

There are two basic emotions at the center of the counterparty risk storm: greed and fear. Greed will go a long way, but when fear takes over, like it did with Bear Stearns, Lehman Brothers and others, the financial system goes down quickly. It's not clear if there's a floor to the elevator. What is clear, however, is that no one is immune.

What's also clear is that we're all at risk—sell side and buy side alike. We're inextricably intertwined. If one thread unravels, others will follow.

Let's not make our Battle for Wall Street a thing of the past. Let's stay ahead of the nine-year financial crisis cycle. Let's be proactive and build a firewall to protect against counterparty exposure.

And a good place to begin? Pay a little today into a general fund and hopefully avoid paying more—much more—tomorrow. The downturn in each cycle comes sooner than you think. Sounds like a decent insurance policy to me.

Sell-Side Commercial Banks—A New Battlefield

Let's start with the sell-side landscape that has been flattened by the credit crisis.

Are we looking at a commercial banking environment dominated by four mega-institutions? I would say yes. It appears that the credit crisis, with intervention from the government, has led the sell side down a path that may have inadvertently created four banking axes, providing a safe haven to institutions that were falling on the battlefield. The surviving warriors in this case are Bank of America, Citigroup, JPMorgan and Wells Fargo.

JPMorgan started the roundup of collapsing institutions when it bailed out Bear Stearns and, subsequently, Washington Mutual. Next came Bank of America's arranged marriage with Merrill Lynch. Citigroup followed suit with its plan to acquire Wachovia. Wells Fargo, previously sitting on the sidelines, joined the skirmish with Citigroup to acquire Wachovia. As I write this, Wells Fargo won the battle.[12]

I wouldn't be surprised to see a few more axes show up on the radar screen. It would make commercial sense for a number of regional banks who survived 2008 to join forces and cement their viability.

Let's focus on the Big Four that are still on the banking battlefield: Citigroup, JPMorgan, Bank of America, and Wells Fargo. These power brokers will continue to grab market headlines well beyond 2008.

When reexamining Citigroup's history, it should have been the center of the universe, the clear winner on the sell side. But it fell behind.

Some believe that its overwhelming financial size worked against it. Others believe its underwhelming managerial culture worked against it.

Ironically, going forward, if Citigroup, under the leadership of Vikram Pandit, wants to be the supreme commander on the Street, then it needs the winning combination of size and culture.[13] Speaking of size, if there's another big bank collapse, the government may well direct it to Citigroup.

Unlike Citigroup, it appears that JPMorgan has the managerial culture as well as the breadth to catapult it into an enviable position. From a cultural standpoint, Jamie Dimon is young enough to be a truly effective leader for a long time. From a size perspective, Bear Stearns adds scale to JPMorgan's corporate, investment banking and prime brokerage franchises, while Washington Mutual meaningfully expands its consumer deposit base and geographic footprint.

History could prove that JPMorgan bought Bear Stearns and Washington Mutual because the government asked it to. Financial results could prove that JPMorgan acquired Bear Stearns and Washington Mutual because they were great deals.

Like JPMorgan, Bank of America is well supported by the two pillars of managerial culture and financial franchise. In a cultural sense, chairman/CEO Ken Lewis understands the value proposition of positioning Bank of America as "America's consumer bank" and recognized strategic opportunities in the financial chaos of 2008, namely in its acquisition of Merrill Lynch. In a franchise sense, the Merrill Lynch transaction enhances Bank of America's current strength—consumer footprint—and creates new strengths—an international footprint.[14]

Similar to Bank of America, Wells Fargo's culture is something to stand up and cheer about. Its laser-like focus in consumer banking has kept the ship moving forward in the choppy waters of the credit crisis. Leading the charge at Wells is Richard Kovacevich, who engineered the very clever Wells Fargo/Norwest Corporation merger in 1998, which in a sense solidified the future of both firms. Now, in thinking about size, with its Wachovia acquisition, Wells should be the largest consumer deposit franchise in the U.S. Culture and size: a winning combination at Wells Fargo.

What does the future hold for the sell-side regional banks living outside these banking axes? I would say the mortality of a number of them is in question.

The credit crisis has burned through many of the troubled players of significant size, such as Washington Mutual. This blaze will eventually work its way to the regional banks. The savings and loan crisis of the 1980s took down more than 2,000 depository institutions.[15] If the present follows the past, we're looking at another 2,000 financial institutions—and it appears that Arizona, California, and Nevada institutions could well be at the head of the checkout counter.[16]

And to make the future landscape a bit more interesting, let me toss out one last sell-side banking group, one that has not been heard from for awhile, one with the capital wind at its sails: Japanese banks.

Back in the 1980s, the Japanese banks, as well as their investment banks, were on a spending/investment spree for U.S. sell-side banks. In the 1990s, they retreated to the sidelines as they got caught in their own real estate/economic bubble. Fortuitously, they sat out the "banks go wild" strategy of acquiring subprime mortgages.

The Japanese banks are back with strong balance sheets and plenty of cash. Overlay that with access to $14 trillion in Japanese household savings,[17] a liquidity pool that the U.S. sell-side banks would like at their disposal as they navigate through the credit crisis.

And, Japanese banks are looking at the convergence of opportunities in the U.S. and lack of opportunities at home.[18] One such U.S. opportunity—and a precursor to others—was the Mitsubishi UFJ Financial Group's investment in Morgan Stanley in October 2008. I would say to those sitting at the international liquidity table, such as sovereign wealth funds, China and India: "Make room for one more player: the Japanese banks."

Sell-Side Investment Banks—A Reconfigured Battlefield

On the other side of the sell-side coin is investment banking. September 2008 will be remembered as a time when a number of U.S.-based investment banks surrendered to the credit crisis. Lehman Brothers fell on the battlefield; Merrill Lynch limped off of it into the hands of Bank of America, and lastly, Morgan Stanley and Goldman Sachis shifted their strategies, becoming commercial bank holding companies.[19]

Why commercial bank holding companies? These firms closed their doors on their traditional investment banking status as they recognized that their financial models were too risky. They opened their doors to a new commercial banking status to latch onto the safe haven of consumer bank deposits.

To see why that made sense, look no further than commercial banks Bank of America, Citigroup, JPMorgan, and Wells Fargo, whose consumer deposit bases helped them maneuver through the credit crisis.

So what does the future have in store for Goldman Sachs and Morgan Stanley?

Going forward, Goldman Sachs should be a clear winner on both the buy and sell sides. From a buy-side vantage point, Goldman should continue to be a dominant hedge fund player. In fact, many observers believe it is really a hedge fund disguised as a sell-side firm. From a sell-side standpoint, it should continue to be at the top of its game in managing balance sheet risk.

And whether you look at Goldman from the buy side or the sell side perspective, it is amazing to see what its alumni are doing in terms of populating buy-side firms. There is no question that trend will continue—a trend that will certainly not bring joy to the hearts of the sell side.

In thinking about Morgan Stanley's destiny, some of its observers believe it's a flip of the coin. On one hand, kudos to John Mack and his team for building out an impressive footprint for the future: more global reach, more alternative asset management and more debt products.

On the other hand, as I write this, some believe the winds of investor confidence, including hedge funds, are blowing against it.[20] It is in the unfortunate position, according to the rumor mill, of being next in line, after Lehman and Merrill, to say goodbye. My take on the situation is that there should always be a place on the Street for a firm like Morgan Stanley. I believe both the government and the markets will come to realize that two small capital market firms—Goldman and Morgan Stanley—make commercial sense.

What will investment banking look like as it rises from the ashes of the credit crisis? I believe it will center around three models.

The first model will be guys who resemble hybrid commercial and investment banks. Going forward, this group, with cash flows of consumer deposits and institutional financing, will try to emerge, after the credit crisis, as the kings of finance. Credit Suisse, Goldman Sachs, and JPMorgan are a few names that fall into this category.

The second group will be the guys who are still standing after the turmoil. They are the guys who played the winning hand of traditional client servicing and not the losing hand of leverage and balance sheet risk. Going forward, they will resemble the major independent investment banks of old, before those firms lost their way into enormous leverage and aggressive trading. Greenhill & Co.,[21] Jefferies Group, and Lazard are just a few names that land in this second group.[22]

The third band of soldiers will be the new guys on the block. They represent another one of those cycles where we start creating small, boutique-type firms—firms that look like hedge funds, but actually operate like investment banks. I'd refer to these firms as boutiques in the trading space, as opposed to the boutiques in the merger-and-acquisition space we saw in past cycles—mainly Greenhill and Evercore Partners.

These trading boutiques would resemble the old boutique Grantchester Securities. Grantchester, through the vision of Bill Begley, was a product of the high-yield days.[23] The opportunity is there to build these kinds of businesses again—and you don't need tons of balance sheet to do it.

At some point, a number of the sovereign wealth funds pumping billions into places like Citigroup may just look around and say, "Let's back the new kids who can compete with the old guard." Think about it this way: These capital folks put in, say, $5 billion, behind these new firms, and bingo, these trading institutions now have a $20 billion balance sheet and they're players in the market. Not bad.

As a number of these major sell-side firms continue to look inward in an attempt to restore their balance sheets in light of the 2007–2008 credit crisis, there will be players who may be less talked about today but will be the subject of much more chatter tomorrow. Macquarie Group, a major Australian investment bank, is one of them: They could step up to the plate and look outward to buy, buy, and buy again.

Take the following hypothetical example: Macquarie buys a commercial bank, and that commercial bank buys an investment bank. Now what you have is a financial juggernaut that comes not from the U.S. or the European Union, but from commodity-driven money. Going forward, we can't discount the massive amounts of money flowing into these commodity-based economies and creating sell-side financial giants of their own.

And a last sell-side banking point: The future winners will be the ones who have strong balance sheets, who keep their talent in the farm system a little longer, and who continue to innovate and find ways to reconnect with the buy side.

Buy Side—A Shifting Battlefield

What will the future look like for hedge funds? What's the forecast?

First, hedge fund assets and strategies will continue to proliferate—there's no doubt about it. The only doubt is whether their sometimes esoteric strategies—strategies that can't be diligenced—can survive. I suspect these strategies will still be part of the mix but will become less popular. The more these guys play the computer modeling tune, the more the investment community could say that it's a temporary sort of dislocation, at best.[24]

I also suspect people will have less confidence in computer-technology investing and have more confidence in core-value investing.[25] Hopefully, hedge funds will get away from trades on miniscule margin products leveraged 20 to 1, 30 to 1, and get back to core value investing—namely, credit analysis and less leverage. Let's cross our fingers that they get back to picking winners and losers. That's where their energy should be directed.

Second, the world does not need 10,000 hedge funds.

I believe a number of funds will disappear. Leading the "out of business, gone fishing" list will be the small and underperforming hedge funds, as well as those that fall below scale or critical mass—and say to themselves, "The economics don't make sense—I've made a few dollars in better times, but it's time to get out, thank you very much."

But the hedge funds will not be down and out for long. I suspect these funds will actually reappear over time. I foresee three cycles in the lives of hedge funds: down, up, and down again. We could lose 20 percent of these 10,000 hedge funds over the next few years. As we know, the barriers to entry for starting a hedge fund are almost nonexistent, and more will appear on the horizon. How many Bear Stearns or

Lehman or Merrill Lynch guys are going to start a hedge fund? How many more sell-side guys are going to? They pop up like mushrooms on the forest floor—but the weak ones are not going to survive.

The migration of talent from the sell side to the buy side will continue to flourish.

Will it flourish to the point of 10,000 hedge funds again? Unlikely. Those days are behind us. At the end of a few years, after this buildup, the old hedge fund tune will be replayed once again: too many hedge funds chasing too few opportunities. And with that, the size of the industry will shift down once again. Welcome to the roller-coaster world of hedge funds.

Third, the larger hedge funds will get even larger. History has shown that hedge funds are very effective in gathering assets. The problem is that size, in and of itself, is a deterrent. Moving the performance needle in a big hedge fund will be a challenge.

There's only one player I can think of who has consistently been able to win on size, and win more times than not on high returns—and that's Warren Buffett from Berkshire Hathaway. You could argue that Goldman Sachs gets it right more often than not. But the roster of those who can boast both size and performance is a small one, at best.

Fourth, hedge funds will continue to expand into private equity, just like the venture capital guys I knew early on in my career. They were once pure venture capital, but today a number of them have transitioned into private equity. Just look at hedge fund giant D. E. Shaw and its evolution into private equity.

And it works both ways—look at how many private equity guys have moved into hedge funds. The most interesting part of the Blackstone Group from where I sit isn't the high profile of their private equity portfolio—it's their hidden jewel . . . its hedge funds.

Look at how Carlyle Group has evolved—it's fully integrated these days, with a private equity castle, a venture capital castle, and an asset management castle, all together in one sandbox.

Carlyle even found itself under the falling knife of the subprime crisis. Carlyle created a mortgage fund and took it public—but it didn't even make its first birthday. The fund went down and sustained billions in write-offs. And one important variable that took the fund down was over-leverage. [26]

The mind-set of leveraging up to the gills has to stop. The invest-ment community could take to heart a line from the movie *Network*, which would go a long way toward altering its mind-set: "We're not going to take it anymore."

Going forward, the clear winners in the hedge fund space will be the big players like D. E. Shaw, who stay within the band of private assets—hedge funds and, to a lesser degree, private equity. The notion, however, of hedge funds blending into great, big multi-line firms and overrun-ning the sell side is unlikely. There aren't many people who are capable of running those kinds of firms well. Citadel is a rare exception—and could be a clear winner in 2008 and beyond.

Even hedge funds going into private equity can hit the wall. Good example: the hedge fund Cerberus Capital's private equity investment in Chrysler. As I'm writing this, it doesn't look like a winner. A lot of peo-ple who run hedge funds well are by definition traders, not managers.

Sell-side firms can breathe a little easier now, but one caveat to the sell side: Don't lose sight of a certain company which falls not in the hedge fund camp, but rather in the more traditional one. That company is BlackRock.

BlackRock is a truly integrated institution run by traders and man-agers. Over the next several years, it will be a magnet for market share and market talent. BlackRock is a clear winner, with a seat at the power table. Sell side, don't catch your breath for too long.

What does the future look like for private equity firms? How its future plays out is actually the product of an evolution over three generations.

Looking back, the first generation of private equity firms were run by people who tried to arbitrage between inefficient companies, where value could be obtained with the best possible exit.[27] Then came the second generation, who basically said, "We just want to buy, collect fees, move on, raise another fund, and on and on."

In today's generation, a number of private equity firms have become what I've hoped they'd become: relative value buyers.

Those private equity firms, grounded in the principles of core invest-ing, should be clear winners in the years ahead. They will be able to broaden their businesses and be successful in putting multiple product lines in place. At least three names in that category come to mind: Apollo Management, Blackstone, and Warburg Pincus. And with vertically inte-grated businesses, private equity firms will be a force to be reckoned with.

And sell-side firms who have kept one eye on private equity players as cash cows and one eye on private equity firms as competitors, may want to start viewing the private equity world as a formidable competitor. Again, sell side—don't catch your breath for too long.

A last buy-side point: The future winners will be the ones who continue to maintain a high profile with endowments, financial entrepreneurs, prime brokers, and—over time—sovereign wealth funds.

Yes, sovereign wealth funds will shift from being equal opportunity spenders to buy-side advocates. And, as they're keeping a high profile with that, they may want to maintain a low profile involving those computer-driven investment strategies.

The Bottom Line on the Battle

The sell side and buy side will continue to position themselves along the lines of a baseball analogy.

As I mentioned in the introduction, the sell side will play the role of baseball's nine-position players, having to pitch and hit all the time. And it will not stop there. Sell-side guys will say, "We want to play more than nine positions. We want to be the parking lot attendant, the hot dog vendor—we want it all."

The buy side will play the role of baseball's designated hitter. It will attract hitters from the sell-side farm system, acknowledge its fans in the stands with the letter E—entrepreneurs, endowments, electronic exchanges—wait for their best pitch, and drive the ball (drive the trade).

Tomorrow's winners from both teams will be those who effectively orchestrate the obvious variable of liquidity and maintain a mindset of the less obvious variable of credit and value.

In the context of both sides' ongoing power gambit, there is one thing we can count on. The names of the sell-side and buy-side players sitting at the power table may change, but the high-stakes financial game they're playing will not.

Finally, the team declaring victory at the financial power table in 2008 . . . the buy side.

Notes

Introduction: Let the Battle for Wall Street Begin

1. Joseph Weber, "Warren Buffett, Goldman's White Knight." *BusinessWeek*, September 25, 2008; www.msnbc.msn.com/id/26887422/.
2. "2007: The Yale Endowment." Yale University; www.yale.edu/investments/Yale_Endowment_07.pdf.
3. "CalPERS Names Senior Portfolio Managers for Infrastructure, Internal Global Equity." Office of Public Affairs, CalPERS, September 25, 2008; www.calpers.ca.gov/index.jsp?bc=/about/press/pr-2008/sep/names-senior-portfolio-managers.xml.

Chapter 1: Sea of Liquidity

1. "UBS and PaineWebber Announce Merger Completion Date." UBS, October 20, 2000; last updated October 18, 2005, 4:20 p.m.; www.ubs.com/1/e/media_overview/media_global/search1/search10?newsId=59210.
2. "Chase and J.P. Morgan Agree to Merge." CNN, September 13, 2000; http://money.cnn.com/2000/09/13/deals/chase_morgan/chasemorgan.htm.
3. "AXA Closes Sale of DLJ to CSFB." *Insurance Journal*, November 6, 2000; www.insurancejournal.com/news/international/2000/11/06/10620.htm.
4. "Dresdner, Wasserstein Talk." *CNN Money*, September 12, 2000; http://money.cnn.com/2000/09/12/deals/dresdner/.

5. Danny Hakim, "The Markets: Market Place; Alliance Capital Linking Up with Bernstein." *New York Times*, June 21, 2000; http://query.nytimes.com/gst/fullpage.html?res=950CEEDF1031F932A15755C0A9669C8B63.

6. "Credit Suisse Swallows DLJ." *CBC News*, November 10, 2000; www.cbc.ca/money/story/2000/08/30/dlj000830.html.

7. "DLJ Names Bennett Goodman to Expanded Role in Leveraged Finance." *Business Wire*, July 13, 2000; www.allbusiness.com/banking-finance/financial-markets-investing-securities/6470138-1.html.

8. "DLJ High Yield Bond Fund Announces Portfolio Weightings." *Business Wire*, August 25, 1998; http://findarticles.com/p/articles/mi_m0EIN/is_1998_August_25/ai_21053812.

9. "Description and Inclusion Rules of the CSFB High Yield Index." *Credit Suisse First Boston Corporation*; www.styleadvisor.com/support/download/hyidx_desc.pdf.

10. Peter Truell. "Nationsbank Deal Expected for Montgomery Securities." *New York Times*, June 30, 1997; http://query.nytimes.com/gst/fullpage.html?res=9502E3DE1F31F933A05755C0A961958260.

11. Peter Behr, "GE to Acquire Control of Broker Kidder Peabody." *Washington Post*, April 25, 1986; http://pqasb.pqarchiver.com/washingtonpost_historical/access/126224522.html?dids=126224522:126224522&FMT=ABS&FMTS=ABS:FT&date=APR+25%2C+1986&author=By+Peter+Behr+Washington+Post+Staff+Writer&pub=The+Washington+Post&desc=GE+to+Acquire+Control+Of+Broker+Kidder%2C+Peabody&pqatl=google.

12. John Mauldin, "Are There Too Many Hedge Funds?" *Millennium Wave Advisors*; http://news.goldseek.com/MillenniumWaveAdvisors/1120856013.php.

13. "The Various Types of CMOs." Securities Industry and Financial Markets Association; http://www.investinginbonds.com/learnmore.asp?catid=11&subcatid=58&id=3.

14. "Robert Kapito: Executive Profile and Biography." *BusinessWeek*, http://investing.businessweek.com/businessweek/research/stocks/people/person.asp?personId=403417&symbol=BLK.

15. "Speaker List: Future of Asset Allocated Funds Conference." *Plansponsor.com*, 2008; ww2.plansponsor.com/assetallocation/speaker.html.

16. Renee Schultes, "Volatility Accelerates Rise of the Risk Manager." *Dow Jones Financial News Online, U.S. Edition*, September 20, 2007; www.efinancialnews.com/usedition/index/content/2448755641.

17. "Hoover's Profile: BlackRock, Inc." *Hoover's, Inc.*, 2008; www.answers.com/topic/blackrock-inc.

18. "BlackRock, Inc. Company Profile." *Reuters*, 2008; www.reuters.com/finance/stocks/companyProfile?symbol=BLK.N.

19. "BlackRock and Merrill Lynch Investment Managers to Combine, Forming One of the World's Largest Independent Investment Management Firms."

Merrill Lynch press release, February 15, 2006; www.ml.com/index.asp? id=7695_7696_8149_63464_64119_64465.

20. Juan Lagorio and Lilla Zuill. "AIG to Keep Core Insurance, Sell Assets to Pay U.S. Loan." *Reuters*, October 3, 2008; www.guardian.co.uk/business/ feedarticle/7843879.

21. "Could Warren Buffett Rescue AIG?" *StreetInsider.com*, September 15, 2008; www.streetinsider.com/Insiders+Blog/Could+Warren+Buffett+Rescue+ AIG%3F/3988186.html.

22. Ieva M. Augstums and Stephen Bernard. "AIG Plans Sale of Business Units to Repay Debt." *The Associated Press*, October 4, 2008, http://ap.google .com/article/ALeqM5joDo_vKoTtP08QzUNctxgOLlW21QD93JLHPG0.

23. See note 20.

24. Christopher Condon, "Reserve Primary Money Fund Falls Below $1 a Share (update 4)." *Bloomberg.com;* www.bloomberg.com/apps/news?pid= 20601087&sid=a5O2y1go1GRU&refer=home.

25. "The 2000–02 Nasdaq Bear Market vs. Nikkei." Lowrisk.com, July 2, 2002; www.lowrisk.com/nasdaq-nikkei.htm.

Chapter 2: Financial Information in a Digital Age

1. "MarketWatch Profile: NASDAQ Omx Group Inc." *MarketWatch, Inc.*, 2008; www.answers.com/topic/nasdaq.

2. "Melamed Sells Stake in His Firm." *New York Times,* February 21, 1991; http://query.nytimes.com/gst/fullpage.html?res=9D0CE0DF143FF932A157 51C0A967958260&scp=1&sq=Melamed%20Sells%20Stake%20in%20His%2 0Firm&st=cse.

3. See note 1.

4. "NASDAQ Timeline/Milestones." *Nasdaq,* 2008; www.nasdaq.com/ newsroom/presskit/timeline.stm.

5. Nina Mehta, "Algos Get Serious." *Traders Magazine,* June 5, 2007; www .westwatercorp.com/documents/Westwater_JimLeman_AlgosGetSerious.pdf.

6. "The Rise and Rise of Algorithmic Trading and Its Implications for Best Practice Implementation." *Euromoney,* May 2007; www.euromoney.com/.

7. Aaron Luccheti. "Firms Seek Edge through Speed as Computer Trading Expands." *Wall Street Journal,* December 14, 2006; www.batstrading.com/ news_article_pdf/Firms%20Seek%20Edge%20Through%20Speed%20As%20 Computer%20Trading%20Expands.pdf.

8. "BATS Trading Averages More than a Billion Shares a Day in July." *Kansas City Business Journal*, August 12, 2008; http://kansascity.bizjournals.com/ kansascity/stories/2008/08/11/daily20.html.

9. Robert Daly, "Pipeline Takes Aim at Information Leakage," *Waters Trading Technology Week*, December 12, 2003; www.exad.com/News/ViewArticle .aspx?ArticleID=25.

10. Sara Kugler, "Forbes Doubles Bloomberg Wealth Estimate." *Washington Post*, September 21, 2007; www.washingtonpost.com/wp-dyn/content/ article/2007/09/21/AR2007092102029.html.

11. "Michael Bloomberg." *FinFacts Ireland*, 2005; www.finfacts.ie/busbloomberg.htm.

12. Chris Smith, "The Stadium's Silver Lining." *New York*, June 12, 2005; http:// nymag.com/nymetro/news/politics/columns/citypolitic/12024/.

13. "Mayor Michael R. Bloomberg Biography." Carnaval.com; www.carnaval .com/cityguides/newyork/Mayor/mayorB.htm.

14. Vault Company Snapshot: Bloomberg LP, 2008. www.vault.com/ companies/company_main.jsp?product_id=657&ch_id=306&co_ page=2&tabnum=2&v=1.

15. "Tomorrow's Front Page Now." *Bloomberg News*, 2008; http://about.bloomberg .com/news/news.html.

16. See note 13.

17. David S Bennahum, "Terminal Velocity." *Wired*, July 2, 2004; www.wired .com/wired/archive/7.02/bloomberg_pr.html.

18. "The Banks that Robbed the World." *BBC News*, June 9, 2004; http://news .bbc.co.uk/2/hi/business/3086749.stm; "Timeline of Enron's Collapse. *Washington Post*, September 30, 2004; www.washingtonpost.com/wp-dyn/ articles/A25624-2002Jan10.html.

19. Jon Merriman and William J. Febbo. "Due Diligence 2.0." *The Deal*, 6(5), February 18–24.

20. "Barclays ETF." *ETF Global Investor*, 2008; www.etfglobalinvestor.net/ barclays-etf.php.

21. "Barclays Family." Morningstar.com; http://quicktake.morningstar.com/ FundFamily/BestWorst.asp?Country=USA&Symbol=11558.

22. Justin Fox, "The Best Investors You've Never Heard of: Here's How Barclays Global Beats the Market—and Why You Can't." *Fortune*, June 16, 2003; http://money.cnn.com/magazines/fortune/fortune_archive/2003/ 06/16/344194/index.htm; Mark Hulbert, "One Way to Let Mutual Funds Trade throughout the Day." *New York Times*, January 9, 2005; www.nytimes .com/2005/01/09/business/09strat.html.

23. David Gauthier-Villars, Carrick Mollenkamp, and Alistair MacDonald, "French Bank Rocked by Rogue Trader." *Wall Street Journal*, January 25, 2008.

24. "Société Générale Posts $4.91 Billion Loss." Associated Press, February 21, 2008; www.msnbc.msn.com/id/23272321/.

25. "Blame the Risk Manager?" *Wall Street & Technology*, March 1, 2008.

26. David Gauthier-Villars, Carrick Mollenkamp, and Alistair MacDonald. "French Bank Rocked by Rogue Trader." *Wall Street Journal,* January 25, 2008.

27. Ibid.

28. Ibid.

29. Ibid.

30. See note 25.

31. Ibid.

32. Heather Smith. "Kerviel Says He Won't Be Made SocGen 'Scapegoat.'" Bloomberg, February 5, 2008; www.bloomberg .com/apps/news?pid=20601087&sid=aXjXl4EinzZU&refer=home.

33. Kennedy, Simon. "SocGen jumps after revealing underlying profit" Marketwatch. October 14, 2008. http://www.marketwatch.com/news/ story/socgen-jumps-after-revealing-14/story.aspx?guid={DB02E6DB-8925-42ED-9374-EC84A7EED1A8}&dist=msr_22.

Chapter 3: Prime Brokerage Meeting Hall

1. "Business Definition for: Global Custody." *BNET Business Network,* 2008; http://dictionary.bnet.com/definition/global+custody.html.

2. Hoover's Profile: Deutsche Bank AG. *Hoover's Inc.,* 2008; www.answers .com/topic/deutsche-bank-ag-usa.

3. "NatWest Sells Equity Unit to Bankers Trust. *New York Times,* December 3, 1997; http://query.nytimes.com/gst/fullpage.html?res=9804E6D8173DF930A35751 C1A961958260.

4. John Schmid, "S&P Acts as Investment Banking Woes Fester: Deutsche Bank Slips from Top of Ratings." *International Herald Tribune,* August 27, 1998; www .iht.com/articles/1998/08/27/db.t.php.

5. "NatWest Sells Troubled Equities Business." *BBC News,* December 2, 1997; http://news.bbc.co.uk/2/hi/business/36346.stm.

6. Mark de Cambre. "Morgan Stanley Not Out of the Woods Yet." *New York Post,* October 3, 2008; www.nypost.com/seven/10032008/business/morgan_ stanley_not_out_of_the_woods_yet_131966.htm.

Chapter 4: Hedge Funds: Buy-Side Player, Sell-Side Foe

1. Michael J. Aitken, "Principal Trading and the Fiduciary Relationships between Brokers and Their Clients"; www.sirca.org.au/Papers/1991004.pdf.

2. Yalman Onaran, "Wall Street Trading Gets Zero Value from Lehman, Merrill Owners." *Bloomberg,* September 8, 2008; www.bloomberg .com/apps/news?pid=20601109&refer=home&sid=aPBMl6mTFuks.

3. "About AQR." AQR Capital, 2004; www.aqrcapital.com/about.htm.

4. "Goldman & Morgan Alumni Launch Eton Park, a Multi-Strategy Fund." *Daily News,* November 4, 2004; www.highbeam.com/doc/1P2-10023944.html.

5. "Who We Are: Managing Members." Farallon Capital, 2004; www.faralloncapital.com/farallon/members_andrew_jm_spokes.htm.

6. "About Us: Directors and Executive Officers." Fortress Investments; www.fortressinv.com/site_content.aspx?s=17#Garonzik.

7. "Company Description." GLG Partners, 2008; www.glgpartners.com/about_glg/company_description.

8. "Our Team: Daniel Och." Och-Ziff Capital Management Group, 2007; www.ozcap.com/ourTeam/Och_Daniel.html.

9. "Sears Holdings Elects Richard C. Perry, Founder of Perry Capital, to Board." Sears Holdings Corporation, September 26, 2005; www.prnewswire.com/cgi-bin/stories.pl?ACCT=104&STORY=/www/story/09-26-2005/0004131665&EDATE=.

10. Andrew Ross Sorkin, "Hold Those Punches. Goldman May Be the Good Guy." *New York Times.* October 30, 2005; www.nytimes.com/2005/10/30/business/yourmoney/30deal.html.

11. Patrick Hosking, "Millionaire Duo Ride on BlueCrest of a Wave." *TimesOnline,* May 13, 2006; http://business.timesonline.co.uk/tol/business/article717295.ece.

12. "FrontPoint Acquires Ivory Capital Group." *Los Angeles Times,* July 30, 2003; http://articles.latimes.com/2003/jul/30/business/fi-wrap30.1.

13. "Executive Profile: Timothy R. Barakett." *BusinessWeek,* 2008; http://investing.businessweek.com/businessweek/research/stocks/private/person.asp?personId=783323&privcapId=4663262&previousCapId=875839&previousTitle=RIT%20Capital%20Partners%20plc.

14. Duen-Li (Tony) Kao, "Risk Analysis of Hedge Funds versus Long-Only Portfolios." General Motors Asset Management Working Paper, October 2001; http://ssrn.com/abstract=280389 or DOI: 10.2139/ssrn.10.2139/ssrn.280389.

15. "2 and 20." *Financial Reference.com,* September 29, 2005; www.financialreference.com/blog/2005/09/29/2-and-20/.

16. Katherine Burton, "Hedge Funds Raise Fees as Returns Decline 50 Percent from 1990s." *Bloomberg.com,* January 17, 2006; www.bloomberg.com/apps/news?pid=10000103&sid=ah8Nqrtqez9Q&refer=news_index.

17. Matt Krantz, "Nasdaq Lumbers into Bear Market Territory." *USA Today,* February 6, 2008; www.usatoday.com/money/markets/2008-02-06-nasdaq-bear_N.htm.

18. "Fifth Anniversary: Nasdaq's Record All-Time Closing High 5,048.62." *FinFacts.com,* March 8, 2005; www.finfacts.com/irelandbusinessnews/publish/article_1000766.shtml.

19. Anne Tergesen, "A Fee Frenzy at Hedge Funds." *BusinessWeek,* June 6, 2005; www.businessweek.com/magazine/content/05_23/b3936115_mz070.htx.

20. "130/30 Primary: Merrill 130/30 Poll Corroborates Earlier Polling, but Also Finds Some New Surprises." *AllAboutAlpha,* January 14, 2008; http://allaboutalpha.com/blog/2008/01/14/13030-primary-merrill-13030-poll-corroborates-earlier-polling-but-finds-some-new-surprises/.

21. "Annual Report: 2007." Berkshire Hathaway, Inc.; www.berkshirehathaway.com/letters/2007ltr.pdf.

22. Andrew Ross Sorkin, "Kenneth Griffin, Founder of Citadel Investment, Bashes His Peers." *International Herald Tribune,* May 13, 2008; www.iht.com/articles/2008/05/13/business/sorkin.php.

23. Jenny Anderson, "Will a Hedge Fund Become the Next Goldman Sachs?" *New York Times,* April 4, 2007; http://dealbook.blogs.nytimes.com/2007/04/04/will-a-hedge-fund-become-the-next-goldman-sachs/.

24. Marcia Vickers, "A Hedge Fund Superstar." *Fortune,* April 3, 2007; http://money.cnn.com/magazines/fortune/fortune_archive/2007/04/16/8404298/.

25. Michael Covel, "Kenneth Griffin." *Turtle Trader,* February 14, 2005; www.turtletrader.com/trader-griffin.html. "Citadel Investment Group." Jobs for PhDs. 2008. http://jobs.phds.org/employer/jobs/1161/citadel-investment-group.

26. Chris Murphy, "Where Tech Is the Business." *Finance Tech,* October 21, 2004; www.wallstreetandtech.com/data-management/showArticle.jhtml;jsessionid=TUGBKI1FD4FQ2QSNDLOSKHSCJUNN2JVN?articleID=51000184&_requestid=590757.

27. See note 24.

28. "Griffin's Citadel LP Raises Stake in Titan International (TWI) to 5.27%." StreetInsider.com, September 5, 2007; www.streetinsider.com/13Gs/Griffins+Citadel+LP+Raises+Stake+in+Titan+International+(TWI)+to+5.27%25/2927575.html.

29. "Asset Allocation." CalPERS, August 13, 2008; www.calpers.ca.gov/index.jsp?bc=/investments/assets/assetallocation.xml.

30. "Facts at a Glance: General." CalPERS, August, 2008; www.calpers.ca.gov/eip-docs/about/facts/general.pdf.

31. "CalPERS Casts Its Lot with Apollo." *Fierce Finance,* September 12, 2007; www.fiercefinance.com/story/calpers-casts-its-lot-apollo/2007-09-12.

32. Roy Mark, "CalPERS Invests $425 Million in the Carlyle Group." Internetnews.com, February 1, 2001; www.internetnews.com/bus-news/article.php/2101_576721.

33. Swagata Gupta and Jessica Hall. "CalPERS buys minority stake in Silver Lake." *Reuters,* January 9, 2008; www.reuters.com/article/innovationNews/idUSWNAS598220080109.

34. "CalPERS Hikes Potential Allocations to Corporate Governance and Hedge Funds," CalPERS press release, June 18, 2007; www.calpers.ca.gov/index.jsp?bc=/about/press/pr-2007/june/allocations-corp-gov-hedge-funds.xml.

35. Christine Williamson, "CalPERS Harbors Hedge Fund Hope." *Pensions and Investments,* January 21, 2008.

36. "CalPERS and Texas Teachers Ready to Form Strategic Hedge Fund Partnerships." *Investhedge,* February 2008 (newsletter); www.hedgefund intelligence.com/ih/Article.aspx?ArticleID=1861638&PositionID=109877.

37. Ibid.

38. "Bank of New York." Casey, Quirk & Associates Study, 2007.

39. Riva D. Atlas, "Pension Plans Pouring Billions into Hedge Funds." *International Herald Tribune,* November 27, 2005; www.iht.com/articles/2005/11/27/business/web.1127walsh.php.

40. Ibid.

41. "Facts at a Glance: Investment." CalPERS, August 2008; www.calpers.ca.gov/eip-docs/about/facts/investme.pdf.

42. "California Bill Aims at Calpers, Calstrs' Private Equity Relationships." Dow Jones Newswires, February 2008; www.efinancialnews.com/assetmanagement/pensionfunds/content/2349896154.

Chapter 5: Private Equity: Buy-Side Player, Sell-Side Friend

1. Heidi N. Moore, "Buyout Debt: Now Available in Stores." *Wall Street Journal,* April 18, 2008; http://blogs.wsj.com/deals/2008/04/18/financing-for-big-buyouts-free-at-last/?mod=WSJBlog.

2. "Bain Capital. Inc." Behind the Buyouts, a Project of the Service Employees International Union, 2008. www.behindthebuyouts.org/bain-capital/.

3. "The Blackstone Group." Behind the Buyouts, a Project of the Service Employees International Union, 2008. www.behindthebuyouts.org/blackstone/.

4. "Kohlberg, Kravis, Roberts, and Company." Behind the Buyouts, a Project of the Service Employees International Union, 2008. www.behindthebuyouts.org/kkr/.

5. "TPG: Formerly Texas Pacific Group." Behind the Buyouts, a Project of the Service Employees International Union, 2008. www.behindthebuyouts.org/tpg/.

6. "Bausch & Lomb Agrees to Buyout Offer." Associated Press, May 16, 2007; www.msnbc.msn.com/id/18697545/.

7. Jason Lopez, "SunGard Goes Private in $11.3 Billion Buyout." *CIO Today,* March 28, 2005.

8. Heidi N. Moore, "Private Equity: The List of the Fallen." *Wall Street Journal,* March 27, 2008; http://blogs.wsj.com/deals/category/the-deal/the-first-data-buyout/.

9. "Buyout Firms Surf Wave of Liquidity." December 26, 2006; http://waterindustry.org/New%20Projects/investment.-12.htm.

10. "Warburg Pincus May Profit on Turmoil with MBIA Deal." TheDeal.com December 10, 2007; www.thedeal.com/dealscape/2007/12/warburg_pincus_may_profit_on_t.php.

11. Peter Lattman. "WaMu Fall Crushes TPG." *Wall Street Journal,* September 27, 2008; http://online.wsj.com/article/SB122247093070880789.html.

12. Steve Bergsman, Maverick Real Estate Investing: The Art of Buying and Selling Properties Like Trump, Zell, Simon, and the World's Greatest Land Owners. Hoboken, NJ: John Wiley and Sons, 2004. Roger Tjong, "Distressed Debt Draws Investors. *Stanford Business Magazine,* November 2002; www.gsb.stanford.edu/news/bmag/sbsm0211/trends.shtml.

13. Zac Bissonnette, "Carlyle Group Launches a Hedge Fund." BloggingBuyouts .com, April 5, 2007; www.bloggingbuyouts.com/2007/04/05/carlyle-group-launches-a-hedge-fund/. Thomas Heath, "Carlyle Fund's Assets Seized." *Washington Post,* March 13, 2008; www.washingtonpost.com/wp-dyn/content/article/2008/03/13/AR2008031300061.html.

14. "Blackstone Raises $10.9 Billion Real Estate Fund." Reuters, April 1, 2008; www.reuters.com/article/innovationNews/idUSWNAS652320080401.

15. "Apollo's $1 Billion Bet on Distressed Debt." *New York Times,* March 12, 2008; http://dealbook.blogs.nytimes.com/2008/03/12/apollo-said-to-have-poured-1-billion-into-distressed-debt/.

16. "Ross Acquires Option One Mortgage for $1.1 Billion." cnbc.com, March 17 2008. www.cnbc.com/id/23671169.

17. "Assured Guaranty Ltd. Announces Commitment by Wilbur Ross to Purchase Up to $1 Billion . . ." Reuters, February 29, 2008; www.reuters .com/article/pressRelease/idUS123605+29-Feb-2008+BW20080229.

18. "American Home Mortgage Names W.L. Ross as Successful Bidder for American Home's Servicing Business." Business Wire, October 5, 2007; http://findarticles.com/p/articles/mi_m0EIN/is_2007_Oct_5/ai_n21027282.

19. "Citadel Boosts E-Trade Stake with $2.5 Billion Investment." Trading Markets. com, November 30, 2007; www.tradingmarkets.com/.site/news/Stock%20News/873463/.

20. "Can Deutsche Bank Debt Sale Ease Crunch." *Financial News,* April 15, 2008; www.efinancialnews.com/homepage/content/2350370198.

21. "Citi Up on Plan to Sell Leveraged Loans." *AP,* April 9, 2008; http://news.moneycentral.msn.com/provider/providerarticle.aspx?feed=AP&date=20080409&id=8458118.

22. Tom Taulli, "DE Shaw: Jumping More Aggressively into Private Equity?" Blogging Stocks.com, May 1, 2007; www.bloggingstocks.com/2007/05/01/de-shaw-jumping-more-aggressively-into-private-equity/.

23. "Private-Equity Firm to Buy Chrysler—Report." *MarketWatch,* May 13, 2007; www.marketwatch.com/news/story/private-equity-firm-cerberus-

buy-chrysler/story.aspx?guid=%7BDA1EEB74-B726-4AFB-8D03-7AEACF8FC89C%7D.

24. Zac Bissonnette. "Carlyle Group Launches a Hedge Fund." BloggingBuyouts. com, April 5, 2007; www.bloggingbuyouts.com/2007/04/05/carlyle-group-launches-a-hedge-fund/.

25. Tom Bawden, "Texas Pacific to Boost Income by Playing Markets." *The Times,* August 19, 2004; http://business.timesonline.co.uk/tol/business/article471405.ece.

26. Gwen Robinson. "Relative Values: Private Equity vs. Hedge Funds." *Financial Times,* July 9, 2007; http://ftalphaville.ft.com/blog/2007/07/09/5757/relative-values-private-equity-vs-hedge-funds/.

27. Lucas Mearian, "SunGard Agrees to $11.3B Buyout." ComputerWorld. com, March 28, 2005; www.computerworld.com/securitytopics/security/recovery/story/0.10801.100696.00.html.

28. Gwen Robinson, "JC Flowers Moves on Shinsei Bank." *FinancialTimes,* November 20, 2007; http://ftalphaville.ft.com/blog/2007/11/20/9028/jc-flowers-moves-on-shinsei-bank/.

29. "Fund of Funds." Fort Washington Investment Advisors, 2007; www.fortwashington.com/privateequity/fundoffunds.asp.

30. "Hellman and Friedman—Team: Matthew Barger." 2008; www.hf.com/team/Team.aspx?membercode=mBarger.

31. "Texas Pacific Group Inc.—Company History." FundingUniverse.com; www.fundinguniverse.com/company-histories/Texas-Pacific-Group-Inc-Company-History.html.

32. "The Cypress Group: Jeffrey P. Hughes." www.cypressgp.com/bio_jeff_hughes.html.

33. "AEA Investors LLC: Partners"; www.aeainvestors.com/biopartner.htm.

34. Stacy-Marie Ishmael, "Fortune's Private Equity Power List—and a Critique." *Financial Times,* February 21, 2007; http://ftalphaville.ft.com/blog/2007/02/21/2651/the-private-equity-power-list/.

35. "Blackstone Eyes Seven Billion Dollars in IPO, China Deal." *The Raw Story,* May 21, 2007; http://rawstory.com/news/afp/Blackstone_eyes_seven_billion_dolla_05212007.html.

36. Paul Tharp, "Blackstone Buys Hilton for $20B." *New York Post,* July 4, 2007; www.nypost.com/seven/07042007/business/blackstone_buys_hilton_for_20b_business_paul_tharp.htm.

37. Terry Pristin, "After Acquiring Equity Office, Blackstone Begins Selling It." *New York Times,* February 10, 2007; www.nytimes.com/2007/02/10/business/10real.html?partner=rssnyt&emc=rss.

38. Ibid.

39. Michael Quint, "Nikko Acquires 20% of Blackstone Group." *New York Times,* December 13, 1988; http://query.nytimes.com/gst/fullpage .html?res=940DE5DD1F3AF930A25751C1A96E948260.

40. "Blackstone Raises Record Private Equity Fund." Blackstone Group Press Release, July 16, 2002; www.blackstone.com/news/press_releases/07-16-02. pdf.

41. "Crestwood Midstream Partners, LLC Announces the Blackstone Group and GSO Capital Partners LP as New Investors." Business Wire, June 25, 2008; http://findarticles.com/p/articles/mi_m0EIN/is_2008_June_25/ai_ n27508175; http://www.blackstone.com./private_equity/index.html.

42. Guy Paisner, "Foresight Paves Way for Record Fund." *Financial News,* August 22, 2005; www.efinancialnews.com/usedition/index/content/539146.

43. "China to Invest Three Billion Dollars in Blackstone." *AFP,* May 21, 2007; http://business.maktoob.com/NewsDetails-20070423095138-China_to_ invest_three_billion_dollars_in_Blackstone.htm.

44. Tennille Tracy, "Blackstone-China: Let 100 Conspiracies Bloom." *Wall Street Journal,* May 21, 2007; http://blogs.wsj.com/deals/2007/05/21/ blackstone-china-let-100-conspiracies-bloom/.

45. "Silver Lake Aims to Make a Splash." *Financial Times,* October 12, 2005. www .silverlake.com/pdfs/2005-10-12.pdf.

46. "Evercore Partners: The Team." Evercore Partners, 2008; www.evercore.com/ userdetail/index.php?userid=76.

47. "Global Conference 2008: Speakers." Milken Institute, 2008; www.milkeninsti- tute.org/events/gcprogram.taf?function=bio&EventID=GC08&SPID=3431.

48. "Fortress Investment Group: Officers and Directors." Reuters; www.reuters .com/finance/stocks/companyOfficers?symbol=FIG.N&viewId=bio.

49. "About Us: Directors and Executive Officers." Fortress Investment Group; www.fortressinv.com/site_content.aspx?s=17#Nardone.

50. "About Us: Directors and Executive Officers." Fortress Investment Group; www.fortressinv.com/site_content.aspx?s=17#Briger.

51. Ann Cullen, "When Hedge Funds Meet Private Equity." *Working Knowledge for Business Leaders,* Harvard Business School, February 20, 2006; http:// hbswk.hbs.edu/archive/5215.html.

52. Mark DeCambre,, "Fortress War Chest Up by $1B." *New York Post,* June 20, 2008; www.nypost.com/seven/06202008/business/fortress_war_chest_up_ by_1b_116402.htm?dbk.

53. "Nomura to Buy Stake in Fortress Investment." *New York Times,* December 19, 2006; http://dealbook.blogs.nytimes.com/2006/12/19/nomura-to-buy -stake-in-hedge-fund-firm-fortress/.

54. "Hedge Fund to Stake Out Public Terrain." *CNNMoney,* September 15, 2006; http://money.cnn.com/2006/09/15/markets/hedgefund_ipo/index.htm.

55. Alex Halperin, "Investors Storm Fortress IPO." *BusinessWeek,* February 9, 2007; www.businessweek.com/investor/content/feb2007/pi20070209_895342 .htm?chan=top+news_top+news+index_businessweek+exclusives.

56. "Bear Stearns, Fortress Talked but Dismissed Tie-up: Report." Reuters, January 10, 2008.

Chapter 6: Entrepreneurs to Endowments: Buy-Side Catalysts

1. "Liquidnet: Leadership." Liquidnet, 2008; www.liquidnet.com/cont/about/ topManagement.jsp.

2. Ivy Schmerken, "Liquidnet Founder Seth Merrin Calls for Greater Cooperation between Exchanges and ATSs." *Wall Street & Technology,* June 11, 2008.

3. Ibid.

4. "Testimony on Regulation NMS before the Securities and Exchange Commission." www.404.gov/rules/proposed/s71004/testimony/nmsliquidnet.pdf.

5. Mairin Burns, "TH Lee Scores Big in Liquidnet Sale." *Private Equity Insider,* February 25, 2005; www.ftpartners.com/news/PEInsiderLeeScoresBig.pdf.

6. "Liquidnet: Our Services." 2008; www.liquidnet.com/cont/howLiquidnetWorks/ howLiquidnetWorks.jsp.

7. "Liquidnet Founder and CEO Seth Merrin Wins Ernst & Young's Entrepreneur of the Year..." Reuters, July 11, 2008; www.reuters .com/article/pressRelease/idUS149179+11-Jul-2008+PRN20080711.

8. Alexa Jaworski, "Liquidnet Plans to Go Public." SecuritiesIndustries.com, July 3, 2008; www.securitiesindustry.com/news/22593-1.html.

9. Barnaby J. Feder, "Business Technology: Sophisticated Software Set for Exotic Financial Trades." *New York Times,* March 30, 1994. http://query.nytimes .com/gst/fullpage.html?res=9B01E1D6173FF933A05750C0A962958260.

10. Dan Safarik, "Direct Market Access—The Next Frontier." *Wall Street & Technology,* February 28, 2005; www.wallstreetandtech.com/advancedtrading/ showArticle.jhtml?articleID=60404150.

11. "DMA: Overview." HCL Technologies, 2008; www.hcltech.com/ financial-services/capital-market-services/DMA/.

12. Roger Aitken, "Buy-Side Freedom Lets Them Go It Alone." *Financial Times,* July 2006; www.ftmandate.com/news/fullstory.php/aid/1172/Buy-side_ freedom_lets_them_go_it_alone.html.

13. See note 8.

14. "Knight Capital Group Completes Acquisition of EdgeTrade, a Leading Agency-Only Trade ..." Reuters, January 15, 2008; www.reuters.com/article/ pressRelease/idUS136629+15-Jan-2008+PRN20080115.

15. "Merrill Lynch to Buy Wave Securities." *Waters,* January 24, 2006; http://db.riskwaters.com/public/showPage.html?page=312309.

16. See note 10.

17. Jenny Anderson, "Shhh. Liquidnet Is Trading Stocks in Huge Blocks." *New York Times,* February 23, 2005; www.nytimes.com/2005/02/23/business/23place.html.

18. "Lava Trading Inc. Secures $30 Million in Financing Led by TA Associates." *Business Wire, April 9, 2002;* http://findarticles.com/p/articles/mi_m0EIN/is_2002_April_9/ai_84587867.

19. Constance Loizos, "Sequoia Scores Windfall from the YouTube Deal." *Oakland Tribune,* October 13, 2006; http://findarticles.com/p/articles/mi_qn4176/is_20061013/ai_n16787077.

20 "The Bank of New York, Eze Castle Software and GTCR Golder Rauner Join Forces to Form New Company Focused on Trade Execution, Order Management and Related Services." *Business Wire,* June 30, 2006; http://findarticles.com/p/articles/mi_m0EIN/is_2006_June_30/ai_n26913229.

21. Gregory J. Millman, "ECN: A New Force in the Stock Markets?" *Financial Executive,* May 1, 2002; www.allbusiness.com/technology/computer-software/183122-1.html.

22. "Lava Solutions for the Sell Side." Lava Trading, 2008; www.lavatrading.com/solutions/sellside.php.

23. "Citigroup to Buy Lava Trading." Finextra.com, July 2, 2004; www.finextra.com/fullstory.asp?id=12111.

24. "Goldman Sachs Completes Spear, Leeds & Kellogg Transaction." Goldman Sachs Press Release, November 1, 2000; www.goldmansachs.com/our-firm/press/press-releases/archived/2000/2000-11-01.html.

25. Ivy Schmerken, "Will Citigroup Acquisition Spoil Lava Trading's Neutrality?" *Wall Street & Technology,* July 8, 2004; www.wallstreetandtech.com/news/trading/showArticle.jhtml?articleID=22104423.

26. "Deutsche Bank, Goldman Sachs and JPMorgan Finalise Agreement to Sell Credit Derivatives Reference Entity Database to Mark-it Partners." www.markit.com/information/news/press_releases/2003/august/29.html.

27. Ibid.

28. Ibid.; "Markit Launches Real-Time Service To Enhance Price Discovery." www.markit.com/information/news/press_releases/2007/july/10.html.

29. "About Markit." Markit Group Limited, 2008; www.markit.com/information/about.html.

30. Eric.Reguly, "He Wants to Rule Brittania—and More." Globeandmail.com, December 3, 2007; https://secure.globeadvisor.com/servlet/ArticleNews/story/gam/20071203/RMARKIT03.

31. "Gary Coull." *The Times,* October 30, 2006; http://www.timesonline.co.uk/ tol/comment/obituaries/article617186.ece. "Bloomberg and CLSA Join Forces to Form Global Tradebook" PRNewswire. May 19, 1999. http:// www.in4reach.com/1.html.

32. "Bloomberg Tradebook Completes Build-Out of European Interactive Electronic Trading Platform." PR Newswire, 2008; www.prnewswire .co.uk/cgi/news/release?id=62902.

33. "GTCR Closes Investment in BNY ConvergEx Group." *BusinessWire,* October 2, 2006; www.allbusiness.com/services/business-services/3928801-1.html.

34. Craig Karmin, "Yale Endowment's Performance: A+." *Wall Street Journal,* September 27, 2007; http://dtscapital.com/wp-content/uploads/2007/09/ swensen-wsj.pdf.

35. Geraldine Fabrikant, "Yale Endowment Grows 28%; Topping $27 Billion." *New York Times,* September 27, 2007; www.nytimes.com/2007/09/27/ business/27yale.html?_r=1&scp=1&sq=Yale%20Endowment%20Grows%20 &st=cse&oref=slogin.

36. Geraldine Fabrikant, "For Yale's Money Man, a Higher Calling." *New York Times,* February 18, 2007; www.nytimes.com/2007/02/18/business/ yourmoney/18swensen.html.

37. Nicholas A. Vardy, "How to Invest Like Yale." *Global Guru;* www .theglobalguru.com/article.php?id=40&offer=guru001.

38. See note 35.

39. Svea Herbst-Bayliss, "Education Endowments' Taste for Hedge Funds Shifts." Reuters, January 17, 2008; www.reuters.com/article/fundsFundsNews/ idUSN1722768320080117.

40. Zachary M. Seward, "Harvard's Billion-Dollar Man Departs." *Forbes,* June 29, 2005; http://www.forbes.com/2005/06/29/harvard-management-meyer- cx_zs_0629harvard1.html.

41. Thomas Kaplan, "Swensen's Raise Tops $1 Million." *Yale Daily News,* November 15, 2007; www.yaledailynews.com/articles/view/22491.

42. Robert Quigley, "Finance Guru Makes a Killing with Eli Cash." *Yale Herald,* February 1, 2008; XLV(3); www.yaleherald.com/article.php?Article =6126. Boyd, Roderick. "Harvard Stunned By the Defection Of Fund Manager." NY Sun. January 12, 2005. http://www.nysun.com/business/ harvard-stunned-by-the-defection-of-fund-manager/7552/.

43. Robert Weisman, "Harvard Portfolio Managers' Pay Drops." *Boston Globe,* December 22, 2005.

44. Ibid.

45. Roderick Boyd, "Harvard Stunned by the Defection of Fund Manager." *New York Sun,* January 12, 2005; www.nysun.com/business/harvard-stunned- by-the-defection-of-fund-manager/7552/.

46. Lars Toomre, "Jack Meyer and Convexity Capital Management: Largest Hedge Fund Launch Ever." Toomre Capital Markets LLC, February 5, 2006; www.toomre.com/node/286.

47. Peter Grant and Rebecca Buckman, "Fatter Pay Lures University Endowment Chiefs; Stanford Loses Fund Manager; McCaffery Leaves for Start-Up with Paul Allen Seed Capital." *Seattle Post-Intelligencer,* June 27, 2006; http://blog. seattlepi.nwsource.com/review.asp?entryID=105006&commentID=8609.

48. Svea Herbst-Bayliss, "Education Endowments' Taste for Hedge Funds Shifts." Reuters, January 17, 2008; www.reuters.com/article/fundsFundsNews/idUSN1722768320080117.

49. "Thomson Sells Stake in Tradeweb to Nine Broker-Dealers for $180 Million." TheTradeNews.com, October 11, 2007; www.thetradenews.com/trading/fixed-income-trading/1294.

Chapter 7: Exchanges: Sell-Side Voice, Buy-Side Electronics

1. "New York Stock Exchange—NYSE"; Investopedia, www.investopedia.com/terms/n/nyse.asp.

2. Larry Tabb, "The NYSE Floor: A Question of Control." *Wall Street & Technology,* February 27, 2005; www.wallstreetandtech.com/electronic trading/showArticle.jhtml;jsessionid=JAWZ0BFR0M0Y0QSNDLRSKH0C JUNN2JVN?articleID=60403815&_requestid=257810.

3. "Exchanges in Battle with Dark Pools." Reuters, April 23, 2008; www.reuters .com/article/reutersEdge/idUSN2132782920080423?pageNumber=4&virtu alBrandChannel=10003.

4. Branden Moskwa, "Executing a Stock Market Trade." Article Alley, February 10, 2007; www.articlealley.com/article_128028_19.html.

5. Ben White, "Two Plus Two Equals What?" *Washington Post,* May 1, 2005; www.washingtonpost.com/wp-dyn/articles/A27256-2005Apr30_2.html.

6. David Harper, "Getting to Know Stock Exchanges." Investopedia, www .investopedia.com/articles/basics/04/092404.asp.

7. Wendy Cole, "Quicker on the Draw in a Wall Street Showdown." *Time,* October 16, 2000; www.time.com/time/magazine/article/0,9171,998255,00 .html?promoid=google.

8. Ibid.

9. "Archipelago and NYFIX Millennium Announce Reciprocal Order Routing Agreement." BNET, January 30, 2002; http://findarticles .com/p/articles/mi_m0EIN/is_2002_Jan_30/ai_82316753.

10. "CEO Network Chat: Gerald Putnam." *Forbes,* August 7, 2003; www.forbes .com/2003/08/07/0807chat_transcript.html.

11. See note 9.

12. "Archipelago to Acquire Pacific Exchange's Parent." *Los Angeles Times,* January 5, 2005; http://articles.latimes.com/2005/jan/05/business/fi-px5.

13. "Archipelago Opens Office in London." BNET, August 15, 2001; http://findarticles.com/p/articles/mi_m0EIN/is_2001_August_15/ai_77225410.

14. Jennifer Bayot, "Nasdaq to Acquire Instinet in $1.9 Billion Deal." *New York Times,* April 22, 2005; www.nytimes.com/2005/04/22/business/22cnd-nasdaq.html.

15. Joseph Weber, "Taking Aim at the Big Board." *BusinessWeek,* November 8, 2004; www.businessweek.com/magazine/content/04_45/b3907123_mz020.htm.

16. Liz Moyer, "Careful What You E-Mail!" *Forbes,* October 26, 2005; www.forbes.com/2005/10/25/goldman-emails-archipelago-cx_lm_1026goldman.html.

17. "Taking Aim at the Big Board." *BusinessWeek.* November 8, 2004; www.businessweek.com/magazine/content/04_45/b3907123_mz020.htm.

18. "NYSE Euronext Registration Statement." *EDGAR Online,* October 30, 2006; http://sec.edgar-online.com/2006/10/30/0001047469-06-013276/Section28.asp.

19. Naween A. Mangi, "Q&A 'Difference between an ECN and ESE Is Determined by Regulators.'" *Daily Times,* February 22, 2003; www.dailytimes.com.pk/default.asp?page=story_22-2-2003_pg5_7.

20. Grace Cheng, "Trading through a Market Maker vs. an ECN." Investopedia, www.investopedia.com/articles/forex/06/ECNmarketmaker.asp.

21. Ibid.

22. Walter Hamilton, "For NYSE Unit, It's Get Tough or Get Out." *Los Angeles Times,* September 11, 2005; http://articles.latimes.com/2005/sep/11/business/fi-nyse11.

23. "International Securities Exchange LLC: Company Overview." *International Securities Exchange,* 2008; www.ise.com/WebForm/viewPage.aspx?categoryId=140&header5=true&menu0=true.

24. "Why Trade FOREX?" www.fxonline.co.jp/en/beginners/whyforex.html.

25. "About the Options Exchange." http://advancedtrading.firstlightera.com/EN/Microsites/1/ISE/OptionsExchange.

26. "History of Leadership." *International Securities Exchange,* 2008; www.ise.com/WebForm/viewPage.aspx?categoryId=141&header5=true&menu0=true&link0=true.

27. Steve Goldstein, "Deutsche Boerse's Eurex in Talks to Buy ISE for $2.8 billion." *MarketWatch,* April 30, 2007; www.marketwatch.com/news/story/deutsche-boerses-eurex-talks-buy/story.aspx?guid=%7BBBFD7C97A-CD1A-4F75-B965-C1342C09A58D%7D.

28. Nandini Sukumar and Edgar Ortega, "Deutsche Boerse Plans to Buy ISE for $2.8 Billion." *Bloomberg,* April 30, 2007; www.bloomberg.com/apps/news?pid=20601087&sid=aLdPzxiN4ygY&refer=home.

29. "ICE: Technology. Innovation. Liquid Markets." *IntercontinentalExchange,* www.theice.com/history.jhtml.

30. www.theice.com/history.jhtml; www.theice.com/customers.jhtm.

31. Leah McGrath Goodman, "ICE Capades." *Trader Monthly,* June/July 2007; www.secinfo.com/dsVsf.u5Pm.htm. "CME/CBOT Merger Creates World's Biggest Derivatives Exchange" *Seeking Alpha.* October 18, 2006.

32. Diana B Henriques, "After Facing Scrutiny, Commodities Trading Accepts Regulations." *New York Times,* July 25, 2008; www.nytimes.com/2008/07/25/ business/worldbusiness/25ice.html?ref=business.

33. Ivy Schmerken, "New Futures Exchange Takes a Name: ELX Electronic Liquidity Exchange." *Wall Street & Technology,* March 12, 2008; www .wallstreetandtech.com/exchanges/showArticle.jhtml?articleID=206903283.

34. Jeremy Grant, "Eurex Move on Forex Signals Clash with CME." *Wall Street Journal,* June 9, 2005; www.marketwatch.com/News/Story/Story.aspx?guid= %7B6523E8FD-859E-4991-9D14-DA5690FEAD33%7D&siteid=mktw.

35. See note 33.

36. Luke Jeffs, "Project Turquoise." *Financial News,* October 17, 2007; www .efinancialnews.com/usedition/index/content/2348965310.

37. Phil Wahba, "'Dark Pools' Are Tempting Morsels for Major Stock Exchanges." *International Herald Tribune,* April 23, 2008; www.iht.com/ articles/2008/04/23/business/col24.php.

38. "Thain and O'Neal: Two Cool Customers." *New York Times,* November 14, 2007;http://dealbook.blogs.nytimes.com/2007/11/14/thain-and-oneal-two-cool-customers/index.html.

39. "NYSE/Archipelago Merger Gains Final SEC Approval." *NYSE Euronext,* www.nyse.com/press/1141083887100.html.

40. Jeffrey Kutler, "NYSE Buys Stake in Emerging-Markets Trading Platform." Securitiesindustry.com, September 18, 2006; www.securitiesindustry .com/news/18365-1.html?CMP=OTC-RSS.

41. "NYSE—Euronext Corporate Time Line." New York Stock Exchange; www .nyse.com/pdfs/NYSEEuronextTimeline-web.pdf.

42. "ICE Announces Definitive Agreement to Acquire YellowJacket." http:// www.prnewswire.com/cgi-bin/stories.pl?ACCT=104&STORY=/www/ story/01-31-2008/0004746770&EDATE=.

43. Liz Peek, "'Dark Pools' Threaten Wall Street." *New York Sun,* October 16, 2007; www.nysun.com/business/dark-pools-threaten-wall-street/64598/.

44. "Eurex and ISE Complete Merger." Deutsche Boerse Group, December 20, 2007; http://deutsche-boerse.com/dbag/dispatch/en/listcontent/gdb_ navigation/investor_relations/60_News/10_Press_Releases/Content_ Files/13_press/December_2007/pm_news_eurex-ise_201207.htm.

45. "CME Group Announces Completion of Combined CME/ CBOT Trading Facility." Reuters, May 19, 2008; www.reuters .com/article/pressRelease/idUS104046+19-May-2008+PRN20080519.

46. Zachery Kouwe, "CME to Buy NYMEX for $9.5B." *New York Post,* March 17, 2008; www.nypost.com/seven/03172008/business/cme_to_buy_nymex_ for_9_5b_102375.htm.

Chapter 8: Sovereign Wealth Funds: Sell Side Today, Buy Side Tomorrow

1. Katrin Bennhold, "Sovereign Wealth Funds Seek Balance against Western Regulation." *International Herald Tribune,* January 24, 2008: www.iht.com/ articles/2008/01/23/business/fund.php.co.uk/2/hi/business/36346.stm.

2. "S&C Chairman H. Rodgin Cohen Interviewed by *The Deal* about Recent Involvement in Negotiating Sovereign Wealth Funds." Sullivan & Cromwell LLP, www.sullcrom.com/news/detail.aspx?news=637.

3. Laura M. Holson. "Private Sector: Master of Facts, Legal and Musical." *New York Times,* July 9, 2000; http://query.nytimes.com/gst/fullpage.html?res=9B 04E3DC1738F93AA35754C0A9669C8B63&sec=&spon=&pagewanted=1.

4. "China Investment Corp Buys $5 Bln in M. Stanley Units." Reuters, December 19, 2007; www.reuters.com/article/etfNews/idUSN1957628320071219. "Merrill Lynch Will Sell Stake to Temasek Holdings" Reuters. December 25, 2007. http://www.cnbc.com/id/22395384/

5. "Citi to Sell $7.5 Billion of Equity Units to the Abu Dhabi Investment Authority." Citigroup, November 26, 2007; www.citi.com/citigroup/press/ 2007/071126j.htm.

6. Shu-Ching Jean Chen, "Singapore Investment Arm to Sink Billions into UBS." *Forbes,* December 10, 2007; www.forbes.com/2007/12/10/ubs-gic-singapore-markets-equity-cx_jc_1210markets03.html.

7. "Hedge Fund." Sullivan & Cromwell LLP, www.sullcrom.com/practices/ detail.aspx?service=134.

8. Peter Lattman, "Sullivan & Cromwell's H. Rodgin Cohen Names Joseph Shenker His Heir Apparent." *Wall Street Journal,* February 16, 2006; http:// blogs.wsj.com/law/2006/02/16/sullivan-cromwells-h-rodgin-cohen-names-joseph-shenker-his-heir-apparent/.

9. "Sullivan & Cromwell's Rodgin Cohen on Sovereign Wealth Funds." *The Deal,* March 7, 2008; www.sullcrom.com/files/News/746091c0-e8c5-4956-b093-a0d96646d6d4/Presentation/NewsAttachment/a38ebb19-4c1b-4cfa-b260-f6279a4407d2/sovereigninterests.pdf.

10. Ibid.

11. "Sovereign Wealth Funds and Office FX Reserves." *Morgan Stanley Research: Economics,* September 14, 2006, p. 2.

12. "The Overflowing Bathtub: The Running Tap and Sovereign Wealth Funds." *Merrill Lynch Economic Analysis,* October 5, 2007, p. 1.

13. "Merrill Lynch Enhances Its Capital Position by Raising Up to $6.2 Billion from Investors. Temasek Holdings and Davis Selected Advisors." Merrill Lynch, December 24, 2007; www.ml.com/index. asp?id=7695_7696_8149_74412_86378_87784.

14. Christine Harper, "Morgan Stanley Posts Loss. Sells Stake to China." Bloomberg, December 19, 2007; www.bloomberg.com/apps/news?pid= 20601103&sid=aw_wuZ3QM5eU&refer=us.

15. Andrew Ross Sorkin and David Barboza, "China to Buy a Stake in Blackstone." *New York Times,* May 21, 2007; www.nytimes.com/2007/05/21/ business/worldbusiness/21yuan.html?n=Top/Reference/Times%20 Topics/Subjects/C/Currency.

16. Leo Lewis and Gary Duncan, "America to Press for Restrictions on Potent Sovereign Wealth Funds." *Times Online,* October 15, 2007; http://business. timesonline.co.uk/tol/business/industry_sectors/banking_and_finance/ article2658402.ece.

17. Joseph B. Treaster, "Dubai to Buy Large Stake in Nasdaq." *New York Times,* September 20, 2007; www.nytimes.com/2007/09/20/business/worldbusiness/ 20exchange.html.

18. Herbert Lash, "Sovereign Funds May Be Savior of U.S. Finance." Reuters, November 29, 2007; www.reuters.com/article/reutersEdge/id USN2964029420071129.

19. Hilary Whiteman, "The Rise of the SWF." CNN.com, January 20, 2008; http://edition.cnn.com/2008/BUSINESS/01/17/sovereign.funds/.

20. "Sovereign Wealth Fund" compiled by Kevin Plumberg, edited by Derek Caney, "FACTBOX—Soft Market Sours Sovereign Wealth Fund Deals." Reuters, March 20, 2008; www.reuters.com/article/companyNews/ idUSN2038825420080320.

21. Arild Strømmen, "Transparency and Trust: Keys to the Norwegian Pension Fund," Norway.org, January 24, 2008; www.norway.org/policy/gpf/norwegian +pension+fund+global.htm.

22. See note 20.

23. Jesse Westbrook and Peter Cook, "Kuwait Sovereign Fund May Boost Citi, Merrill Stakes." Bloomeberg, May 1, 2008; www.bloomberg.com/ apps/news?pid=20601087&refer=home&sid=aHwjxvO2RV3s.

24. Rita Raagas De Ramos, "Agreement on Sovereign Wealth Funds." *BusinessWeek,* March 25, 2008; www.businessweek.com/globalbiz/content/

mar2008/gb20080325_139235.htm?chan=top+news_top+news+index_ global+business.

25. "Mapping Global Capital Markets: Fourth Annual Report." McKinsey & Company, January 2008; www.mckinsey.com/mgi/publications/Mapping_ Global/slideshow/slideshow_1.asp.

26. Ceyla Pazarbaşıoğlu, Mangal Goswami, and Jack Ree, "The Changing Face of Investors." *International Monetary Fund,* March 2007, www.imf.org/external/ pubs/ft/fandd/2007/03/pazar.htm.

27. "The World Factbook." United States Central Intelligences Agency. November 6, 2008. www.cia.gov/library/publications/the-world-factbook/print/ us.html.

28. "Remarks by Acting Under Secretary for International Affairs Clay Lowery on Sovereign Wealth Funds and the International Financial System." *U.S. Department of the Treasury,* June 21, 2007. www.ustreas.gov/press/releases/ hp471.htm.

29. "IMF Intensifies Work on Sovereign Wealth Funds." International Monetary Fund. March 4, 2008. www.imf.org/external/pubs/ft/survey/so/2008/ POL03408A.htm.

30. Stanley Reed, "Abu Dhabi's Citigroup Bargain." Business Week. www. businessweek.com/globalbiz/content/nov2007/gb20071127_878991. htm?chan=rss_topStories_ssi_5.

31. Madlen Read, "Citi falls on worries about cash levels." *USA Today,* March 4, 2008, www.usatoday.com/money/economy/2008-03-04-903564521_x.htm

32. David Ellis, "Citigroup's $10 Billion Loss Is Worst Ever." CNN Money, January 15, 2008; http://money.cnn.com/2008/01/15/news/companies/citi- group_earnings/index.htm?postversion=2008011515.

33. "Citigroup Posts $5.1 Billion Loss Due to Hefty Write-downs." *International Herald Tribune,* April 18, 2008; www.iht.com/articles/2008/04/18/business/ 19citigroup.php.

34. "Citi CEO Pandit Made $165 Million Off Sale of Old Lane Fund." *Financial Week,* March 14, 2008; www.financialweek.com/apps/pbcs. dll/article?AID=/20080314/REG/788282036/1036.

35. "Citigroup to Close Hedge Fund that Was Founded by its CEO." *International Herald Tribune,* June 12, 2008. www.iht.com/articles/2008/ 06/12/business/12citi.php.

36. "Citi to Acquire Old Lane Partners, L.P." Citigroup press release, April 13, 2007; www.citigroup.com/citigroup/press/2007/070413a.htm.

37. Ibid.; Eric Dash, "Vikram Pandit's Payout from Citigroup: $216 Million." *International Herald Tribune,* March 14, 2008; www.iht.com/ articles/2008/03/14/business/14citi.php.

38. Eric Dash, "Citigroup Closing Its Tribeca Fund." *TNewYork Times,* September 6, 2007; www.nytimes.com/2007/09/06/business/05cnd-fund.html.

39. Heidi N. Moore, "Vikram Pandit, Citigroup's Chess Master." Online Financial News, May 8, 2008; www.efinancialnews.com/homepage/content/2450595389.

40. Andrew Ross Sorkin, "More Shuffling in Citi's International Operations." *New York Times,* April 11, 2008; http://dealbook.blogs.nytimes.com/2008/04/11/more-shuffling-in-citis-international-operations/.

41. Kevin Lim and Jan Dahinten, "Singapore's GIC Warns of Global Recession, Crisis." *Economic Times,* April 21, 2008; http://uk.reuters.com/article/telecomm/idUKSP3132820080421.

42. "Merrill Lynch Economists Expect Sovereign Wealth Fund Assets to Quadruple by 2011." Merrill Lynch press release, October 12, 2007; www.ml.com/index.asp?id=7695_7696_8149_74412_82725_83576.

Chapter 9: Sell-Side Casualties, Buy-Side Implications

1. Sue Kirchhoff, "Mortgage Lender Files for Chapter 11." *USA Today,* April 2, 2007; www.usatoday.com/money/perfi/housing/2007-04-02-new-century-bankruptcy_N.htm.

2. David Ellis, "Countrywide Rescue: $4 Billion." CNNMoney, January 11, 2008; http://money.cnn.com/2008/01/11/news/companies/boa_countrywide/.

3. Landon Thomas Jr., "Bear's Cayne to Quit as Chief Executive." *New York Times,* January 8, 2008; www.nytimes.com/2008/01/08/business/08bear.html.

4. Robert L. Jackson and Ronald J. Ostrow, "U.S. Prosecutors Expected to Seek Indictments Against Milken, Drexel in 4–6 Weeks." *Los Angeles Times.* September 9, 1988; http://pqasb.pqarchiver.com/latimes/access/59880091.html?dids=59880091:59880091&FMT=ABS&FMTS=ABS:FT&date=Sep+09%2C+1988&author=ROBERT+L.+JACKSON%3B+RONALD+J.+OSTROW&pub=Los+Angeles+Times+(pre-1997+Fulltext)&desc=U.S.+Prosecutors+Expected+to+Seek+Indictments+Against+Milken%2C+Drexel+in+4-6+Weeks&pqatl=google. Moore, Heidi N. "Bear Stearns: The Drexel Burnham Lambert Precedent" *Wall Street Journal.* March 14, 2008. http://blogs.wsj.com/deals/2008/03/14/bear-stearns-the-drexel-burnham-lambert-precedent/?mod=googlenews_wsj.

5. Zarroli, Jim. "Little Sympathy for Bear Stearns." NPR, March 20, 2008; www.npr.org/templates/story/story.php?storyId=88690002.

6. "Failing to Heed the Lessons of Enron." Workplace Prof Blog, March 18, 2008; http://lawprofessors.typepad.com/laborprof_blog/2008/03/failing-to-heed.html.

7. Jacqueline Doherty, "Bracing for a Bear of a Week." *Barron's,* March 17, 2008; http://online.barrons.com/article/SB120553465607937899.html.

8. "The Fall of Bear Stearns: A Quickie Guide." *New York,* March 18, 2008; http://
   nymag.com/daily/intel/2008/03/a_quickie_guide_to_the_fall_of.html.

9. David Barboza and Jeff Gerth, "On Regulating Derivatives: Long-Term
   Capital Bailout Prompts Calls for Action." *New York Times,* December 15,
   1998; http://query.nytimes.com/gst/fullpage.html?res=9A03E2D7143DF936
   A25751C1A96E958260&sec=&spon=&pagewanted=all.

10. Don Amerman, "Sandy Weill 1933–." Reference for Business.com, 2008;
    www.referenceforbusiness.com/biography/S-Z/Weill-Sandy-1933.html.

11. Stephen Taub and David Carey with Alison M. Smith, "Ace Greenberg Is the
    Legendary CEO of Bear Stearns." Street Stories, October 11, 2005; www
    .streetstories.com/ag_fw_top100.html.

12. "Good-Bye, Bear Stearns." *Marketwatch,* May 29, 2008; www.marketwatch.
    com/news/story/bear-stearns-shareholder-vote-wake/story.aspx?guid
    =5E784C24-168C-42CD-A216-C9179F8D0925.

13. "Jerome Kohlberg; Limited Partner, Kohlberg & Co." *Goliath,* 2008; http://
    goliath.ecnext.com/coms2/gi_0199-3265091/Jerome-Kohlberg-Limited-
    partner-Kohlberg.html.

14. Katrina Brooker, "Starting Over." *Fortune,* January 31, 2002; www
    .mutualofamerica.com/articles/Fortune/2002_01_31/starting_over.asp.

15. Ibid.

16. Gretchen Morgenson, "Bear Stearns Says Battered Funds Are Worth Little."
    New York Times, July 18, 2007; www.nytimes.com/2007/07/18/business/
    18bond.html.

17. Daniel Burns, "12 Key Dates in the Demise of Bear Stearns." Reuters.com,
    March 17, 2008; http://blogs.reuters.com/from-reuterscom/2008/03/17/12-
    key-dates-in-the-demise-of-bear-stearns/.

18. Bryan Burrough, "Bringing Down Bear Stearns." *Vanity Fair,* August 2008;
    www.vanityfair.com/politics/features/2008/08/bear_stearns200808;   Julie
    Creswell and Vikas Bajaj, "$3.2 Billion Move by Bear Stearns to Rescue
    Fund." *New York Times,* June 23, 2007; www.nytimes.com/2007/06/23/
    business/23bond.html.

19. Tom Bawden, "Bear Stearns Will Fight to Keep Fund Afloat with $3.2bn
    Rescue." *The Times,* June 23, 2007; http://business.timesonline.co.uk/tol/
    business/industry_sectors/banking_and_finance/article1975073.ece.

20. Jake Zamansky, "Bear Stearns Announces Third Hedge Fund Collapse; A Sign of
    Things to Come?" Zamansky & Associates blog. January 10, 2008; http://zamansky.
    blogspot.com/2008/01/bear-stearns-announces-third-hedge-fund.html.

21. Elizabeth MacDonald, "Details of the Bear Stearns Hedge Fund
    Indictments." FOX Business, June 19, 2008; http://emac.blogs.foxbusiness.
    com/2008/06/19/details-on-the-bear-stearns-hedge-fund-indictments/;

"Bear to Close Third Hedge Fund after 40% Decline." FINalternatives, January 10, 2008. http://www.finalternatives.com/node/3246.

22. Andrew Ross Sorkin, "JPMorgan in Negotiations to Raise Bear Stearns Bid." *New York Times,* March 24, 2008; www.nytimes.com/2008/03/24/business/24deal.html.

23. Landon Thomas Jr., "Buffett Said to Consider Bear Stake." *New York Times,* September 27, 2008; www.nytimes.com/2007/09/27/business/27wall.html?ref=business.

24. Andrew Ross Sorkin, "Bear Stearns and Citic Securities to Form Joint Venture." *International Herald Tribune,* October 22, 2007; www.iht.com/articles/2007/10/22/business/citic.php.

25. Landon Thomas Jr., "Ailing Firm Gets Tonic from China." *New York Times,* October 23, 2007; www.nytimes.com/2007/10/23/business/23place.html.

26. Bradley Keoun and Jody Shenn. "Bear Stearns Removes Spector after Debt Market Losses (Update3)." Bloomberg.com, August 6, 2007; www.bloomberg.com/apps/news?pid=20601087&refer=home&sid=ahOOA5zLaqqg.

27. Kate Kelly, "Bear CEO's Handling of Crisis Raises Issues." *Wall Street Journal,* November 1, 2007; http://online.wsj.com/article/SB119387369474078336.html.

28. "Inside the Demise of Bear Stearns." *Crossing Wall Street.* March 18, 2008; www.crossingwallstreet.com/archives/2008/03/inside_the_demi.html.

29. Robin Sidel, Greg Ip, Michael M. Phillips, and Kate Kelly, "The Week that Shook Wall Street: Inside the Demise of Bear Stearns." *Wall Street Journal,* March 18, 2008; http://online.wsj.com/article/SB120580966534444395.html.

30. Heidi N. Moore, "Can What Happened to Bear Happen to Other Banks?" *Wall Street Journal,* March 18, 2008; http://blogs.wsj.com/deals/2008/03/18/repos-just-where-do-the-other-banks-stand/.

31. Robert Peston, "How Hedge Funds Sank Bear Stearns." BBC News, March 14, 2008; www.bbc.co.uk/blogs/thereporters/robertpeston/2008/03/how_hedge_funds_sunk_bear_stea.html.

32. Elizabeth Spiers, "Bear Run." *Slate,* March 18, 2008; www.slate.com/id/2186792/.

33. Roger Lowenstein, "Bleakonomics." *New York Times,* March 30, 2008; www.nytimes.com/2008/03/30/magazine/30wwln-lede-t.html.

34. "Fingers Crossed." *The Economist,* June 26, 2008; www.economist.com/finance/displaystory.cfm?story_id=11637798.

35. "JP Morgan Works to Retain Bear Hedge Fund Clients." *Fierce-Finance,* March 25, 2008; http://www.fiercefinance.com/story/jp-morgan-works-to-retain-bear-hedge-fund-clients/2008-03-25.

36. Robert Salomon, "Rescue for Bear or Bailout for JPMorgan?" March 18, 2008; http://blog.robertsalomon.com/2008/03/18/rescue-for-bear-or-bailout-for-jp-morgan/.

37. "Historical Prices for JPMorgan." Yahoo!, http://finance.yahoo .com/q/hp?s=JPM&a=02&b=13&c=2008&d=02&e=18&f=2008&g=d.

38. Duff McDonald, "The Heist." *New York,* March 24, 2008. http://nymag .com/news/features/45320/

39. Ibid.

40. Ibid.

41. Ibid.

Chapter 10: Buy-Side Casualties, Sell-Side Implications

1. "FIG: Investment Profile for Fortress Investment Group." Yahoo!, http:// finance.yahoo.com/q/pr?s=FIG.

2. Lars Toomre, "Fortress Investment Group IPO Prices at $18.50 per Share." February 9, 2007; www.toomre.com/FIG_Prices.

3. Ibid.

4. Alex Halperin, "Investors Storm Fortress IPO." *BusinessWeek,* February 9, 2007; www.businessweek.com/investor/content/feb2007/pi20070209_ 895342.htm?chan=top+news_top+news+index_businessweek+exclusives.

5. William Hutchings, "Renaissance Makes First Loss in 20 Years." Dow Jones Financial News Online, January 11, 2008; www.efinancialnews .com/usedition/index/content/2349548843.

6. Roddy Boyd, "AQR's Quant Loses Luster." *New York Post,* December 6, 2007; www.nypost.com/seven/12062007/business/aqrs_quant_loses_luster_ 753667.htm.

7. "Hedge Fund AQR's Flagship Fund Down 15 pct in 2008." Reuters, February 22, 2008; www.reuters.com/article/etfNews/idUSN2239142420080222.

8. Katherine Burton,. "Lampert, Wood Show Risk of 'Concentrated' Hedge Funds (Update1)." Bloomberg, May 9, 2008; www.bloomberg.com/ apps/news?pid=20601087&sid=azobDABpF9ZU&refer=home.

9. Svea Herbst-Bayliss, "Prominent Hedge Funds Nurse Heavy Losses in 2008." Reuters, January 23, 2008;www.reuters.com/article/fundsFundsNews/ idUSN23863620080123.

10. Alistair Barr, "Two Goldman Sachs Hedge Funds Suffer Losses." *MarketWatch,* August 9, 2007; www.marketwatch.com/news/story/two- goldman-sachs-hedge-funds/story.aspx?guid=%7B7647E3E0-8989-4E74- 844F-C491E5299F53%7D.

11. "Tough Times for Big-Name Funds." *New York Times Dealbook,* February 12, 2008; http://dealbook.blogs.nytimes.com/2008/02/12/bad-bets-and-accounting-flaws-bring-staggering-losses/.

12. Jenny Strasburg, and Katherine Burton, "Sowood Funds Lose More Than 50% as Debt Markets Fall." Bloomberg, July 31, 2007; www.bloomberg.com/apps/news?pid=20601087&sid=a5He2yClHjJE&refer=home.

13. "Sowood to Shutter after Citadel Sale, 50% NAV Drop." Finalternatives.com, July 31, 2007; www.finalternatives.com/node/2205.

14. Susan Thompson, "Peloton Partners to Liquidate and Close Shop." *Times Online,* March 5, 2008; http://business.timesonline.co.uk/tol/business/industry_sectors/banking_and_finance/article3492287.ece.

15. "A Brief History of the Hedge Fund Industry." *Vault Online,* 2008; www.vault.com/nr/newsmain.jsp?nr_page=3&ch_id=261&article_id=23801470&cat_id=2853.

16. Richard Wilson, "New Hedge Funds." http://richard-wilson.blogspot.com/2008/02/new-hedge-funds-hedge-fund-startups.html.

17. Jonathan Davis, "Amaranth: How to Lose $6 Billion in a Fortnight." *The Spectator,* October 25, 2006; www.spectator.co.uk/print/the-magazine/business/25964/amaranth-how-to-lose-and366-billion-in-a-fortnight.thtml.

18. Scott Krady, "Fewer New Hedge Funds Are Born." Efinancialcareers.com; http://news.campus.efinancialcareers.com/NEWS_ITEM/newsItemId-14354; See note 16.

19. Jim Rohwer, with Tony Paul and Neel Chowdhury, "Asia's Meltdown." CNNMoney.com, February 16, 1998; http://money.cnn.com/magazines/fortune/fortune_archive/1998/02/16/237678/index.htm.

20. Brian,Pinto, Evsey Gurvich, and Sergei Ulatov, "Lessons from the Russian Crisis of 1998 and Recovery." World Bank, February 2004; www1.worldbank.org/economicpolicy/documents/mv/pgchapter10.pdf.

21. Michael Maiello, "Small-Time Crooks." *Forbes,* October 2, 2003; www.forbes.com/2003/10/02/cz_mm_1002hedge_print.html.

22. "The World According to Mark Rubinstein; www.derivativesstrategy.com/magazine/archive/1999/0799qa.asp.

23. Marin Arnold, "Carlyle Capital to Be Wound Up." *Financial Times*, March 17, 2008; www.ft.com/cms/s/0/117e5cb0-f409-11dc-aaad-0000779fd2ac.html?nclick_check=1.

24. "John J. Mack, 1944–." www.referenceforbusiness.com/biography/M-R/Mack-John-J-1944.html.

25. "Morgan Stanley Investment Management Launches Alternative Investment Partners Absolute Return Fund; New Fund of Hedge Funds Offers a

Management Team with Established Track Record of Success." *Business Wire,* June 9, 2006; http://findarticles.com/p/articles/mi_m0EIN/is_2006_June_9/ai_n26891964.

26. Lauren Silva, "BlackRock Talks Reportedly End." *Fierce Finance,* February 1, 2006; www.fiercefinance.com/story/no-deal-for-morgan-stanley-blackrock/2006-02-02.

27. "Morgan Stanley Buys Seventh Hedge Fund Stake." FINalternatives, April 2, 2008; www.finalternatives.com/node/3991.

28. Christine Harper and Jenny Strasburg, "Morgan Stanley Expands, Buying Hedge-Fund Stake." *Bloomberg News,* October 31, 2006; www.iht.com/articles/2006/10/30/bloomberg/bxhedge.php.

29. Benjamin Peretz and Michael Dworkis, "Avenue Capital Group Founder Discusses Distressed Investing with Wharton Hedge Fund Network." *Wharton Journal,* September 24, 2007; http://media.www.whartonjournal.com/media/storage/paper201/news/2007/09/24/News/Avenue.Capital.Group.Founder.Discusses.Distressed.Investing.With.Wharton.Hedge.F-2986330.shtml.

30. "Morgan Stanley Buys Stake in Hedge Fund Traxis." Finalternatives.com, November 14, 2007; www.finalternatives.com/node/2897.

31. "Traxis Partners LLC Barton Biggs." Stockpickr.com, August 5, 2008; http://stockpickr.com/port/Traxis-Partners-LLC-Barton-Biggs/.

32. "Morgan Stanley Investment Management Takes Minority Stake in Hawker Capital." Reuters, April 1, 2008; www.reuters.com/article/pressRelease/idUS122402+01-Apr-2008+BW20080401.

33. "Morgan Stanley Investment Management Acquires Stake in Lansdowne Partners." Morgan Stanley Press Release, November 1, 2006; www.morganstanley.com/about/press/articles/3821.html.

34. Ibid.

35. "Morgan Stanley to Acquire FrontPoint Partners." Morgan Stanley press release, October 31, 2006; www.morganstanley.com/about/press/articles/3820.html.

36. "Long-Term Partners. May 2003," www.risk.net/public/showPage.html?page=11683.

37. Landon Thomas Jr. "Morgan Stanley in Deal for Hedge Fund Manager." *New York Times,* November 1, 2006; www.nytimes.com/2006/11/01/business/01wall.html.

38. Stanley Reed, Diane Brady, Jason Bush, and Frederik Balfour, "Morgan Stanley's Mack Attack." *BusinessWeek,* June 21, 2006; www.businessweek.com/investor/content/jun2006/pi20060621_288903.htm.

39. Cormick Grimshaw, "The New [Quantitative Finance] Math." *Market Pipeline,* April 7, 2008; http://marketpipeline.blogspot.com/2008/04/new-quantitative-finance-math.html.

40. Ibid.

41. "Chief Scientist." D. E. Shaw Research; www.deshawresearch.com/chiefscientist.html.

42. "Lawrence H. Summers to Join the D. E. Shaw Group." D. E. Shaw Research, October 19, 2006; www.deshaw.com/articles/20061019.pdf.

43. "Strategic Alliance between Bank of America and D. E. Shaw & Co. Creates New Force in Global Financial Markets." *Business Wire,* March 13, 1997; http://findarticles.com/p/articles/mi_m0EIN/is_1997_March_13/ai_19204434.

44. Liz Moyer, "D. E. Shaw's Second Marriage." *Forbes,* March 13, 2007; www.forbes.com/business/2007/03/13/shaw-lehman-merger-biz-cx_lm_0313shaw.html.

45. "People: David Coulter." Warburg Pincus, 2008; www.warburgpincus.com/people/ViewEmployee,employeeid.29.aspx.

46. "James River Group Reaches Agreement with the D. E. Shaw Group in $575 Million Transaction." November 12, 2007; www.insuranceheadlines.com/Insurance-News/National-Insurance-News/4154.html.

47. Landon Thomas Jr., "Lazard I.P.O. Seeks to Raise $850 Million." *New York Times,* December 18, 2004; www.nytimes.com/2004/12/18/business/18lazard.html.

Chapter 11: Regulatory Implications

1. "The Savings and Loan Crisis and Its Relationship to Banking." www.fdic.gov/bank/historical/history/167_188.pdf; Andrew Cave, "Federal Reserve Defends $3.6bn Rescue of LTCM." *UK Telegraph,* October 2, 1998; www.telegraph.co.uk/htmlContent.jhtml?html=/archive/1998/10/02/cnfed02.html.

2. "Moody's President Will Step Down at End of July." *International Herald-Tribune,* May 8, 2008; www.iht.com/articles/2008/05/08/business/08moody.php.

3. Aaron Lucchetti and Serena Ng, "S&P President Corbet Is Replaced." *Wall Street Journal,* August 31, 2007; http://online.wsj.com/article/SB118851936423414088.html?mod=hps_us_whats_news.

4. F. William Engdahl, "The Financial Tsunami Part IV: Asset Securitization—The Last Tango." *Financial Sense Editorials,* February 8, 2008; www.financialsense.com/editorials/engdahl/2008/0208.html.

5. Dan Ackman, "Merrill Covers Its Eyes, Fires Enron Bankers." *Forbes,* September 19, 2002; www.forbes.com/2002/09/19/0919topnews.html; Thomas A. Fogarty and Edward Iwata, "Links between Reports, Banking Fees Cited." *USA Today,* April 23, 2003; www.usatoday.com/money/industries/brokerage/2003-04-28-banks3_x.htm.

6. Shanny Basar, "Spitzer Reaches Agreement with Remaining Banks under Global Settlement." *Financial News,* August, 2003; http://findarticles.com/p/articles/mi_hb5555/is_200308/ai_n21930930.

7. R. Alton Gilbert, "Requiem for Regulation Q: What It Did and Why It Passed Away." http://research.stlouisfed.org/publications/review/86/02/Requiem_Feb1986.pdf.

8. Yongil Jeon and Stephen M. Miller, "Deregulation and Structural Change in the U.S. Commercial Banking Industry." *Eastern Economic Journal,* Summer 2003; http://findarticles.com/p/articles/mi_qa3620/is_200307/ai_n9247642.

9. Peter J. Wallison, "Groundhog Day: Reliving Deregulation Debates." *AEI Online,* October 19, 2006; www.aei.org/publications/pubID.25034/pub_detail.asp.

10. "The History of Forex." *Forex Fanatic,* http://forexfanatic.com/the-history-of-forex/.

11. Susan Pulliam and Serena Ng, "Default Fears Unnerve Markets." *Wall Street Journal,* January 18, 2008, p. A1.

12. Evelyn M. Rusli, "Citigroup's Write-Down Disaster." *Forbes,* January 15, 2008; www.forbes.com/2008/01/15/citigroup-merrill-closer-markets-equity-cx_er_ra_0115markets45.html.

13. "Wall Street Write-Downs: Closing In on $100 Billion." *Financial News,* January 15, 2008; http://blogs.wsj.com/deals/2008/01/15/wall-street-write-downs-closing-in-on-100-billion/.

14. "Margin Requirement." *Columbia Encyclopedia,* 6th ed., 2008; www.encyclopedia.com/doc/1E1-marginre.html.

15. "Leveraged Loans: Decidedly Not the Same as It Ever Was." *Wall Street Journal,* July 23, 2008; http://blogs.wsj.com/deals/2008/07/23/leveraged-loans-decidedly-not-the-same-as-it-ever-was/.

16. Pierre Paulden, "CLO Spreads Rise to Most Since 2003, Cutting LBO Loan Issuance." *Bloomberg,* August 7, 2008; www.bloomberg.com/apps/news?pid=20601009&sid=a6.CiG3p3RwI&refer=bond.

17. "High Yield Spreads." http://bespokeinvest.typepad.com/bespoke/2008/03/high-yield-spre.html.

Chapter 12: Future Implications

1. John Greenwald, "Special Report: Crisis in Banking: Requiem for a Heavyweight." *Time,* January 21, 1991; www.time.com/time/magazine/article/0,9171,972188-2,00.html.

2. Carl Gewirtz, "Has Regulators' Attention: Booming Swap Market." *International Herald Tribune,* March 16, 1992; www.iht.com/articles/1992/03/16/ebon_1.php?page=2.

3. "Concentration of Deposit Liabilities in New England." Federal Reserve Bank of Boston, July 8, 2004; www.bos.frb.org/economic/regional/profile/banking/bcdl.htm.

4. Gretchen Morgenson, "Arcane Market Is Next to Face Big Credit Test." *New York Times,* February 17, 2008; www.nytimes.com/2008/02/17/business/17swap.html?_r=1&oref=slogin.

5. F. William Engdahl, "Credit Default Swaps the Next Crisis." *Financial Sense Editorials,* June 6, 2008; www.financialsense.com/editorials/engdahl/2008/0606.html.

6. "Credit Default Swaps and Bank Leverage." *Naked Capitalism,* April 16, 2008; www.nakedcapitalism.com/2008/04/credit-default-swaps-and-bank-leverage.html.

7. Gabrielle Coppola and Caroline Salas, "Bond Traders Lose 'One-Night Stands' in Credit Crunch." *Bloomberg,* September 10, 2008; www.bloomberg.com/apps/news?pid=20601109&refer=home&sid=apx7VaSD28lU.

8. Pierre Paulden and Jonathan Keehner, "Slow Buyout Market Chases Bankers Away." *Business Report,* May 30, 2008; www.busrep.co.za/index.php?fSectionId=&fArticleId=4428598; Reggie Middleton, "The Next Shoe to Drop: Credit Default Swaps (CDS) and Counterparty Risk—Beware what lies beneath!" *Reggie Middleton's Boom Bust Blog,* May 8, 2008; http://boombustblog.com/component/option,com_myblog/show,The-Next-Shoe-to-Drop--Credit-Default-Swaps-CDS-and-the-Counterparty-Risk-What-lies-beneath.html/Itemid,20/.

9. Robert Glauber, "Can the Crash Happen Again?" NewsHour Online Forum, October 28, 1997; www.pbs.org/newshour/forum/october97/crash_10-27.html.

10. Bob Woodward, "Crash of October 1987 Challenged Fed Chief." *Washington Post,* November 13, 2000; www.washingtonpost.com/ac2/wp-dyn/A1742-2000Nov11?language=printer; http://www.goldensextant.com/SavingtheSystem.html; http://www.sprott.com/pdf/TheVisibleHand.pdf.

11. Ibid.

12. David Mildenberg and Bradley Keoun. "Wells Fargo's $12 Billion Bid Beats Citi to Wachovia." *Bloomberg.* October 10, 2008. www.bloomberg.com/apps/news?pid=20601087&refer=home&sid=aUpv3.YOFyRU.

13. "Big Shake-Up as Citi Combines Two Units. *New York Times,* October 12, 2007; http://dealbook.blogs.nytimes.com/2007/10/12/big-shake-up-as-citigroup-combines-two-key-units/.

14. "Bank of America to purchase Merrill Lynch." *Associated Press.* September 15, 2008. www.msnbc.msn.com/id/26708958/.

15. "Opinions Split About Financial Sector, But More Large Bank Failures Feared." *Trading Markets.com*. July 20, 2008. www.tradingmarkets.com/.site/news/ECONOMIC%20NEWS/1769339/.

16. "Feds Seize Banks In Arizona, California, Nevada; Is Florida Next?" *Strategies of the Condo Vultures*. July 27, 2008. www.realtown.com/condovultures/blog/feds-seize-banks-in-arizona-california-nevada-is-florida-next

17. Worsley, Ken. "Bank of Japan: savings deposits exceed loan balances by a record 145 trillion yen." *japaneconomynews.com*. September 8, 2008. www.japaneconomynews.com/2008/09/08/bank-of-japan-savings-deposits/.

18. Fackler, Martin. "Wall Street Attracts Japanese Banks." *NY Times*. September 24, 2008. www.nytimes.com/2008/09/25/business/worldbusiness/25comeback.html?partner=rssnyt&emc=rss.

19. Andrew Ross Sorkin and Vikas Bajaj. "Shift for Goldman and Morgan Marks the End of an Era." *NY Times*. September 21, 2008. www.nytimes.com/2008/09/22/business/22bank.html?hp

20. Armistead, Louise. "Hedge fund stars in crisis as performance plummets." *Telegraph*. October 18, 2008. www.telegraph.co.uk/finance/financetopics/financialcrisis/3225311/Hedge-fund-stars-in-crisis-as-performance-plummets.html.

21. Vodicka, Michael. "Greenhill & Co." *Zacks Investment Research*. October 9, 2008. www.zacks.com/commentary/8834/Greenhill+&+Co.

22. Masters, Brooke. "Jefferies its head while others all about to lose theirs." *Financial Times*. September 24, 2008. www.ft.com/cms/s/0/fcda291a-89d1-11dd-8371-0000779fd18c.html.

23. Kurt Eichenwald, "As Firms Shift Strategies, the Old Order Moves On; Perella Severing Wasserstein Link." *New York Times*, July 23, 1993; http://query.nytimes.com/gst/fullpage.html?res=9F0CE4D8123BF930A15754C0A965958260.

24. Paul Mungo, "Quant Funds Must Innovate to Regain Investor Confidence." *Financial News*, November 21, 2007; www.efinancialnews.com/usedition/index/content/2449214126/printerfriendly/.

25. Ibid.

26. Julia Werdigier, "Carlyle Capital Asks Lenders to Halt Further Liquidation." *International Herald Tribune*, March 10, 2008; www.iht.com/articles/2008/03/10/business/carlyle.php.

27. Walter Hamilton, "Private Equity Falls to Earth." *Los Angeles Times*, May 26, 2008; http://articles.latimes.com/2008/may/26/business/fi-buyout26.

About the Author

Richard Goldberg is a 25-year Wall Street veteran with Lehman, Lazard, and Wasserstein Perella. He has been a banker to the banks and advised on a number of transformational financial services transactions. He is also a faculty member at Columbia University's School of International and Public Affairs and has taught at Boston College's Carroll School of Management and Brandeis University's International Business School.

Index

Printed and bound by CPI Group (UK) Ltd, Croydon, CR0 4YY

13/04/2025

14656500-0002